More Paleozoic Fossils

Bruce L. Stinchcomb

4880 Lower Valley Road • Atglen, PA 19310

Other Schiffer Books by the Author:
Cenozoic Fossils I: Paleogene. ISBN: 9780764334245. $29.99
Cenozoic Fossils II: The Neogene. ISBN: 9780764335808. $29.99
Jewels of the Early Earth: Minerals and Fossils of the Precambrian. ISBN: 9780764338809. $29.99
Mesozoic Fossils I: Triassic and Jurassic Periods. ISBN: 9780764331633. $29.99
Mesozoic Fossils II: The Cretaceous Period. ISBN: 9780764332593. $29.99
Meteorites. ISBN: 9780764337284. $29.99
Paleozoic Fossils. ISBN: 9780764329173. $29.95
World's Oldest Fossils. ISBN: 9780764326974. $29.95

Library of Congress Control Number: 2012936156

ISBN: 978-0-7643-4030-7
Printed in China

Schiffer Books are available at special discounts for bulk purchases for sales promotions or premiums. Special editions, including personalized covers, corporate imprints, and excerpts can be created in large quantities for special needs. For more information contact the publisher:

Published by Schiffer Publishing Ltd.
4880 Lower Valley Road
Atglen, PA 19310
Phone: (610) 593-1777; Fax: (610) 593-2002
E-mail: Info@schifferbooks.com

For the largest selection of fine reference books on this and related subjects, please visit our website at
www.schifferbooks.com
We are always looking for people to write books on new and related subjects. If you have an idea for a book, please contact us at
proposals@schifferbooks.com

This book may be purchased from the publisher.
Please try your bookstore first.
You may write for a free catalog.

In Europe, Schiffer books are distributed by
Bushwood Books
6 Marksbury Ave.
Kew Gardens
Surrey TW9 4JF England
Phone: 44 (0) 20 8392 8585; Fax: 44 (0) 20 8392 9876
E-mail: info@bushwoodbooks.co.uk
Website: www.bushwoodbooks.co.uk

Contents

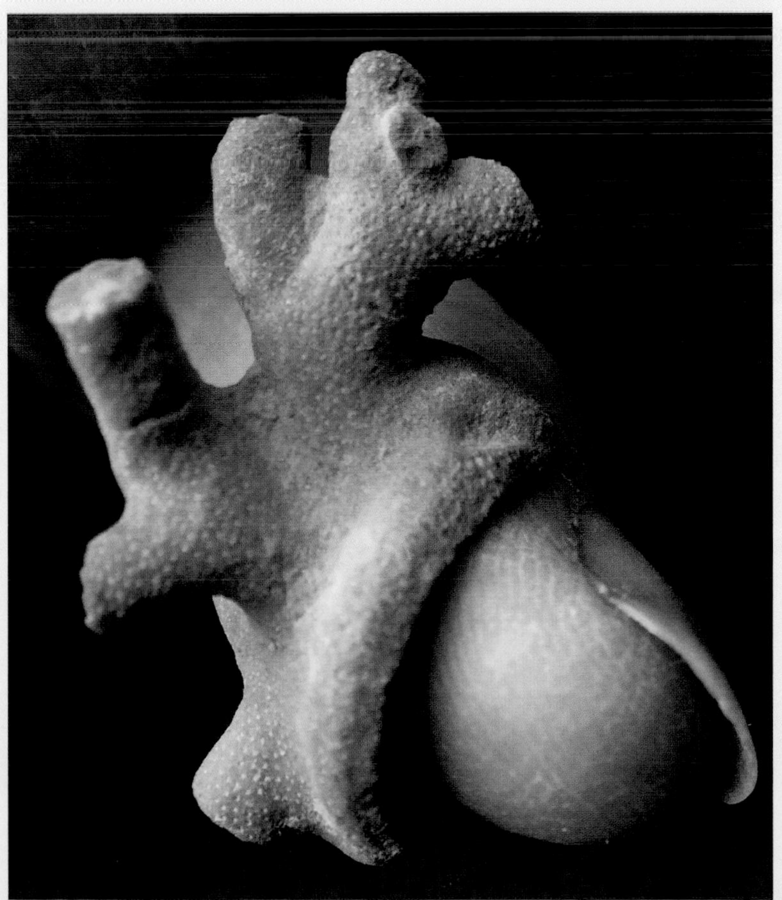

Foreword

The world of the Paleozoic Era was a very different one from that of today! Sediments, seemingly in violation of uniformitarianism, accumulated in a manner significantly different from that of today. Vast, epicontinental seas, in which these sediments were deposited, covered major portions of regions of continental crust. These epicontinental seas were extremely shallow. They do not exist today in anywhere close to the extent that they did in the Paleozoic (seaways covering major parts of continents during the Cretaceous, being a possible exception). What appears to have been responsible for these different conditions? During the Paleozoic, the Earth was (probably) much smaller than it is today. It was mostly covered by continental crust (felsic crust) and, after the Paleozoic, it "cracked" and expanded, the "cracks evolving, with sea floor spreading, into the modern deep seas of today.

Introduction

Ancient=(Paleo), life=(zoic)

Decades of successful space exploration by NASA, with more to come, have pretty well established a lack of evidence for life in the solar system other than of the earth (however the "oceans" of Titan do offer a minuscule chance of some weird form of life and microbes might yet be found on Mars). The development and evolution of the biosphere on the earth appears otherwise to be it for the solar system, and this extremely interesting phenomena has been recorded beautifully by fossils found in the rocks of planet Earth. Often these are both abundant and attractive, offering a natural collectable that has both aesthetics and educational value. It's in this light that this book is presented, as an overview of that part of geologic time when fossils are abundant and highly diversified, yet remote enough in geologic time to offer what in many ways really was "another world."

The Paleozoic Era— A World Before Dinosaurs

This is the author's second book on those fossils found in the "hard rocks" of the Paleozoic Era. Representing the earliest portion of a "clear" animal fossil record, Paleozoic fossils initiate the record of animals with hard parts as well as that of undoubted plants. The fossil record prior to the Paleozoic Era is predominantly one of monerans (in the form of stromatolites and associated microfossils) and in the late Precambrian, one of small eukaryotes and the peculiar and baffling Ediacarian fossils.

Much of the Paleozoic fossil record consists of marine organisms—animals like corals, arthropods, mollusks, and echinoderms. Many of these animals suddenly come onto the scene in the Cambrian Period. These fossils appeared with well mineralized exoskeletons. They were organisms that were capable of leaving a clear and distinct fossil record. The early Paleozoic fossil record of plants is not as clear as is that of animals. Non-vascular plants, such as mosses and liverworts, are presumed to have been living early in the Paleozoic Era; however, the fossil record of these plants is poor and limited. With the rise of vascular plants, with their stems and leaves—containing cellulose—the fossil record becomes much better in that kingdom. This appears to have happened during the Silurian Period but really takes off in the Devonian.

Paleozoic Animals

When one probes Paleozoic rocks for fossils, some distinct facts begin to emerge. One of these is that, although many marine rocks deposited during the Paleozoic Era contain fossils, those present are often small and broken up. Only occasionally does the collectable, nice, complete, larger "eye candy" specimen come along. Another observation is that (generally), the earlier in the Paleozoic one goes, the harder it is to find fossils. Nature seems to guard her paleontological treasures effectively and puts up numerous natural barriers to the collector. Another observation is that the earliest animal fossils of the Paleozoic Era are somewhat peculiar. Peculiar not only as to the organisms represented as fossils themselves, but also the manner in which they occur in the rocks. The author was made aware of this at an early age when he found that as you go south of St. Louis, Missouri, the rocks get progressively older and their fossils become less obvious. With this "going-backward-through-time," he especially wanted to get acquainted with the oldest rocks and their fossil content, rocks containing fossils belonging to the Cambrian Period. The author's first oldest-fossil-bearing-rock experience was encountered at a Boy Scout camp in the early 1950s. It took some real effort however to find some of these fossils, as nature has really concealed them.

The Cambrian is the first (and earliest) period of the Paleozoic Era. Worldwide, the Paleozoic represents the oldest rocks containing (relatively) abundant fossils—especially those of animals containing hard parts. Some of the body plans (phyla) of these early fossils appear odd, while others, in contrast, are similar to marine animals living today. What are usually found, and what occur most frequently, are fossils representative of living phyla, but displaying odd, archaic aspects.

Cambrian fossils and the organisms they represent can really be puzzling at times. Puzzling like the archeocyathids, one of the subjects of the next chapter. Probably the best preserved and now the most extensively studied fossil faunas of the Cambrian are those of the Burgess Shale of Canada and closely following these are fossils of the related Lower Cambrian Chengjiang fauna of China. In both of these occurrences, soft tissues of the organisms are represented, preserved either as a film of graphite (Burgess Shale) or as colored mineralized layers (Chengjiang biota or fauna). How these often peculiar animals relate to modern animals is intensely argued among paleontologists. Their arguments center around whether Cambrian fossils represent extinct life forms that still fit into modern phyla or whether they represent "evolutionary experiments" of which no representatives exist today.

Older strata of "Pre-Cambrian" age, by contrast, lack evidence of the ancestors of these phyla. Animals just seem to appear mysteriously, all at once, at the beginning of the Cambrian Period. This is a phenomenon found to be world wide. Charles Darwin, in his 1859 *Origin of Species*, had some interesting things to say about it, even at that time.

This puzzle of the lack of predecessors of Cambrian organisms and its seemingly well developed animals remain an enigma to this day.

The Cambrian Radiation Event

The animals shown in this text as fossils suddenly appear in strata that reflect what is widely known as the Cambrian Radiation Event. Ever since the fossil record has been seriously investigated, it has been known that many major body plans of animals (phyla) suddenly appear for the first time, in strata of Cambrian age.

Eon	Era	Period	Age my.
PHANEROZOIC	Cenozoic		0
		Tertiary	67
	Mesozoic	Cretaceous	
		Jurassic	
		Triassic	235
	Paleozoic	Permian	280
		Pennsylvanian	
		Mississippian	300
			320
		Silurian	350
		Ordovician	440
			500
			542
Precambrian ↓			

Geologic Time Scale. The Paleozoic Era extends from the Cambrian to the Permian periods.

Typical fossiliferous, slabby Paleozoic limestone interbedded with thin shale layers. The limestone slabs are covered with fossils, including brachiopods, bryozoans, crinoid, and trilobite fragments. Such fossil-rich strata first appears in the Cambrian. There are few older than Cambrian occurrences suggestive of this sudden appearance of fossils. This phenomena greatly puzzled Charles Darwin, who said it was sufficient reason to question his hypothesis (natural selection and evolution). The phenomena is still puzzling today, although earlier fossils are now well known. However, they do not appear to be related to the animals found as fossils in the Cambrian Period and those of the GODE (Great Ordovician Diversification Event), whose shells and other hard parts crowd these beds in southeastern Indiana.

Paleozoic Rock Strata of the Grand Canyon

An impressive sequence of Paleozoic strata exists in the Grand Canyon of Arizona. Strata representative of two geologic periods of the Paleozoic (the Ordovician and Silurian) are totally absent from the canyon, but otherwise the sequence of Paleozoic strata exposed in its walls is impressive.

Paleozoic strata in the Grand Canyon: The lower (inner gorge) of the canyon is cut into Precambrian rocks. These are rocks predating the Cambrian, the oldest period of the Paleozoic Era. In the foreground can be seen Cambrian age strata; in the distance are strata of the late Paleozoic, that is strata from the Mississippian, Pennsylvanian, and Permian periods. (Permian rim rock, the Kaibab limestone, is in the distance to the right.)

Paleozoic Formations exposed in the walls of the Grand Canyon: Few places on earth exhibit strata representative of **such a large part of geologic time** in one place as does the Grand Canyon. Names like Bright Angel Shale, Muav Limestone, Redwall Limestone, and Supai Sandstone are names given to what geologists call formations. Each formation consists of rock types with a similar appearance and which may contain diagnostic fossils as well. In other words, a formation name represents a "handle" by which geologists can recognize and communicate regarding thick sequences of sedimentary rocks.

Precambrian rock near the bottom of the Grand Canyon: These rocks occur **underneath** the thousands of feet of Paleozoic rock making up the upper half of the canyon.

Paleozoic Strata Exposed in Locations Other Than the Grand Canyon

A large portion of North America is underlain by Paleozoic rock strata, some of which contains well preserved fossils.

Different types of rock make up different types of topography. The Redwall Limestone forms steep cliffs. The Bright Angel Shale in contrast forms gentle slopes including a "wide bench" midway down into the canyon and known as the Tonto Platform. Part of the Tonto Platform can be seen in the foreground.

Shale of lowermost (oldest) Cambrian age. The earliest portion of the Paleozoic Era is represented by this strata in the southern part of the Appalachian Mountains. This strata contains some of the earliest trace fossils and trilobites—trilobites being life forms strictly characteristic of the Paleozoic Era. This Cambrian age strata is a few million years older than Cambrian strata of the Grand Canyon. A "complete" geologic rock column doesn't exist at any one place, but rather is a compilation of strata from many localities.

Section of the upper portion of the Grand Canyon, with various rock formations identified. The Kiabab Limestone forms the rim of the canyon, younger rocks of the Mesozoic Era at one time existed here above the Kiabab Limestone, but have long been eroded away.

Conglomerate in the Missouri Ozarks which is essentially of the same age as the shale shown in the previous photo. This conglomerate is from gravel and cobbles deposited in a valley during the latest Precambrian and earliest Cambrian. Such coarse sediment like this, deposited over 500 million years ago would contain no fossils this far back into the geologic past. If it was geologically younger, it might contain fossil wood impressions from land plants, but half a billion years ago there was no known land life.

Coconino Sandstone: This Permian age rock sequence is believed to be a dune deposited sandstone. Unlike strata above and below it (which were deposited in shallow epicontinental seaways), the Coconino Sandstone is non-marine. This information is known partially by the presence of fossils (tracks of land animals) which are found in these rock layers.

Tilted-on-end Cambrian strata in the southern Appalachian Mountains: Tectonic activity that formed the mountains tilted this strata at a high angle. The beds of crumpled shale, which crop out along the Coosa River in Alabama, contain Middle Cambrian trilobites (actually along Weiss Reservoir on the Coosa in northern Alabama).

Collecting fossil graptolites from Upper Cambrian strata near Afton, southern Minnesota. These strictly Paleozoic life forms occur in abundance here in one layer of Cambrian siltstone. Fossils other than graptolites are not found at this locality.

Tilted Upper Cambrian strata at the Cedar Bluff trilobite locality, now covered by the water of Weiss Reservoir. These crumpled shale layers yielded a variety of Upper Cambrian trilobites before being covered by the lake. The white beds are thick layers of the mineral calcite.

Fossiliferous (fossil bearing) layers of siltstone at the previous locality in Minnesota.

Soft Cambrian sandstone beds exposed along bluffs of the St. Croix River in eastern Minnesota. These beds contain trilobites (usually fragmentary), mollusks (monoplacophorans and gastropods), and primitive (inarticulate) brachiopods.

Rubbly Middle Ordovician limestone (Plattin Formation) exposed in a quarry face. On fresh rock like this, it is often difficult to see fossils if they are present. When limestone weathers for a few years, the fossils become more noticeable.

Slabby, fossiliferous Middle Ordovician limestone beds with shale layers. Beds like this can be crowded with fossils, especially brachiopods and bryozoans. These layers were exposed in a barrow-pit south of St. Louis in 1965.

Upper Ordovician strata of the same type and age as shown in previous photo, but exposed here in a road cut in central Kentucky.

Similar slabby, fossiliferous layers of limestone and shale (Decorah Formation) as shown above.

Slabby Upper Ordovician limestone (Cincinnatian) exposed in a road cut in southern Indiana. The person looking at the camera is Dorothy Echols, a paleontologist on the faculty of Washington University from the late 1940s through the 1980s.

Slabby Upper Ordovician limestones, the surfaces of which are covered with large numbers of fossil brachiopods. Clifty Creek, southern Indiana.

Lowermost Silurian strata exposed along the Mississippi River near Cape Girardeau, Missouri. Locally, these outcrops can contain zones of crinoids and starfish, but these are difficult to find.

Silurian dolomite (or dolostone) exposed in a quarry in Illinois. Access to such quarries once was not a problem; however, more recent concerns for landowner liability have closed many of them (as well as other lands) formerly available for fossil collecting.

Silurian dolomite exposed in a road material quarry in central Manitoba. Dolomites locally can contain nice fossils. The loose rock at the base of the quarry face might yield fossils; however, loose boulders in the upper portion of the face could make this a hazardous place to look, unless one keeps a watch for falling rocks. Many of the upper face rocks shown here are loose and ready to fall.

Upper Silurian and Lower Devonian strata exposed along the Ohio River at "Falls of the Ohio," near Louisville, Kentucky.

Middle Devonian strata exposed in the Brooks Range of Alaska: Fossil corals and brachiopods are locally abundant here. These strata have been tilted by orogenic (mountain building) forces within fairly recent geologic time. Originally these rocks, like most of the Paleozoic strata shown here, were deposited in warm, shallow seas.

Middle Devonian strata near Arkona, Ontario: Brachiopods, trilobites, and corals are the most commonly found fossils in these beds of shale and slabby limestone.

Lower Mississippian slabby limestone exposed in a recent excavation (2010). Fossils on the slabs become more obvious as the slabs are exposed to weathering.

Lower and Middle Mississippian limestone exposed in a quarry face: Fossils in a vertical face are difficult to see and collect. If this rock was along a stream and allowed to weather, fossils present on the horizontal surfaces (bedding planes) would be more obvious and accessible.

Upper Mississippian (Chesterian) limestone and shale exposed in a road cut in the southern Ozarks near Leslie, Arkansas. Alternating beds of limestone and shale can have fossils on the surfaces (bedding planes) of the limestone slabs. Rock dumped to the left as fill material when the road cut was made might be a better place to search for fossils as weathered slabs are often present.

Pennsylvanian limestone exposed along the Grand River in Missouri. River-outcrops like this can be excellent places to find and collect fossils. Numerous outcrops like this often occur along rivers and weathering along a river can bring out the fossils in a superior manner. Such outcrops are often difficult to get to, however, without the use of a small boat like a canoe or kayak.

Vendozoans

Early in the twentieth century some peculiar fossils, presumed to be Cambrian in age (as they came from strata near the bottom of the local "stack") were found and described from German Southwest Africa (now Namibia). Similar fossils were found in eastern Australia's Flinders Range in the late 1940s and a little later in England. In both instances these fossils, although different from other undoubted Cambrian ones, were still considered as **Cambrian in age** and at first they were of only minor concern to paleontology. In the 1960s, additional fossils were found in the Flinders Range of northeastern Australia and these were demonstrated to be older than the Cambrian. The strata in which they were found was overlain by that of Cambrian age, strata containing archeocyathids. Archeocyathids (covered in the next chapter) represent a type of fossil found worldwide near the bottom of Cambrian strata. Shortly after these finds surfaced, similar vendozoan fossils were found in Newfoundland. These vendozoans were without question of Precambrian age. Not only did the strata in which they occur lie well below that yielding Cambrian fossils, but a profound **unconformity** separated Cambrian beds from the older strata containing the vendozoans. These Newfoundland fossils were also similar to those previously found in England in the 1950s. These finds made paleontologists realize that what were found were from soft bodied but tough, leathery-like organisms which lived in abundance **prior to the Cambrian Period**. These tough, leathery-like organisms seemed to have nothing in common with either the "shelled" organisms of the Cambrian or with the soft, fleshy, and delicate organisms preserved in the Burgess shale. Interpretations as to just what these late Precambrian fossils are (now known as vendozoans or as the Ediacarian Biota) is still hotly debated.

Precambrian strata (rocks formed before the Cambrian) in the Lake Superior region. These ferruginous (iron bearing) layers of fine sandstone are characteristic of many Precambrian sedimentary rocks. Thin bedded strata like this of Paleozoic age might be expected to produce either fossil tracks or trails (trace fossils) or even impressions of marine animals. This strata, being about a billion years old, lacks fossils, as do most Precambrian rock layers, except for fossil stromatolites.

Late Precambrian strata (Ochoee Series) in the southern Appalachians: Younger than strata in the above photo, these black carbon-rich shales also lack fossils. The Ochoee Series is some 700 million years old, similar strata 600 million years old in North Carolina do yield fossils known as vendozoans, which come from what is now referred to as the Ediacarian Stage of the latest Proterozoic (Late Precambrian).

Vendozoans on bedding planes of meta-mudstones of Ediacarian age. Mistaken Point, Cape Race, Newfoundland. Vendozoans were soft bodied (leather-like) organisms that lived in the late Precambrian; most appear to have gone extinct before the Cambrian Period of the Paleozoic Era.

Impression of a vendozoan from Ediacarian strata of the Ediacarian Hills of the Flinders Range, Australia.

Stromatolite: A type of trace fossil produced by the life activities of cyanobacteria. Stromatolites are the oldest known fossils.

The Author and Paleozoic Fossils

Most of this book deals with fossils recovered as a consequence of the author's ramblings over Paleozoic terrain in his native Missouri—a state in the fossil-rich US Midwest that has strata representative of all of the periods of the Paleozoic Era (although the Permian is weakly represented). These ramblings led to the exploration of a range of exposed geologic strata, including examinations of road cuts, quarries, and other cuttings exposed as a consequence of land development. Geologic ramblings also were done by traversing many of the Midwest's waterways by canoe, including sponsoring expeditions of the Outdoor Club at Florissant Valley Community College, where the author often lead multi-day "expeditions."

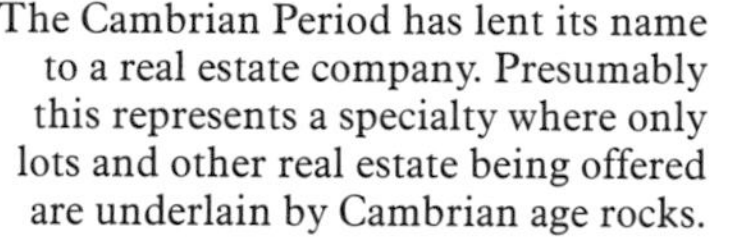

The Cambrian Period has lent its name to a real estate company. Presumably this represents a specialty where only lots and other real estate being offered are underlain by Cambrian age rocks.

These expeditions traversed many of the beautiful Ozark waterways, which unfold what otherwise are almost inaccessible outcrops of Cambrian and Lower Ordovician strata. Many of these outcrops were never before seen or examined by a geologist. As a consequence of this, the rich "fossil treasure trove" of the Cambrian radiation event was tapped into, as was that of the Lower Ordovician and its rather unique molluscan faunas characteristic of the Ozark Uplift.

Fossils, Fossil Collecting, and the Law

Concern over some of the issues and legalities discussed here in the past would have appeared to be almost nonsensical—fossils are part of the natural environment and that is (or was) open to all. Increased concerns for legalities and (seemingly) more emphasis upon a "letter of the law" mindset have made legal issues with regard to fossils and fossil collecting a serious consideration.

Regarding fossils found on private land, the matter is pretty clear. One needs to get permission from the landowner to collect them! With public land however, a much more "sticky wicket" situation has developed. Part of this is a consequence of increased population and other demographics. Another, however, appears to be a consequence of ignorance regarding the difference between **archeology** and **paleontology**. Beside the fact that archeologists deal with phenomena relative to humans, the public is often unaware (along with land managers involved in protecting the publics interest in this land) of differences in the magnitudes of time represented by these two entirely different fields of science (but often "lumped" together by the public). Archeology deals with time spans that are (at most) a few millions of years, being the study of the artifactual record of human activity. Where archeology (and related human paleontology) begins is controversial and depends both on how you define what is a human and whether specific fossils can be considered as humanity's ancestors—the time span involved (at most) being some six million years! Paleontology (and the fossils studied by paleontologists), on the other hand, extend back to **3.5 billion years**. Fossil remains of humans (hominids) are rare; they deserve protection and all (or at least most) of those found should go to science and museums or other suitable institutions. Many fossils, on the other hand, are common. Whole beds of rock can be composed of them. Fossils also occur over a much larger area than do ancient human-related phenomena.

Trilobite: This animal, an extinct member of the phylum arthropoda, is representative of the Paleozoic Era. Trilobites of various kinds lived throughout the Paleozoic Era—distinct genera and families of them being typical of each period of the Paleozoic (this one is characteristic of the Devonian). The last trilobites lived during the Permian Period and at its end these little "bugs" finally went extinct.

Brachiopod: Brachiopods were the dominant shelled animals of Paleozoic seas. Most went extinct at the end of the Permian, but some survived and still live today. Brachiopods, however, never regained the prominence they had during the Paleozoic.

Late Permian Kiabab Limestone forming the rim of the Grand Canyon.

Late Paleozoic strata spectacularly exposed in the canyon of the San Juan River, upstream from the Grand Canyon. The Permian is the last period of the Paleozoic Era. Most of the life represented by Permian fossils went extinct at the end of the Permian Period (c. 235 million years ago)—the worlds most profound extinction event.

Fossil Collecting on Public Land

In the US, the Archeological Resource Preservation Act of 1977 created problems involving fossils. These problems often arose with land managers, who were concerned that they might be challenged if they made a distinction between artifacts and fossils by permitting fossil (and rock and mineral) collecting. The 2010 Paleontological Resources Act, a public law pushed through by the SVP (Society for Vertebrate Paleontology) and (presumably) specifically referring to vertebrate fossils, is probably going to cause even more problems than those created by the Archeological Act. These problems may place a very effective teaching tool off limits to the interested public. Distinguishing a vertebrate fossil from an invertebrate can sometimes be difficult, even for paleontologists. For example, do graptolites (hemichordates) fall under the law as vertebrates? The common confusion of the stems of crinoids (invertebrates) with fish bones (vertebrates) is also an example. The "problem" regarding fossil collecting on public land was first addressed in the early 1990s by a committee of "stakeholders," which met under the auspices of the National Academy of Sciences (NAS), a group serving to provide Congress with decisions regarding technical and scientific matters. Most of the concerned stake holders (representatives of paleontological societies, academia, fossil dealers, and "rockhounds") agreed that existing policies that had evolved regarding paleontologic collecting on public lands were adequate and functioned well. In other words, if it ain't broke, don't "fix" it. Under this policy, the prime custodians of fossil bearing public land, the US Forest Service and the Bureau of Land Management (BLM), allowed reasonable numbers of invertebrate and plant fossils to be collected non-commercially. Fossil vertebrates, especially large ones like dinosaurs, were not! Stake holders involved in the final decisions included representatives of the Paleontological Society, other organizations representing various rockhound groups and paleontologists from federal agencies such as the US Geological Survey and the Society for Vertebrate Paleontology (SVP). Except for the latter, all other stakeholders agreed that no change of rules regarding the publics fossil collecting interests needed to be changed. The SVP, however, proceeded to push for actual legislation (rather than a general policy agreed upon by land managing authorities) to protect vertebrate fossils with a law similar to the 1977 Archeology Resources Protection Act. Introducing various bills into Congress in the late 1990s and early 2000s, they finally succeeded with the Paleontological Resource Protection Act of 2010, as part of an omnibus bill regarding public lands. In its title it specifies vertebrate fossils, but in the body of the bill this distinction is vague. As is the case with much legislation, final interpretation of the law will ultimately depend upon the courts. Currently many persons, including the author, are hesitant to geologize on federal land in the manner previously done as they don't want to be the first person(s) charged under the new federal law—especially when the distinction between vertebrate and invertebrate fossils can be so tricky.

Wonderful Life: A 1998 book by Steven J. Gould on the Cambrian Radiation Event and its record as recorded in the Middle Cambrian Burgess Shale of British Columbia, Canada. The Burgess Shale was discovered by American paleontologist C. D. Walcott and was one of the earliest discovered Cambrian paleontologic windows on this significant time period in earth's geologic history.

The Chengjiang Biota: This is a Lower Cambrian soft-bodied fauna quite similar to the Middle Cambrian Burgess Shale of British Columbia, Canada. The Cambrian radiation event ("explosion") saw the beginning of many animal phyla. Both Chengjiang and Burgess Shale fossils represent this event with a greater degree of fidelity than do most other Cambrian strata. This is because not only are animals with a hard exoskeleton found but those with rarely preserved soft bodies were also represented. This fauna and the Burgess Shale are referred to as paleontological windows in that they give a more unbiased look at this sudden "flowering" of animal life.

The problems of both archeology and vertebrate paleontology preventing access to fossils is also a common one in many other parts of the world, sometimes to the effect (as in South Africa) of making possession of **all fossils** (in the context of a collection) illegal and a serious crime. Besides being basically unfair (especially when considering the public's access to other natural phenomena on public land like fish and game), such bans on fossil collecting places an excellent "hands on" teaching resource off limits. When this happens, science also loses an opportunity to gain specimens, a few of which might be scientifically important. After all, its been said (John Pojeta, during 1993 NAS discussions) that the "more eyes looking for fossils, the better for science." An exclusive, legalistic approach to this resource is a no-win proposition for essentially all, except perhaps to those with a penchant for control.

Fossil Collecting and the Paleontological Community

The author became interested in fossils as a child in the 1950s. During the 1950s and '60s, he developed an expertise in collecting Paleozoic fossils, primarily those found in Missouri and Illinois, to which he had access. A major opportunity to expand the scope and diversity of specimens in his collection came from contacts made with the late Allen Graffham of Geological Enterprises in Ardmore, Oklahoma. Exchanges of locally collected (US) Midwestern fossils for those from other parts of the globe allowed for expansion of his collection to an international level. At this time a spirit of community of both academics and amateurs pretty much prevailed in the "fossil world." Geological Enterprises exchanged and sold fossil specimens throughout the fossil community, which to a major extent included academics.

Rock and fossil fairs: A variety of fossils show up at fairs like this (MAPS EXPO, 2011). Fossils from all over the world show up at such fairs, as well as ones collected previously, like these in ironstone nodules from the famous Mazon Creek fossil beds of northern Illinois.

Mazon Creek ironstone nodules for sale at MAPS EXPO, containing a variety of fossils (mostly plants).

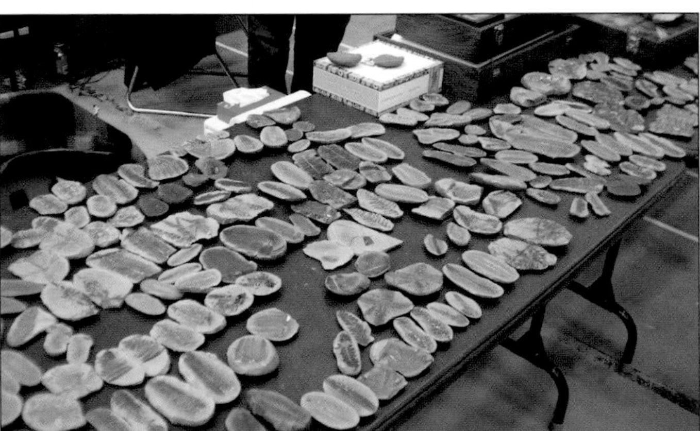

Large numbers of Late Paleozoic fossils in ironstone concretions have been collected from what is known as the "Mazon Creek" locality. These show up frequently at rock and fossil fairs like these fossil plants. Animal fossils in these ironstone nodules generally are rare.

Today, commercial activity in paleontology is often condemned by some in the academic community as not being "scientifically or politically correct." As a consequence, a wedge has been driven between fossil dealers (and sometimes collectors) and the academic community, or at least some parts of it. A specific policy of Geologic Enterprises was that, if a fossil they had was either new to science or had significant scientific value—showing something significantly better than that previously known—it went to science. In other words, **science always came first.** Today many fossil dealers (and some collectors) appear to be overly concerned with the monetary aspects of fossils and some paleontologists also appear to have contempt for collectors. This is a situation that has helped to "drive the wedge" deeper.

Use of This Book and the Internet

Paleontology, and the taxonomy accompanying it, offers a system highly compatible with computers and the Internet. Many taxa included in this work (like paracrinoids) are normally not found in most non-technical works on fossils. A person desirous of additional information on a particular fossil included here can use one of the search engines (like Google) and get a considerable amount of additional information on the desired taxa. This applies to both "high level" taxa, like classes, as well as to the genera mentioned here.

The Internet is a real boon to paleontology!

Value Guide

The uninformed, who see monetary values placed upon fossils that—if you put in the right kind of effort into the process—you can find for yourself, may be attracted to them as a perceived source of easy money. Nothing could be farther from the truth! What has to be considered is a fossils completeness, rarity, and appearance. Fossils can be common. Whole layers of rock can be entirely composed of them. However, these plentiful fossils usually have little or no collector's value. What also has to be considered is the effort and time invested in the preparation of a fossil, which includes removing it from the rock in which it is embedded, polishing, stabilizing, and other time-consuming tasks that are often necessary.

Most fossils also don't look like much when found in the field, Paleozoic fossils especially. They have to be extracted from the enclosing rock, which often can be hard and difficult to do. Others have to be painstakingly cleaned using manual methods or technological devices—such as pneumatic chisels, and air abrasive machines—or by acids or other chemical techniques. Fossil preparation technologies are extensive and the preparation of fossils is a field onto itself. It should be pointed out that most of the specimens in this book fall into the E through G value ranges **after preparation,** which is often time consuming. **Serious work with fossils generally is a labor of love!**

Value range for fossils illustrated in this book.

A $1,000-$2,000
B $500-$1,000
C $250-$500
D $100-$250
E $50-$100
F $25-$50
G $10-$25
H $1-$10

Glossary

Body Fossils: The shell, carapace, bones or other "hard parts" of an animal preserved as a fossil either as an impression, mold or original material. In contrast to **trace fossils.**

Cambrian radiation event: That point in geologic time when fossils become obvious in rocks. This is marked by the seemingly **sudden appearance of animals** with hard parts, such as trilobites, brachiopods, and mollusks. At the same point in geologic time trace fossils (tracks and trails) also become common so this appearance is not just a function of the development of hard parts (which make it easier to form fossils) as trace fossils can be made as easily by an animal lacking hard parts as with those having them. This sudden richness of both trace and body fossils marks the beginning of the Cambrian Period.

Eukaryotes: Life forms made up of cells having a cell nucleus. This is in contrast to **prokaryotes** (Monerans), which are (usually single celled) primitive life forms lacking a cell nucleus.

Lagerstatte (*Conservatat-Lagerstatte*): An area or layer of strata preserving soft parts of fossils not normally preserved. These exceptional fossil beds are also referred to as paleontological "windows."

Monerans: Single-celled organisms (like bacteria and cyanobacteria) lacking a cell nucleus, which are considered much more primitive life forms than are eukaryotes, which have a cell nucleus. Monerans comprised all life on the earth until some 800 million years ago when microbes with a eukaryotic cell nucleus appeared.

Sea Floor Spreading: The concept, now widely accepted and a significant part of plate tectonics, notes that new oceanic crust is formed at mid-oceanic ridges (spreading centers) and that the ocean floor moves, conveyer-belt-fashion, over the underlying mantle to accommodate this spreading.

Stromatolites: Cabbage-like structures formed by the life activities of monerans, especially the cyanobacteria (blue-green algae). Stromatolites represent the oldest fossils, some going back as far into the Precambrian as 3.5 billion years. Stromatolites indicate that life is a very ancient phenomena on the earth! Life appears to have appeared on the planet as early as it possibly could—earth's environment prior to life was a time of intense meteoroid bombardment accompanied by the presence of a magma ocean. A long period of geologic time (almost three billion years) separates the earliest stromatolites from the beginning of the Cambrian. This vast span of time being known as the **Precambrian**. Precambrian rocks, however, until the Paleozoic, yield few other fossils than these "stroms." Stromatolites were still common in shallow waters of the Cambrian and the Lower Ordovician (Ozarkian), after which they became much less common.

Trace Fossils: Tracks, trails, track-ways, and burrows made by organisms interacting with sediment and now preserved as fossils. Unlike body fossils, bias toward an organisms having hard parts is **not** a factor with trace fossils.

Unconformity: A major break in a sequence of strata indicating the passage of a long period of geologic time **when no geologic record was formed**. An unconformity represents a hiatus in a sequence of strata. In this chapter it is mentioned in reference to the hiatus in strata separating vendozoan bearing strata from that of Cambrian age. A major unconformity is also mentioned in the Grand Canyon where Precambrian rocks are separated from those of the Paleozoic era by a major period of erosion and non-deposition of strata.

Uniformitarianism: "The present is the key to the past." A logical underlying concept in natural history involving long time periods when the fundamental workings of the earth, like erosion and weathering, worked about the same as they do today. Uniformitarianism is essentially an embodiment of the concept of the laws of physics and chemistry being consistent over long periods of time.

"Mazon Creek" locality, with its fossil bearing ironstone nodules, 1960. Spoil piles like this from coal strip-mining occurred over large portions of Grundy and Will Counties, Illinois. Fossil bearing plant and animal bearing concretions washed out from these shale piles as they weathered. Spoil piles in the Braidwood area are known for their fossil plants (and non-marine coal-swamp animals). Those further east (pit 11 of the Essex area) are known for their marine animals. Both sites are considered to be among the world's major paleontological windows.

Bibliography

Fedonkin, Mikhail A., James G. Gehling, Kathleen Grey, Guy M. Narbonne, and Patricia Vickers-Rich. 2007. *The Rise of Animals—Evolution and Diversification of the Animal Kingdom.* John Hopkins University Press, Baltimore.

Fortey, Richard, 1997. *Life, A Natural History of the First Four Billion Years of Life on Earth.* Vintage Books, New York. ISBN 0-375-40119-9 and ISBN 0-375-70261-X. **An excellent and readable account for any one who would like to get into this a bit deeper.**

Ludvigsen, Rolf, 1996. *Life in Stone—A Natural History of British Columbia's Fossils.* University of British Columbia Press, Vancouver. ISBN 0-77480578-1.

"Mazon Creek" (Braidwood flora and fauna) fossiliferous ironstone bearing spoil piles, 1960.

Sponges and Archeocyathids

Foraminifera

Foraminifera are shelled protists, single celled organisms in which the cell has a cell nucleus, as is the case with animals and plants. Protista (or protists) are now considered as being a kingdom of organisms separate from the plant and animal kingdoms. Sponges generally are considered as being very primitive members of the animal kingdom. They offer a "link" between protists and animals.

An especially large fusilinid from the Lower Permian of France. (Value range G)

Fossil foraminifera (Fusilinids): These are the tests (shells) of a single celled organism—that is a fossil protist. For a protist, they are **gigantic**. Fusilinids were a type of foraminifera very abundant in the late Paleozoic (Pennsylvanian and Permian periods). During this time, they were so abundant that they sometimes formed entire layers of limestone. They are also quite useful guides to indexing strata as they evolved (and thus diversified) through the entire Phanerozoic. Permian, Torreon, Mexico.

Pebbles from a Missouri River gravel bar near St. Louis, Missouri, containing fusilinids. These came from upstream outcrops where extensive fusilinid bearing limestone beds are common. (Value range H)

Sponges

Sponges are rather strange organisms! Unlike other animals, sponges have no organs or other specialized tissues. Sponges are animals, but very primitive ones. Placed in their own sub-kingdom, the Parazoa, sponges can be considered as a complex of protists supported or "hung" on a scaffolding made of what are known as spicules. Positioned so that all of the individual "protists" (that is sponge cells) are positioned together allowing the circulation of nutrient bearing water through a complex series of pores and canals. To facilitate this distribution of water and its nutrients through pores and canals, sponges use what are known as flagella (tiny whip-like structures moving in unison—flagella are also a characteristic of protists). These flagella convey water through the sponge's body, which is usually vase, cylinder, branching or spherical in shape.

Sponges appear to represent an evolutionary lineage independent from other marine animals, first becoming abundant, like other invertebrates, in the Cambrian Period. Sponges have changed little in half a billion years. They are a very conservative group!

A vase-shaped fossil sponge from the Middle Ordovician. The elongate troughs are known as canals. They convey nutrient bearing water through the sponge's mass to feed individual sponge cells. (Value range E)

Side view of previously shown sponge.

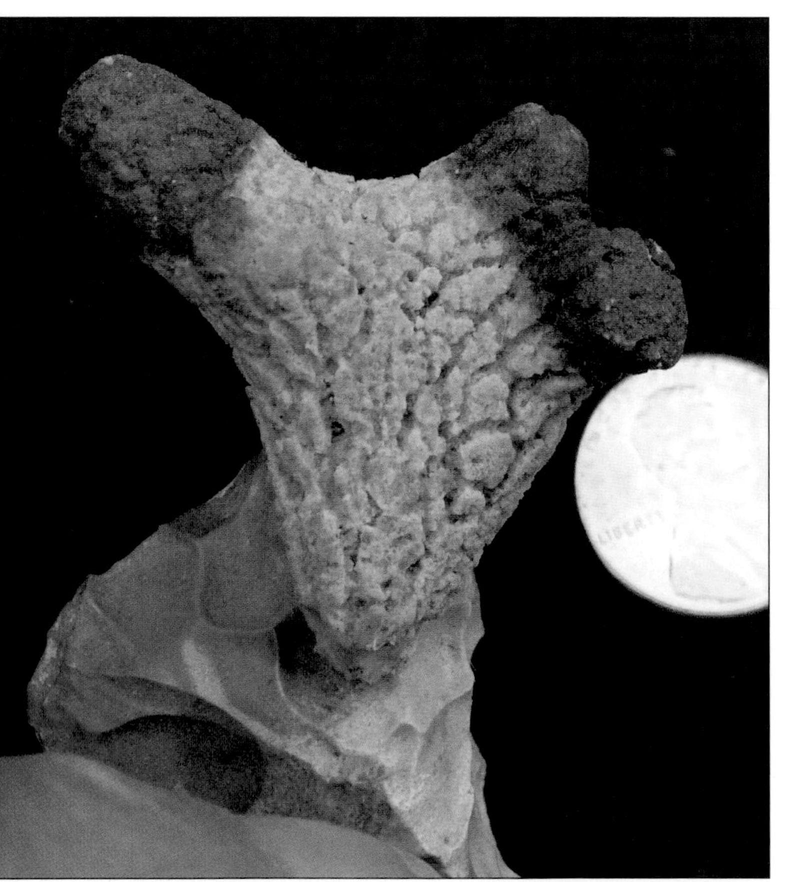

A silicified sponge fossil showing ramifying channels, which carried nutrient bearing water (by means of flagella) through the entire sponge body. Middle Ordovician, Plattin Limestone, Jefferson County, Missouri. (Value range F)

Glass sponge: Middle Devonian, New York. (Value range E)

Sponges can be difficult to spot as fossils. Pores and canals often are not evident—only the vase-shaped form of the sponge being present. Middle Pennsylvanian, Texas. (Value range F)

Archeoscyphia sp. This sponge comes from a zone of them in the Lower Ordovician, Jefferson City Dolomite of southern Missouri. (Value range F)

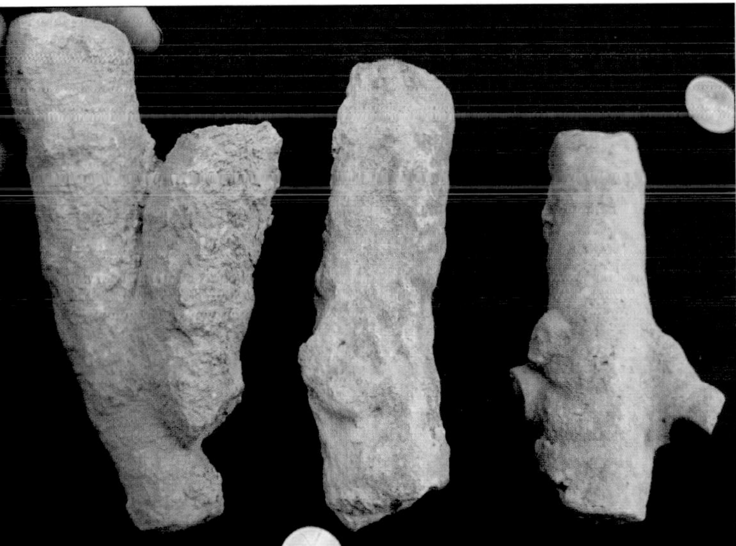

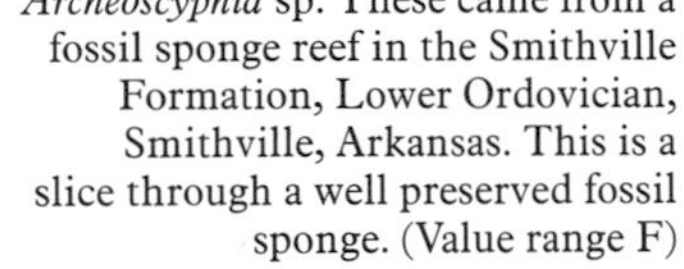

Cylindrical sponges, Lake Bridgeport, Texas. Cylinders are a typical shape of many sponges, both recent and fossil.

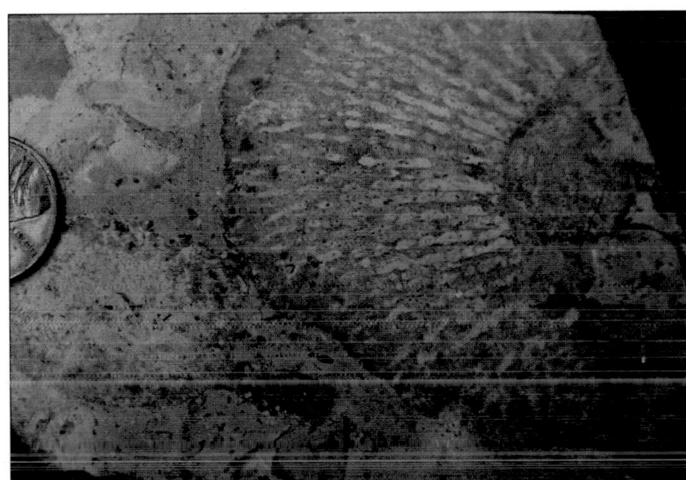

Archeoscyphia sp. Both pores and canals (the latter being the large passageways) show very clearly on these sections of Lower Ordovician sponges from near Smithville, Arkansas. (Value range F)

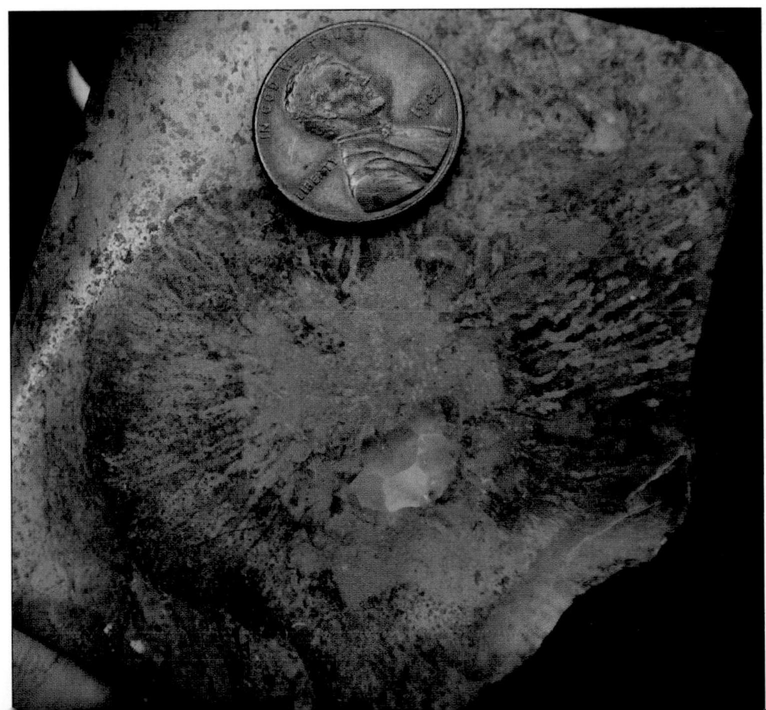

Archeoscyphia sp. These came from a fossil sponge reef in the Smithville Formation, Lower Ordovician, Smithville, Arkansas. This is a slice through a well preserved fossil sponge. (Value range F)

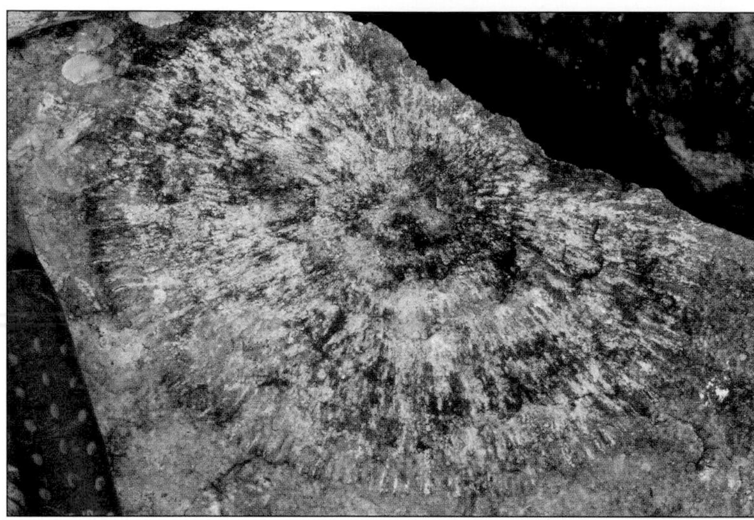

A lithistid sponge on a bedding surface of Chazyan age limestone near Espanola, Ontario. (Handle of rock hammer at bottom left for scale.) This sponge occurs just above Precambrian (Paleoproterozoic) rocks (quartzite).

Sponge bearing outcrop: Paleozoic rocks unconformably, overlie Proterozoic quartzite. (The circular object just below the Ordovician limestone is not a sponge—it's a hubcap!) Outcrop is 20km south of Espanola, Ontario.

Quartzite boulder embedded in sponge bearing limestone in the same outcrop as shown previously. These boulders were ancient when the sponge bearing strata was being deposited. This is a popular geology field trip stop. The white spots on the quartzite boulder were made by impacts of numerous student geology hammers.

Deep Sea Sponges

Fossils are rare in most sedimentary rocks deposited in the open oceans or deep sea environment. This is especially true with Paleozoic deep sea strata, like that found in limited areas of the globe. Sponges can sometimes be found in such Paleozoic rocks, along with fossils of pelagic (floating) life forms such as graptolites.

A carbon film impression of a deep sea sponge from Arkansas. Sponges thrive in shallow water, where most of those found as fossils lived. Sponges, however, are also present on the floor of the deep ocean. This deep sea sponge is preserved as a carbon film somewhat similar to the preservation of fossils found in the famous Burgess Shale, where deep sea fossil sponges also occur.

Tightly folded, deep sea sediments of the Ouachita Mountains of Arkansas, where the above fossil sponge was found. Fossils generally are rare in sediments originating in deep sea environments as these rocks are often metamorphosed and affected by tectonic forces. These tectonic forces were generated when they were incorporated into parts of a continental landmass, as was the case with this sequence of strata. Paleozoic deep sea sediments are also relatively rare—the sequence making up the Ouachita Mountains in Arkansas and eastern Oklahoma being one of the more extensive occurrences.

Stromatoporoids

These puzzling, early Paleozoic fossils were considered for many years to be a type of extinct coral, organisms with which they often are associated. Many stromatoporoids resemble **stromatolites**, those most-ancient-of-fossils produced by communities of cyanobacteria (blue-green algae). Stromatoporoids, however, have a more complex and regular structure than do stromatolites. Structures like astrorhizae and mamelons (star and nipple-shaped protuberances found on the surface of a colony) identify them. Unlike stromatolites, stromatoporoids have never been considered as being non-biogenic, although their taxonomic position has usually been in limbo.

Stromatoporoids come in a variety of forms, the rod-like and peculiar Beatricids being one example. Beatricids are especially characteristic of the Ordovician, being one of the organisms associated with the "Great Ordovician Diversification Event (GODE)," a time of extensive expansion of marine life. Large beatricids are especially characteristic of the Arctic Ordovician fauna of Canada and the western US. This is a fauna associated with sediments deposited in seas that were near the Ordovician equator, which at the time ran through Canada and the northwestern US. Fossils of this fauna are especially noted for their large size.

Stromatolite: **Stromatolites** resemble a category of fossils known as **stromatoporoids,** which belong to a group of sponges known as the sclerosponges. Stromatolites are fossils (biogenic sedimentary structures) produced by the physiological activity of cyanobacteria (also known as blue-green algae). Stromatolites are found in some of the earth's oldest sedimentary rocks! For many decades geologists and paleontologists argued as to whether stromatolites really were produced by organisms as they occur in such ancient rocks. Acceptance of stromatolites as being of biogenic origin means that life is a very ancient phenomena on the earth, a phenomena dating back to at least to 3.5 billion years. Unlike stromatoporoids, stromatolites generally lack any obvious detailed structure that would peg them as organic.

Stromatoporoid with mamelons: Stromatoporoids can be confused with stromatolites. The former commonly have little raised bumps (called mamelons) on their laminae, which are more or less evenly distributed over the surface of the stromatoporoid. Stromatoporoids can also have small star-shaped structures distributed over their surface known as astrorhizae.

Stromatoporoid: Stromatoporoids occur in a manner similar to that of stromatolites, often in reef-like structures. Unlike stromatolites, however, stromatoporoids have always been considered to have been fossil organisms. The phylum to which they belong, however, has been problematic and questioned. Stromatoporoids originally were considered to be related to corals and hence were cidarians (or coelenterates). Today they are recognized as a type of sponge, small living sponges similar to stromatoporoids, having been found in Jamaican sea caves in the 1980s.

Astrorhizae (the small circular structures in the center specimen) on a "nothing fossil:" These peculiar fossils occur associated with stromatolites and sponges and once were considered to be a type of stromatoporoid. Now they are thought to be bryozoans—both bryozoans and stromatoporoids have astrorhizae.

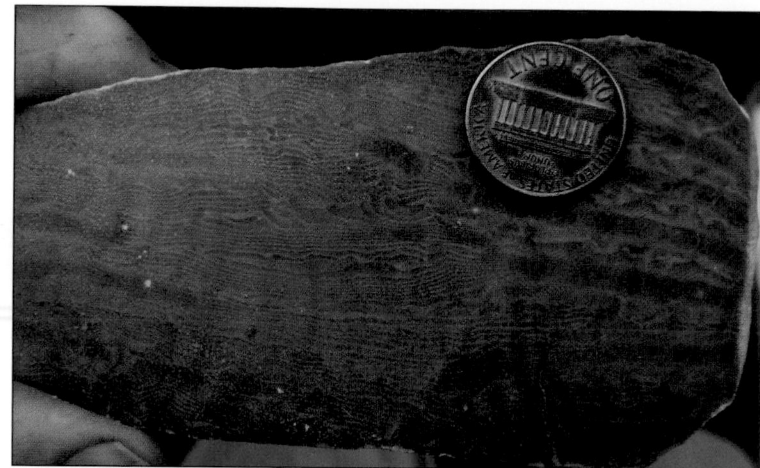

Slice through a stromatoporoid shows a structure formed as a consequence of astrorhizae—stromatolites would lack any such structure. (Value range G).

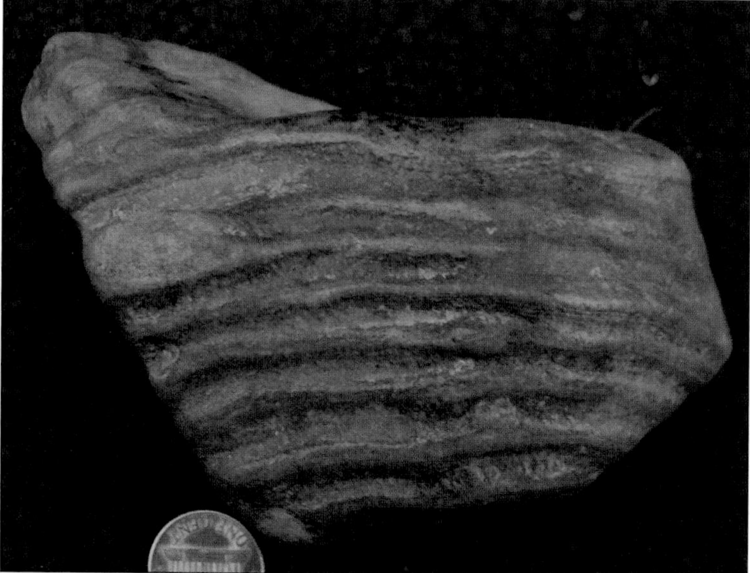

Silicified (replaced by quartz) stromatoporoid found as a glacial erratic. Glacial deposits can contain fossils picked up and carried hundreds of miles by the movement of the glacier. This is a Devonian stromatoporoid, which probably came from Iowa or southern Minnesota, where it was picked up and carried southward by glaciers to the St. Louis, Missouri, area. The regular spacing of layers seen here is more characteristic of a stromatoporoid than it is of a stromatolite. (Value range F)

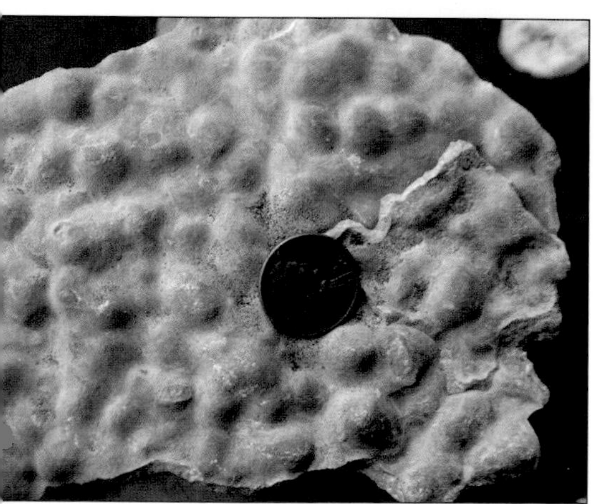

Stromatoporoid surface with large mamelons? Devonian, Iowa City area.

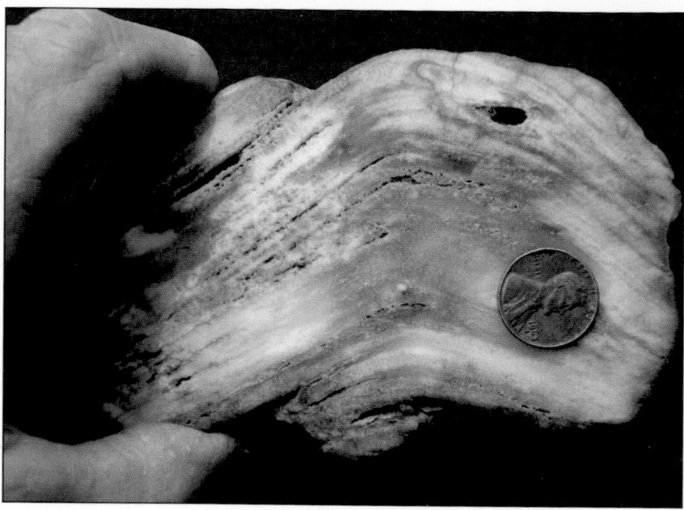

Silicified stromatoporoid found as a glacial erratic in the St. Louis, Missouri, area. Note the radiating structure suggestive of a sponge.

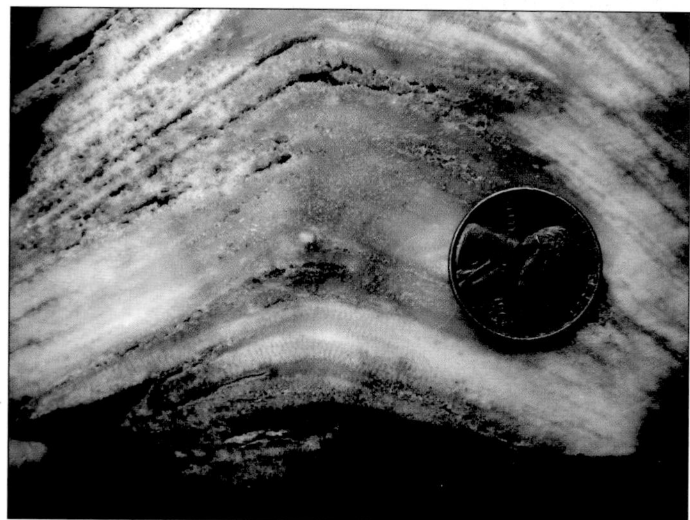

Close-up of silicified stromatoporoid shown in the previous photo.

Silicified stromatoporoids from Silurian strata exposed at the "Falls of the Ohio" near Louisville, Kentucky. These fossils came from the collection of Dr. L. P. Yandell of Louisville, Kentucky, where he collected them in the mid-nineteenth century. Dr. Yandell was a physician, paleontologist, and fossil collector in the nineteenth century who gave his collection to the St. Louis Academy of Science. Stromatoporoids at "Falls of the Ohio" occur with corals, a frequent phenomena in many areas. This is one of the reasons they were considered as a type of coral until recently.

Another silicified stromatoporoid from Silurian strata of the Louisville, Kentucky, area in the Yandell Collection, St. Louis Science Center.

Beatricid: These relatives to stromatoporoids are especially characteristic of the Upper Ordovician of Canada, especially in what is known as the Canadian Arctic fauna. These specimens came from Upper Ordovician strata of Anticosti Island, Quebec. *Courtesy of Peter Groux.* (Value range F)

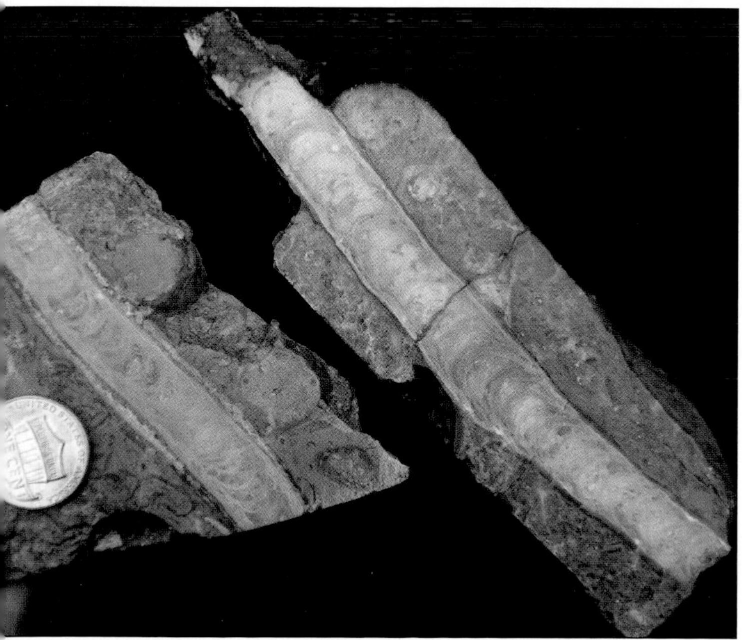

Labecia sp. Beatricids from the Middle Ordovician Plattin Limestone of Missouri. (Value range F)

Archeocyathids

Cambrian fossils can often be puzzling! Their puzzling or problematic nature appears to be a consequence of evolutionary serendipity, evolution having taken many different pathways, only some of which have survived over long time periods to become the phyla and classes of today. Intermediate forms that lived during the Cambrian often becoming extinct sometime between that period and the end of the Paleozoic Era, as is the case with the interesting and attractive **archeocyathids**.

Archeocyathids usually occur, as do corals and sponges, in what can be considered fossil reefs. One of the most prolific of these occur along the coast of Labrador where Lower Cambrian limestone can be full of their graceful "ancient cup skeletons." Some of these have weathered out of the rock in natural relief, while others are best seen by cutting and polishing the hard limestone in which they occur—limestone which resembles marble.

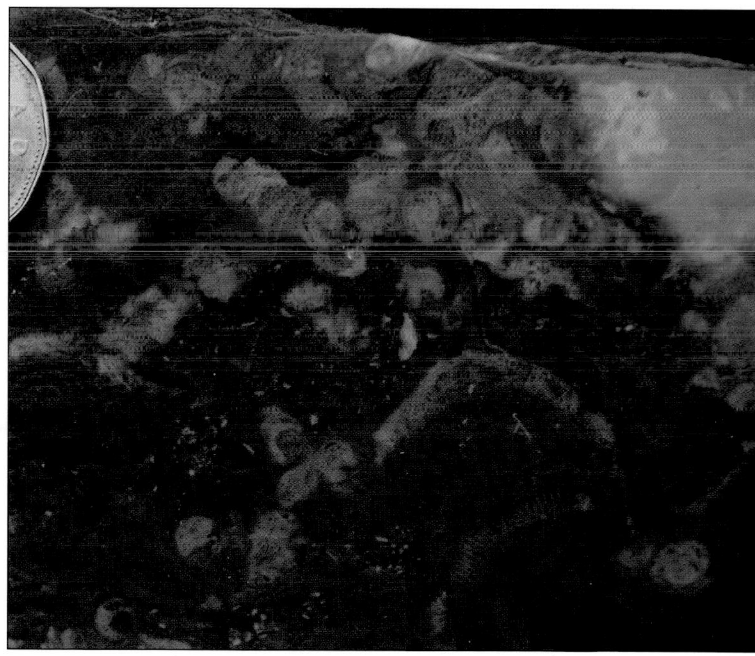

Cambriocyathus sp.: Lower Cambrian of northern Newfoundland, an archaeocyathid. (Value range G)

Cambriocyathus sp. Note the details on the specimen at the left. Archaeocyathids represent one of the enigmas of the Cambrian Period. They are considered as sponges by some paleontologists and as representatives of an extinct phylum by others. Note the perforated outer wall, which is a characteristic not found (with this configuration) in sponges. Lower Cambrian, Wilkawillina Gorge, Flinders Range, South Australia. (Value range F)

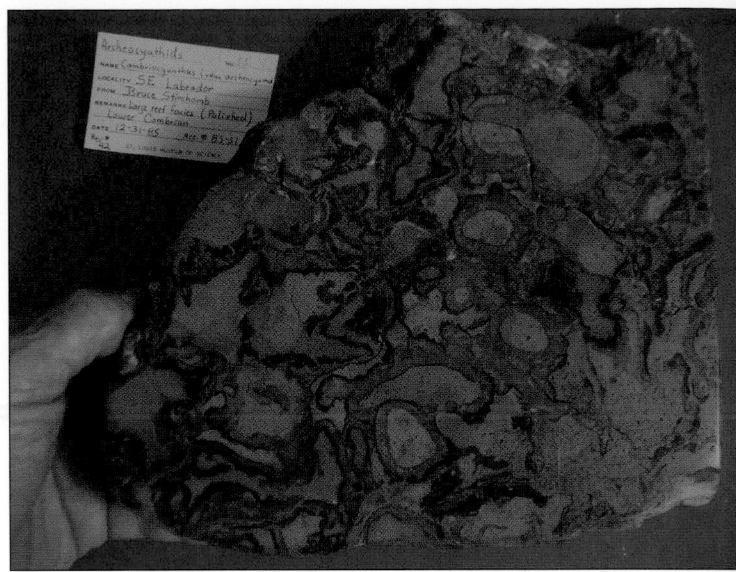

Cambriocyathus sp. Southern Labrador. (Value range F)

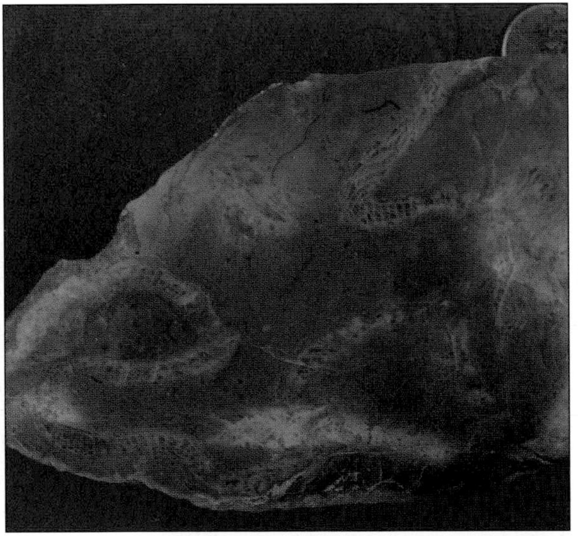

Cambriocyathus sp. A large, folded or crenulated archeocyathid "colony." Lower Cambrian, southern Labrador. (Value range F)

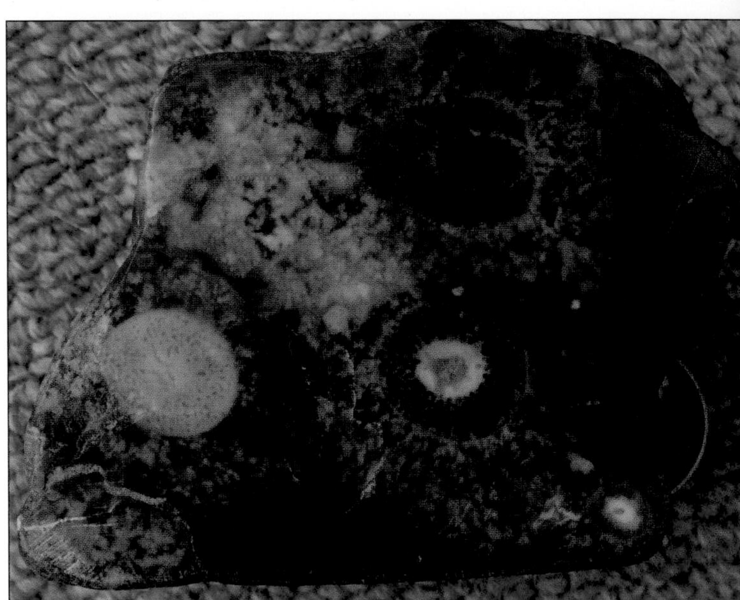

Archeocyathids in red limestone, southeastern Labrador, Fortuna Formation, Lower Cambrian. (Value range F)

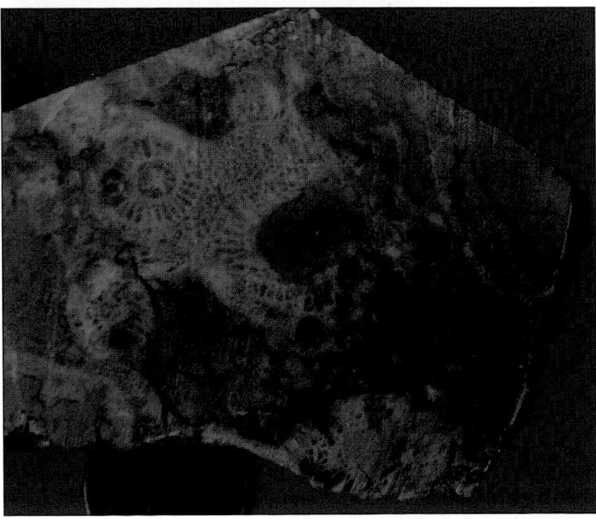

Archeocyathids reproduced by asexual reproduction (cloning). Here an individual has "budded" and formed what could become another archeocyathid colony. Lower Cambrian, Labrador. (Value range F)

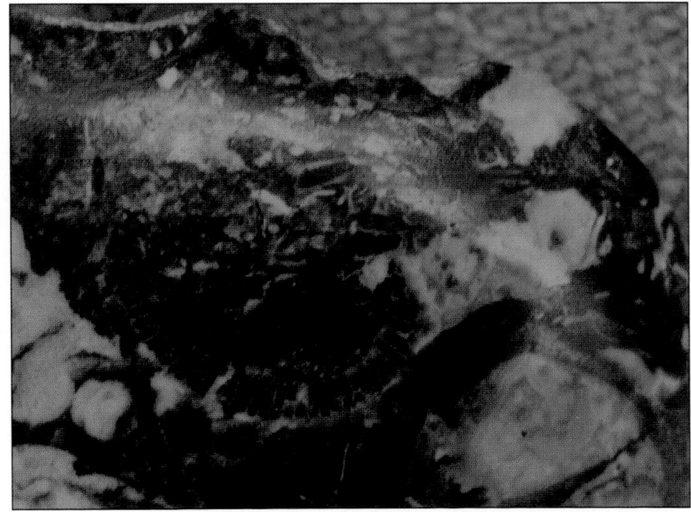

Another form of archeocyathid from the Fortuna formation of Labrador.

Cnidaria

Corals

Fossils of the phylum Cnidaria (or Coelenterata) are some of the most frequently found fossils, especially in marine limestones. Corals have been common elements of marine faunas since the Ordovician period, which ended some 430 million years ago. Appearing in the late Cambrian, corals are commonly not found until the Middle Ordovician when they became both diverse and widely dispersed. The most conspicuous feature of them (both fossil and modern) is the presence of **septa**. Septa are mineralized walls surrounding the gastrial cavity and divide the corallite (the hard part of a coral) into partitions. In Paleozoic corals these septa partitions occur in multiples of four, from which the name for the Paleozoic Order **tetracoralla** (tetra = four) is derived. Post Paleozoic corals have multiples of **six septa** and these are known as hexacorals. Hexacorals first appear in the Triassic Period, after the tetracorals went extinct (at the Permian extinction event).

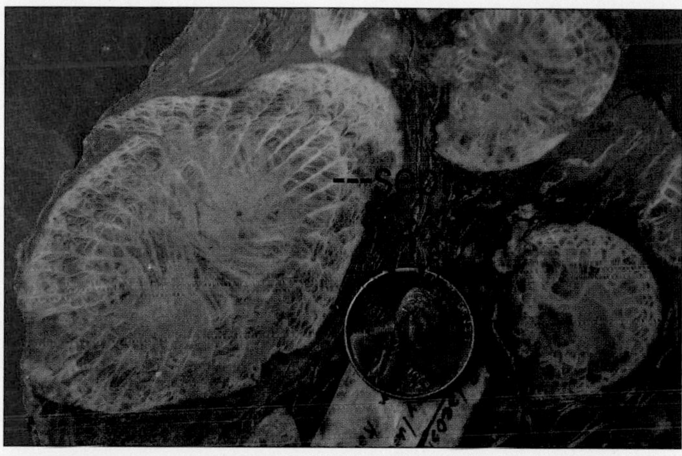

Palaeosmilia sp. Pennsylvanian, eastern Kansas: The two characteristic features of fossil corals are shown here. Septa are the radially arranged walls to which are attached in life what is known as the gastrial cavity. (Value range G)

Corals are some of the most commonly found fossils. Fossils represent hard parts of the coral animal, the hard (mineralized) part of a coral is known as a corallite. These button corals come from the Devonian of New York. (Value range G, single specimen)

Pachyphyllum nevadense. Devonian, Pine Arizona. If the number of septa in a fossil coral occurs in multiples of four (like this), it is a **tetracoral** and it lived during the **Paleozoic Era**. (Value range F)

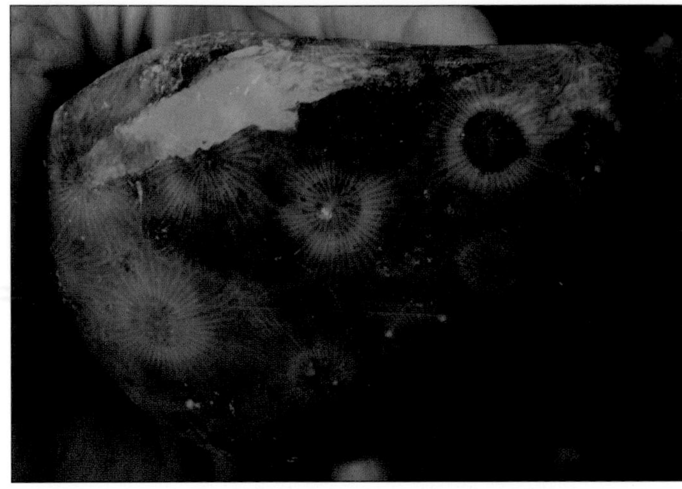

Billingsastraea verneuili. Middle Devonian, Traverse Formation, Michigan. In this coral, individual corallites are not bounded by walls. (Value range F)

Acervularia sp. A peculiar Middle Devonian colonial coral. Callaway Limestone, Callaway County, Missouri.

Lithostrotion proliferium. A widespread Mississippian colonial coral in which the individual corallites are loosely grouped together. (Value range F)

Favosites limitaris. Colonial coral. A colony of the branching form of the common Devonian coral *Favosites*. Middle Devonian, Callaway Limestone, Callaway County, Missouri.

Lithostronella (Acrocyathus) castelnaui. This is a field photo of a small portion of a large colony of this colonial coral. It was exposed in a cut on I-55, Arnold, Missouri, where it was utilized as a field trip stop, where fragments of the reef were periodically collected. The cut and its coral mass were removed in 1985 to accommodate a shopping center; however, a large portion of it was salvaged and now resides in the Bollinger County Missouri Natural History Museum in Marble Hill, Missouri.

Heliophyllum sp. A common solitary Devonian coral. Middle Devonian, Sylvania, Ohio. (Value range G)

Lithostronella castelnaui. A silicified colony of this widespread Mississippian coral. Note the well preserved and pronounced septa. St. Louis Limestone, St. Louis, Missouri. (Value range E)

"Falls of the Ohio" Silurian and Devonian Fossil Corals

Devonian and Silurian strata at Louisville, Kentucky, are full of a variety of fossil corals—corals which are especially characteristic of the Paleozoic and known as tetracorals. These fossil beds now form the basis for the "Falls of the Ohio Fossil Park," a fossil preserve in Louisville. In the nineteenth century, these fossil corals became material for many early fossil collections, fossil collections that provided "hard evidence" not only for the antiquity of the earth and its life, but which also established evidence of the existence of **extinct life forms** existing in the remote geologic past. Superficially, these corals resemble those living today; however, when you look at them closely, they have an anatomy different from modern corals or from corals of the Mesozoic and Cenozoic eras. Paleozoic corals belong to the coral Order Tetracoralla, post Paleozoic corals belong to the Order Hexacoralla, both orders having fundamentally different internal structure.

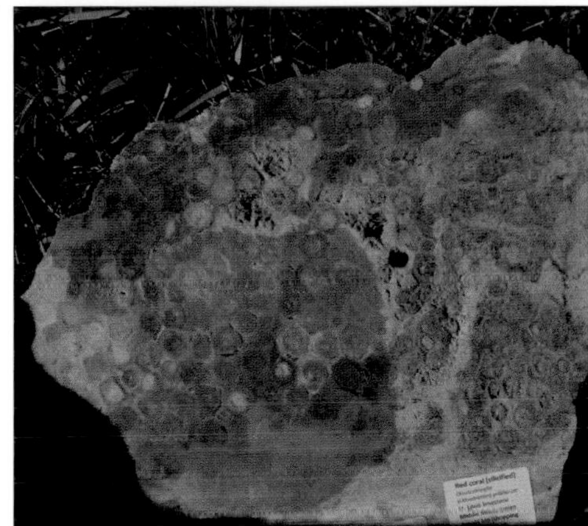

Lithostronella castelnaui. A sawed slab from a silicified mass of Paleozoic coral, St. Louis Formation, Arnold, Missouri. (This is not true red coral; its been replaced with iron bearing silica to give it the red color). Modern red coral is a hexacoral and is not found in the Paleozoic. (Value range F)

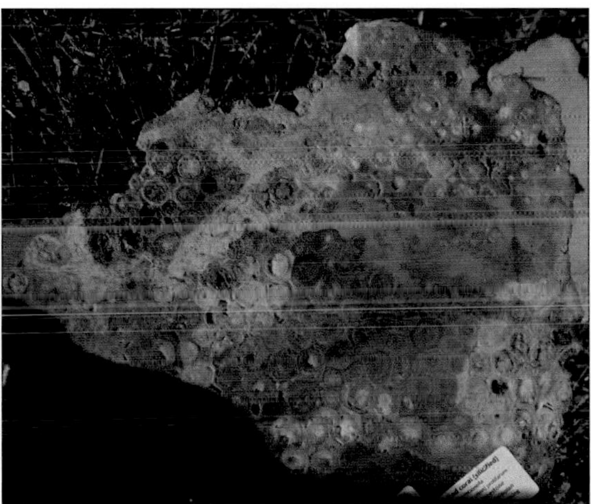

Another sliced section of a *Lithostronella* reef. St. Louis Limestone, Arnold, Missouri. (Value range F)

Fossil coral bearing strata on the south (Kentucky side) of "Falls of the Ohio." The locks in the background have inundated a portion of the fossil coral reefs that was collected by Charles Lyell, Dr. Clapp, and L. P. Yandell. Here the coral bearing rocks are being examined by Dorothy Echols (right) and Courtney Werner (left), both of Washington University, St. Louis. Professor Werner published on these corals (synonymy of mid-Devonian corals of the Falls of the Ohio) in 1937 and regularly visited the fossil coral bearing zones with students on field trips.

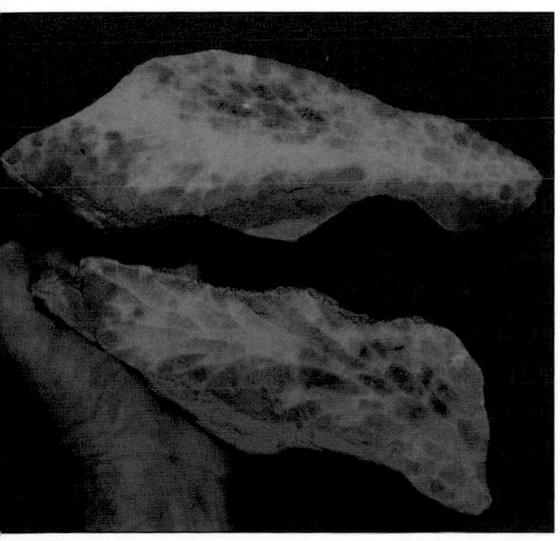

Pleurodictyum sp. A late Paleozoic coral genus. The small colony has been sliced. Fern Glen Formation, Jefferson County, Missouri. (Value range F)

Cathophyllum sp., a solitary rugose coral. A large variety of fossil coral occurs in Lower Devonian strata of the Louisville, Kentucky, area. The following specimens came from the collection of Dr. Lansford P. Yandell, a nineteenth century Louisville physician. Most were collected from late Silurian and early Devonian strata exposed at the "Falls of the Ohio" in the mid-nineteenth century. Dr. Yandell was a member of the St. Louis Academy of Science, to whom he gave his collection. These corals are now part of the collections of the St. Louis Science Center.

Syringopora perelegans. A large mass of this compact Devonian colonial coral from Dr. Yandell's collection.

Lyellia americana. Silurian corals from the "Falls of the Ohio," Louisville, Kentucky. This coral genus is named for Charles Lyell who knew Dr. Yandell and visited with him here in April 1846 during his lengthy trip through the southern states. Lyell spent about two weeks in the vicinity of Louisville, where he geologized with both Lunsford Yandell and with a Dr. Clapp, who also collecte fossils and lived in nearby New Albany, Indiana, across the Ohio River from Louisville. *Courtesy of S Louis Science Center.*

Arachnophyllum striatum (Orbigny). (*Strombodes knotti.*) Falls of the Ohio, Kentucky. Specimen from the collection of L. P. Yandell, the label (presumably in Dr. Yandell's handwriting), identifies the coral strombodes. *Strombodes* is the pre-1850 name for *Arachnophyllum*. *Courtesy of St. Louis Science Center.*

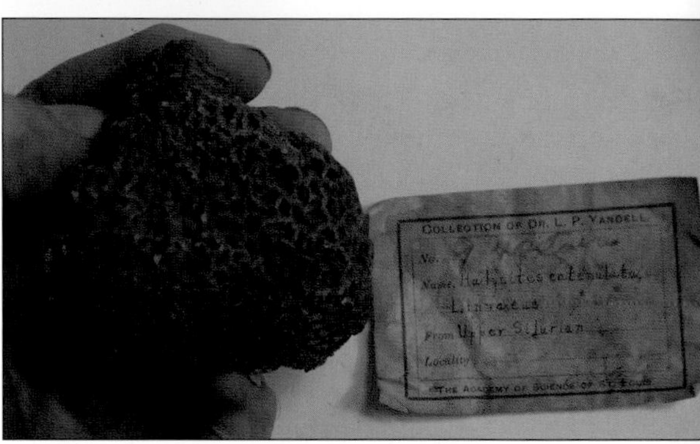

Halysites "catenularia" (Linnaeus). A specimen from L. P. Yandell's collection from Silurian strata at Falls of the Ohio.

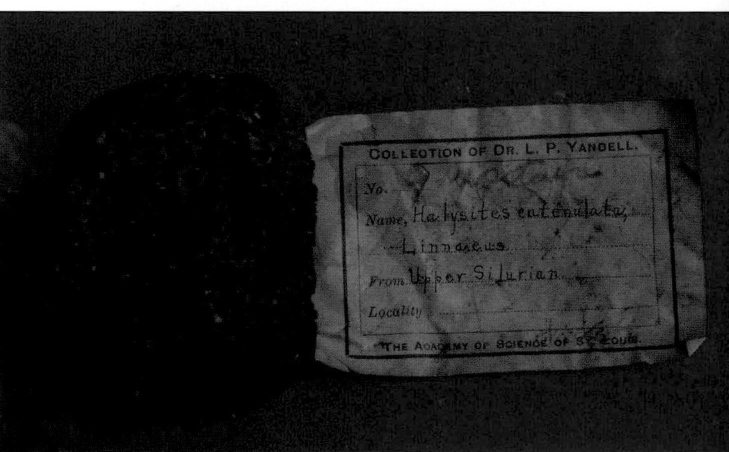

Halysites "catenularia (Linnaeus). Another view of the same specimen as previously shown.

Arachnophyllum striatum. Another specimen of this colonial coral from the "Falls of the Ohio" locality, in the collection of Lunsforth P. Yandell.

Eridophyllum colligatum. Lower Devonian, Falls of the Ohio. Silicified specimen from the collection of Dr. L. P. Yandell.

Favosites limitaris. A specimen from L. P. Yandell's collection from Falls of the Ohio, Louisville, Kentucky. *F. limitaris* is different from the majority of *Favosites* in that it is made up of branching corallites rather than being a solid mass of corallites, which characterize most other species of *Favosites*.

Favosites placenta Rominger. A more typical solid mass of corallites of this widespread Devonian genus.

Favosites limitaris. (Close-up of previous specimen). Most species of *Favosites* are more massive than this. *F. limitaris* has branching and bifurcating corallites which resemble bryozoans.

Favosites sp. Probably *F. placenta*. The **subcarboniferous** (below the Carboniferous) on the Yandell label would be Lower Devonian, the time when *Favosites* was most widespread in southern N. America. Jeff Co. Ky = Jefferson County Kentucky.

Favosites favosus. A branching form of this coral genus from the Yandell Collection. Most specimens of *Favosites favosus* are more globose and massive than this specimen. This specimen today would (probably) be considered *Favosites limitaris*. Niagarian Series, Middle Silurian, Falls of the Ohio.

Favosites sp. Another view of the previous specimens.

Professor Courtney Werner of the Geology Dept., Washington University, in New Albany, Indiana, 1955. Professor Werner had a particular fondness for Kentucky fossils, which included corals. He published on these in the 1930s and also had the Geology Department of Washington University acquire a portion of the Yandell Collection from the St. Louis Academy of Science.

Collecting fossil corals in southern Indiana, May 1960. Courtney Werner at right, Dorthory Echols looking at camera.

Cyathoxenia cyanodon (Horn corals). Dr. Lansford J. Yandell, mentioned previously, donated his fossil collection to the St. Louis Academy of Science, where it was stored on Lindell Avenue for decades. Many of its silver-fish-eaten labels were recopied after the collection was unwrapped from Civil War-Era newspapers by the author when he first worked on them as an early teen in the 1950s. Dr. Yandell's collection contains, besides "Falls of the Ohio" corals and stromatoporoids, numerous crinoid specimens (encrinites), especially specimens from Button Mold Knob near Louisville. Charles Lyell visited this Lower Carboniferous (Mississippian) locality with L. P. Yandell in April of 1846. These fossils may have been collected on that trip!

A Few More Corals and Cnidarid Problematica

Fossil corals are often preserved either in chert or are found replaced with silica. Such fossil corals are often some of the most obvious ones found by persons looking at rocks in creeks and other stream beds.

Amplexus fragilis. A common and attractive Mississippian coral found in Missouri, widely preserved in chert. This coral is especially characteristic of a zone in the Keokuk Formation of Middle Mississippian age. (Value range G)

Amplexus fragilis. Internal impression and silicified mold of this attractive coral. Keokuk Formation, Middle Mississippian, Cedar Creek, Callaway County, Missouri. (Value range G).

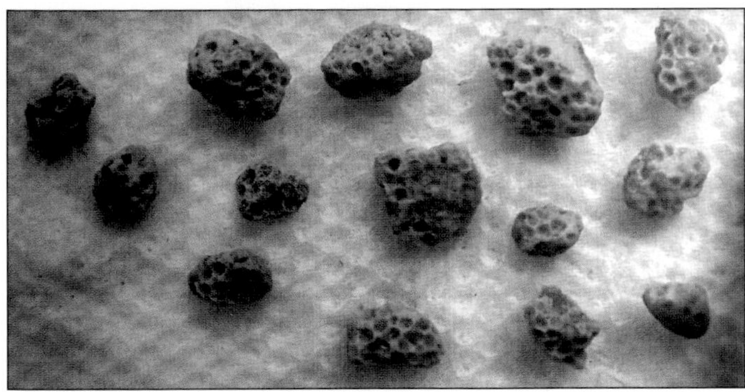

Kinsabia sp. A small, coral-like fossil from the Cambrian. *Kinsabia*, like so many Cambrian fossils, is problematic. It is composed of calcium carbonate and has somewhat of a coral-like morphology, yet no undoubted corals are known until the very end of the Cambrian, where a few rare forms do occur. *Kinsabia* comes from what are either Middle Cambrian or lowermost Upper Cambrian rocks exposed during the failure of the Taum Sauk, Profit Mountain reservoir in 2007, Reynolds County, Missouri.

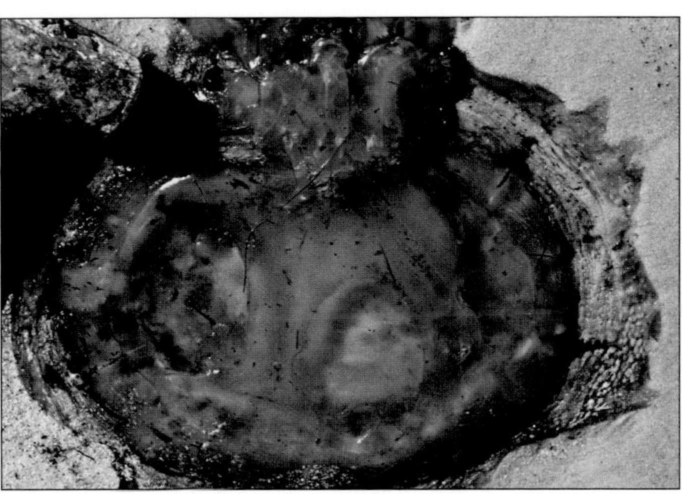

Close-up of stranded jellyfish. The ventral portion of the animal is at the top. Note the ring surrounding the jellyfish and the faint ridges caused by its shrinkage during desiccation.

Medusoids

Medusoids are radially symmetrical impressions of various types presumed to originate from fossil jellyfish (medusa). Found on bedding plane surfaces of sedimentary rocks, medusoids consist of a bewildering variety of forms, their common feature being that they are radially symmetrical. Many of these are actually fossil impressions of soft bodied organisms, some of which (probably most of which) are impressions of medusa. Others, however, are non-biogenic in origin and consist of various types of concretions, water exclusion structures, and other phenomena capable of producing radially symmetrical structures in soft sediments.

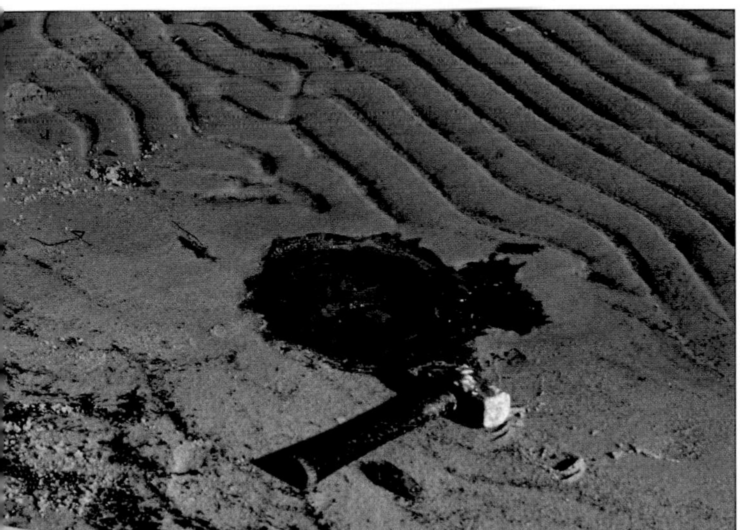

A modern jellyfish (medusa) stranded upon a sand beach. When the unfortunate animal dries out, it is capable of leaving a distinct impression in the sand or other sediment. Jellyfish are usually considered rare fossils, however, a large variety of so-called medusoid fossils occur in rocks of various ages. Some of these may be true jellyfish impressions; others probably are trace fossils and others pseudofossils.

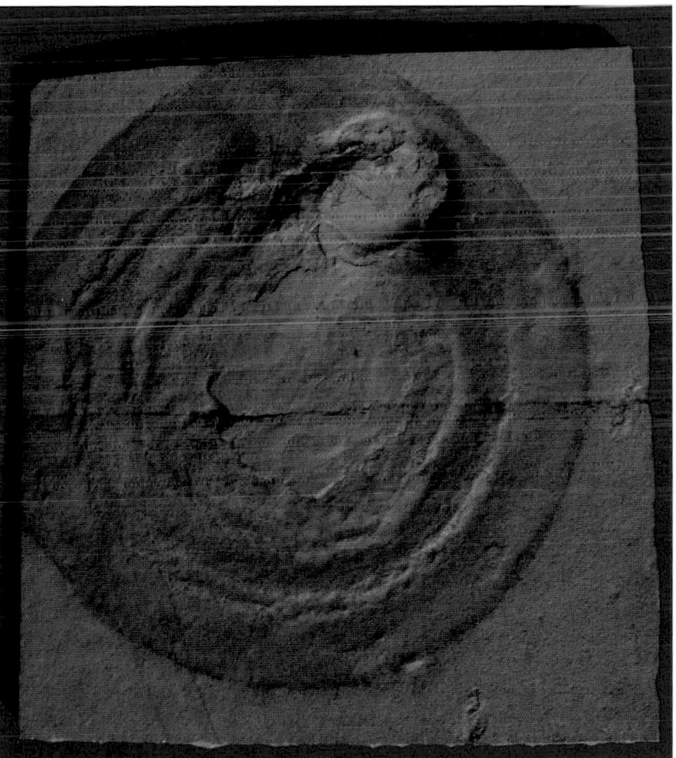

Impression of a stranded jellyfish in lime mud (which has become limestone). Note the surrounding "halo" caused by shrinkage of the jellyfish as it desiccated. The central part of this jellyfish impression (the gonads) corresponds to the top of the previous photo. Upper Jurassic Solnhofen Plattenkalk, Solnenhofen, southern Germany. (Value range D)

Octomedusa pieckorum. A scyphozoan jellyfish in an ironstone concretion, Essex biota, Mazon Creek region, northern Illinois. A variety of what are determined to be fossil medusa are found in these ironstone concretions of the "Mazon Creek" lagerstatten. As is the case with this specimen, soft tissues of an animal are represented by a slight color variation on the opened and slightly weathered surface of the split iron-stone concretion. (Value range F)

Octomedusa pieckorum. A group of concretions from the Essex portion (Essex fauna) of the Mazon Creek area of northern Illinois. Some of the medusoid outlines (they are not impressions) are less distinct—the better the outline, the more desirable the fossil.

Drevotella proteana. A soft-bodied hydroid from the Essex Biota. Hydroids are a class of jellyfish (hydrozoans). (Value range F)

Cyclomedusa sp. A typical medusiform impression in sandstone, They are often rather vague. Mt. Simon Formation, central Wisconsin. (Value range F)

Contorted Middle Cambrian shale yields *Brooksella*, as seen in the following photos, and is exposed along the Coosa River (Weiss Reservoir), Coosa, Georgia.

Brooksella alternata. Part and counterpart in shale from the previously shown locality along the Coosa River. (Value range F)

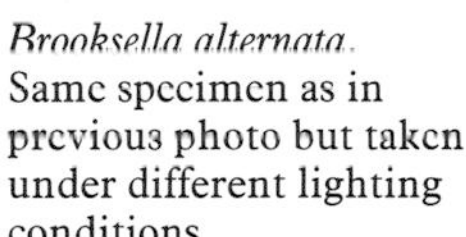

Brooksella alternata. Same specimen as in previous photo but taken under different lighting conditions.

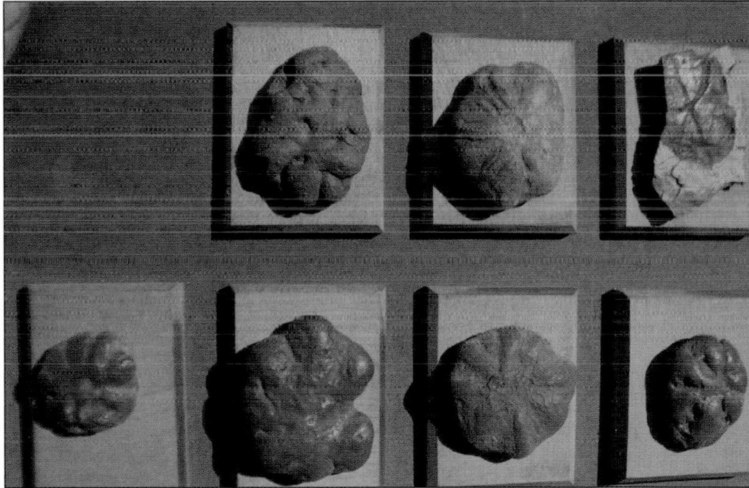

Brooksella alternata Walcott. A group of board mounted specimens of this questionable jellyfish. These fossils are locally known as star pebbles. They occur in hilly areas along the Coosa River, especially in Georgia, where they are associated with weathered beds of the Coosa shale downstream from Rome, Georgia.

Brooksella alternata associated with burrows in a chert concretion. Conasauga (Coosa) Shale, Coosa River (Weiss Lake), Georgia.

"Jellyfish." These peculiar medusoid-like fossils from China appeared on the fossil market in 1998. Rather than being a true jellyfish, they appear (more likely) to be a type of trace fossil. Similar trace fossils occur associated with deep sea sediments in the Ouachita Mountains of Arkansas and eastern Oklahoma. Silurian Period, Xuefeng Mountain, Hunan Province, China. (Value range F)

Dactyloidites asteroides. (Slender form.) These fossils were described as Lower Cambrian medusoids by C. D. Walsott in his 1898 USGS Monograph, "Fossil Medusa." They are now considered to be trace fossils rather than jellyfish. They occur in one layer in a slate quarry that is worked extensively for slate floors and located near the Vermont-New York border. Metawee Slate, Middle Granville, New York. (Value range E)

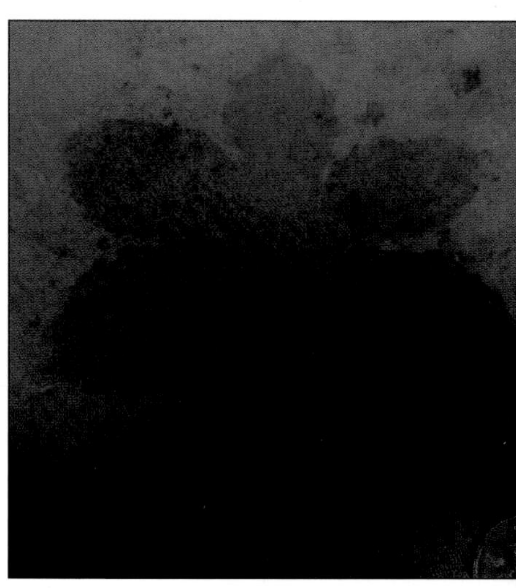

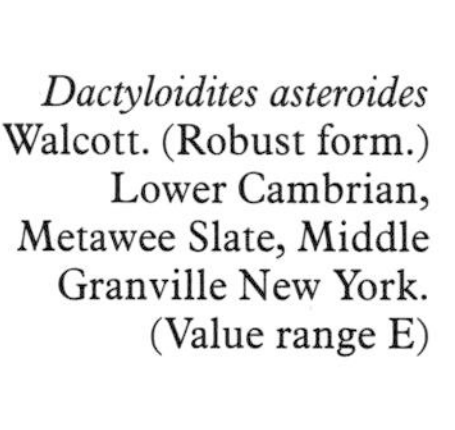

Dactyloidites asteroides Walcott. (Robust form.) Lower Cambrian, Metawee Slate, Middle Granville New York. (Value range E)

"Jellyfish." Another view of what probably are trace fossils.

The fact that the bodies of jellyfish are capable of leaving distinct impressions in sediments is well documented. That jellyfish can be stranded on sediment surfaces, as on a beach or mudflats during low tide, sometimes in vast numbers, has also been widely observed. Radial impressions found on bedding planes, sometimes in considerable numbers, originated from stranded jellyfish. Cnidarians, as part of their life cycle, produce a free floating larval stage which consists of a translucent, delicate floating organism known as a medusa. These range in size from small pelagic stages of coral animals (polyps) to large forms like the Portuguese Man-O-War, a pelagic cnidarian which can reach over fifty feet in length. All of these (or parts of them), are capable of producing the radial impressions illustrated here and seen with some frequency in some Paleozoic rocks.

Pseudofossil "jellyfish." Many phenomena (both manmade and natural) can leave radial medusa-like structures in sedimentary rocks. This medusa-form structure is a manmade one formed by the drill used in quarrying dimension stone. The drill stopping before it could penetrate deeper. This formed a pseudofossil of a type often confused with fossil medusa. Other natural medusa-form pseudofossils are formed from concretion impressions or from sand ejection structures.

Conostichus sp. Single specimen.

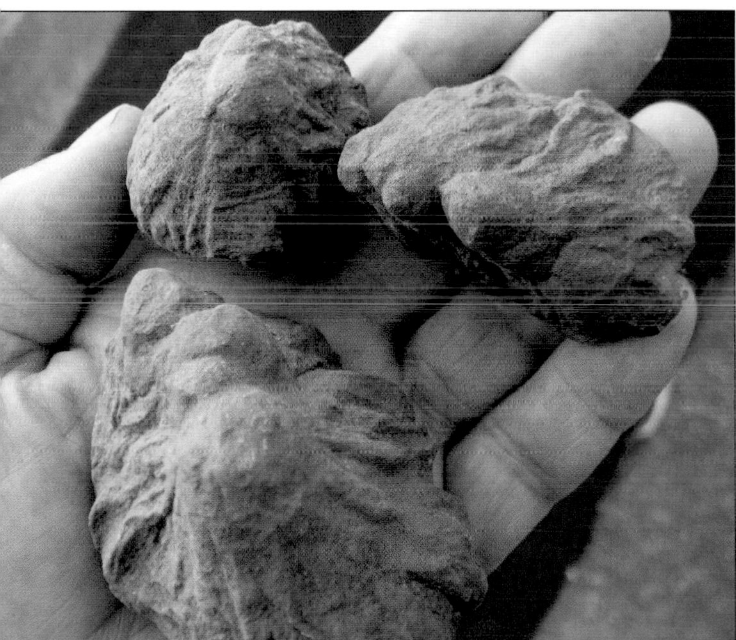

Conostichus sp. These trace fossils are thought by some to be the filled cavity occupied by a sea anemone-like animal. *Conostichus* is also considered by some paleontologists to be a type of sediment-filled worm burrow entrance. Atoka Formation, Lower Pennsylvanian, northwest Arkansas. (Value range G)

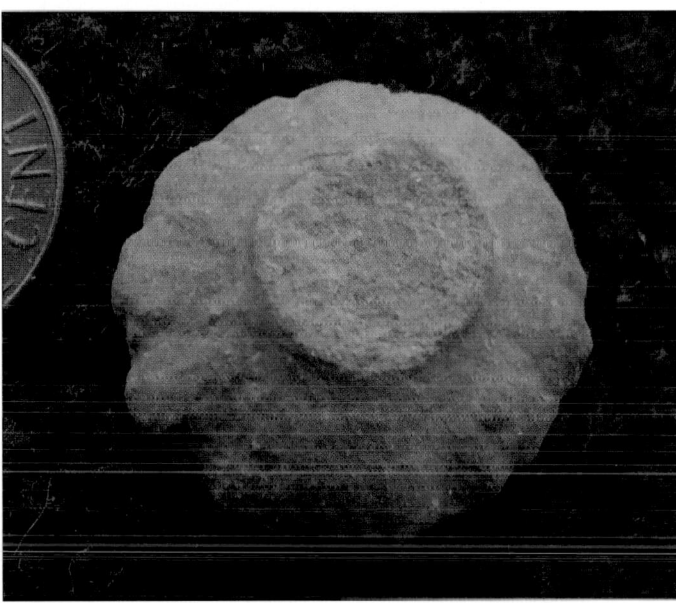

Variations on *Conostichus* are common. This type is associated with extensive worm burrows of the Hannibal Siltstone, Hannibal, Missouri. (Value range G)

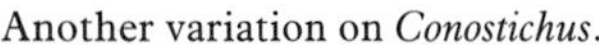

Another variation on *Conostichus*.

Fossil "Worms" and Worm Phyla

"Worms" constitute a diverse group of organisms which have in common an elongate, sinuous body and occupy a wide variety of ecological niches. What usually are referred to as worms are various types of annelids or segmented worms and these appear to have been responsible for many of the trace fossils commonly called worm tracks. Sedimentary rocks often show evidence of burrowing in the sediments, which formed before the sediments became rock. Annelids appear responsible for much of this burrowing (known as bioturbation); however, other "worm phyla" like the sipunculids and phoronids appear also to have been involved in the making of various "worm" trace fossils.

Skolithos linearius. Bedding surface of quartzite (or hard sandstone) of the Chilthowee Group near Montevale, eastern Tennessee. (Light meter is 3.5 inches in length.)

Skolithos

The vertical trace fossils known as Skolithos may have been produced by phoronid worms. Skolithos consists of vertical burrows usually found in sandstone. These burrows are especially abundant in the Cambrian and appear in the earliest of Cambrian strata; however, Skolithos is also found throughout the Paleozoic.

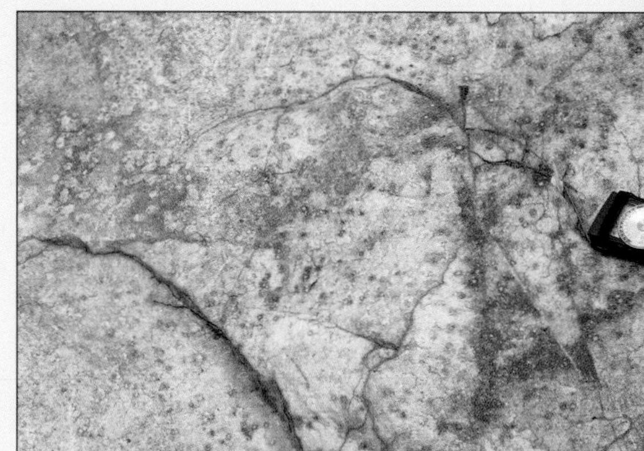

Similar horizontal surface with numerous *Skolithos* burrows. (Basal Lower Cambrian Sandstone, coastal Labrador.)

Skolithos linearius, Chilthowee Mountain, eastern Tennessee. This is one of the earliest, widespread trace fossils. *Skolithos* is hypothesized to have been made by some type of phoronid worm. Many trace fossils appear to be made by annelid worms and some by arthropods. Many members of the various "worm phyla" have the potential for making such tracks and trails. This is a bedding plane surface of the Chilthowee Quartzite (or sandstone) covered with numerous vertical burrows. The Chilthowee Quartzite forms part of a group of strata (Chilthowee Group) which spans (or bridges) the boundary between the Cambrian and Precambrian. The *Skolithos* bearing beds occurring in the upper portion of the sequence is Lower Cambrian in age. Lower beds of the Chilthowee Group being latest Precambrian (Neoproterozoic) in age.

Phycodes sp. Well formed cast of a burrow where the burrow-maker entered on a bedding surface, made a 180 degree turn and then exited the surface near where it entered—all some 530 million years ago. Phycodes has gained a notable reputation by being the fossil marking the beginning of the Cambrian and the Paleozoic Era, separating it from the Precambrian, which lacks this trace fossil, and most others.

A Gallery of "Fossil Worm" Trace Fossils

A wide variety of trace fossils occur in Paleozoic rocks and constitute some of the subject matter of ichnology (the study of tracks and burrows). Many of these trace fossils (ichnofossils) are distinctive and have been given form genera (ichnogenera), even though the taxonomic position of their makers is unknown.

Hormosiroidea sp. The "chain-of-beads" trace fossil is possibly a trace fossil formed from a worm-like animal moving in jerks by peristalsis through an organic-rich layer of sediment—sediment just below the sea bottom. (Value range G)

Helminthopsis sp. (Conspicuous sinuous track.) *Taenidium* (bottom) and *Asterophyllites* sp, the star-shaped trace fossil (upper right). Middle Mississippian, Batesville Sandstone, Leslie, Arkansas. (Value range F)

Scalarituba sp. Slab of this late Paleozoic trace fossil cemented into a masonry wall. Batesville Sandstone, Leslie, Arkansas.

Asterosoma sp. Sandstone boulder covered with this trace fossil. One kind of trace fossil can sometimes merge into another. Some of these filled burrows resemble types of *Phycodes*. Garden City Formation, Middle Ordovician, Wasatch Mountains, eastern Utah.

Outcrop of Cambrian slabby dolomite and shale of the Upper Cambrian Davis Formation. The Davis is a source of numerous (usually rather nondescript) trace fossils generally referred to as worm tracks.

Slab of Upper Cambrian Davis Formation with characteristic "worm tracks."

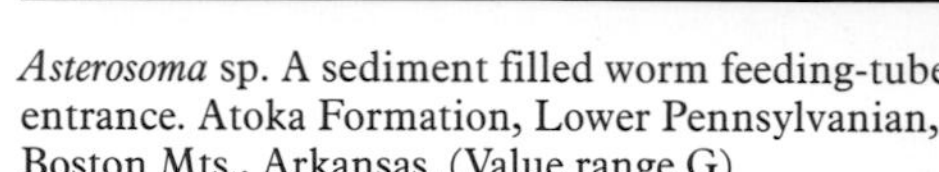

Asterosoma sp. A sediment filled worm feeding-tube entrance. Atoka Formation, Lower Pennsylvanian, Boston Mts., Arkansas. (Value range G)

Conostichus sp. Possibly a worm feeding tube entrance, but also interpreted as the sediment filled impression of a sea anemone. Atoka Formation, Lower Pennsylvanian, Boston Mountains, Arkansas. (Value range G)

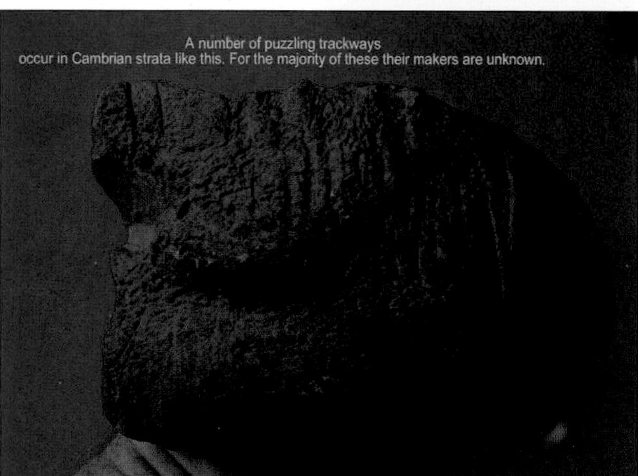

A number of puzzling trackways occur in Cambrian strata like this. For the majority of these their makers are unknown.

A large track of a worm-like (or slug-like) creature. Upper Cambrian, Davis Formation, Ste. Francois County, Missouri.

A variation on *Conostichus*. Atoka Formation, Arkansas. (Value range G)

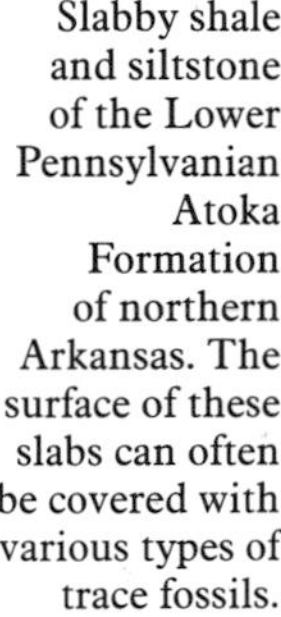

Slabby shale and siltstone of the Lower Pennsylvanian Atoka Formation of northern Arkansas. The surface of these slabs can often be covered with various types of trace fossils.

Asterosoma sp. One of a number of "worm feeding structures" filled in by sediment. These formed when the "worm" entered and left the burrow which was formed in the sediments of the ocean floor. Atoka Formation, northern Arkansas. (Value range G)

Cast of a large burrow of a marine worm similar to *Asterophycus*, but with many more radiating burrows. Fossils like this originally were thought to be impressions of marine plants and hence have the ending phycus (g) = plants. Basal sandstone of late Devonian age, Southern Indiana.

Another view of the above specimen.

Chondrites sp. The "fucoids" of nineteenth century literature. *Chondrites* is a commonly occurring fossil burrow, and is especially characteristic of the Middle and Late Ordovician. Plattin Limestone, Jefferson County, Missouri. (Value range G)

"Worm" Tracks and Burrows in Flysch Deposits

Sediments deposited in a deep sea environment, often on the floor of the open ocean, can contain many worm-like trace fossils. These sediments (or sedimentary rock) can have distinctive trace fossils made by deep sea organisms (often worm-like) burrowing in sediments. Such deep sea sediments are often folded, metamorphosed, and crumpled when thrust laterally onto continental crust and known as flysch—a term first used to describe the peculiar rocks forming much of the Alps of Europe.

Chondrites sp. A group of bifurcating, sediment filled burrows that came from deep-sea Pennsylvanian sediments of the southern Boston Mountains, northern Arkansas. (Value range F)

Arthrophycus sp. A sediment filled burrow similar to the above *Chondrites* burrow but showing "segmentation". Such a pattern is almost certainly the product of peristalsis, a physiological adaptation which enabled the burrower to move through the sediment (somewhat similar to a bowel movement). Platteville Formation, Middle Ordovician, Minneapolis Minnesota.

Close-up of *Arthrophycus* burrow.

Lookout on Mt. Magazine in the Boston Mountains of Arkansas. Deep sea sediments (flysch) deposited in a rapidly subsiding basin make up part of Mt. Magazine, the highest point in the US between the Appalachian Mountains and the Rockies. This deep sea sedimentary sequence has been uplifted to form these quite-rugged mountains. Many of the slabby sandstone and siltstone beds in this area are full of deep-sea trace fossils.

Thin bedded, deep sea sediment (flysch) outcropping at the base of Mt. Magazine, Boston Mountains, Northern Arkansas.

Deep sea sediments exposed along cliffs of the Arkansas River below Mt. Magazine, Northern Arkansas.

Polychete Worms in Ironstone Concretions

Fossil polychetes (annelid worms) occur in ironstone concretions locally in abundance, especially in the marine portions of the "Mazon Creek" fossil beds of the Essex (Pit 11) locality near Essex, Illinois.

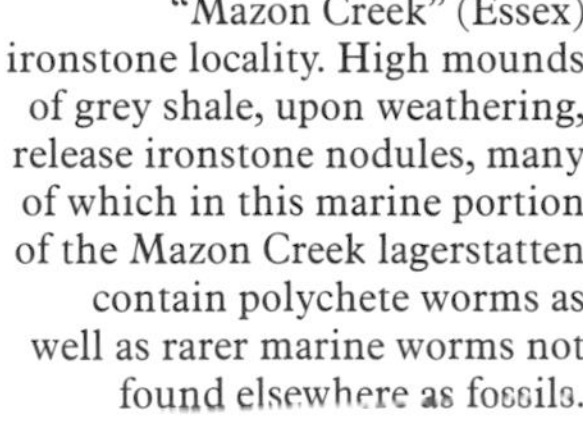

"Mazon Creek" (Essex) ironstone locality. High mounds of grey shale, upon weathering, release ironstone nodules, many of which in this marine portion of the Mazon Creek lagerstatten contain polychete worms as well as rarer marine worms not found elsewhere as fossils.

Esconites sp. Polychete worm. A large number of segmented organisms like this occur in ironstone concretions of the pit 11 (Essex Fauna) of the Mazon Creek Lagerstatten of Northern Illinois. Most of these are various forms of polychete annelids.

Polychete worm.

Polychete worm.

Polychete worm.

Polychete worm.

Polychete worm. (Value range G)

Problematic Fossils (Conularids)

Conularids are problematic organisms that had an exoskeleton composed of chitin, a polysaccharide also composing the exoskeletons of insects. Some paleontologists place conularids in the Cnidaria. Like Tentaculites, conularids appear unrelated to anything living today. This is one of the attractions of Paleozoic life; there are numerous mysteries.

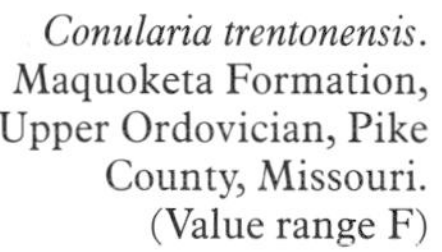

Conularia trentonensis. Maquoketa Formation, Upper Ordovician, Pike County, Missouri. (Value range F)

Conularia missouriensis. Middle Mississippian, Salem Formation, Godfrey, Illinois. (Value range F)

Problematic Fossils (*Tentaculites*)

Tentaculites provides an example of a problematic fossil. Its taxonomic position is unknown and nothing today is living with which it might be compared. *Tentaculites* occurs only in the Silurian and Devonian, usually in slabby limestones.

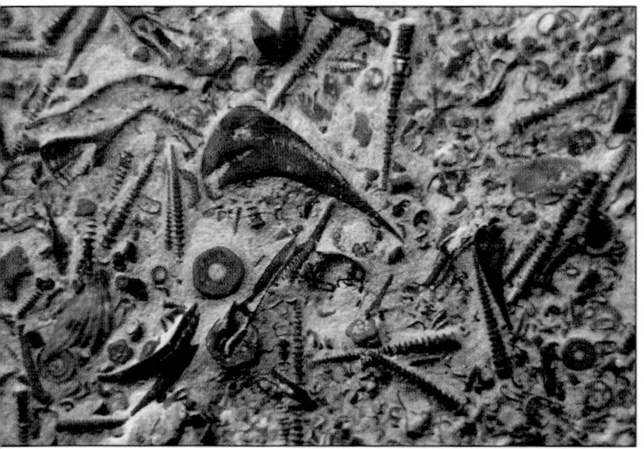

Tentaculites distans. This problematic fossil is considered by some paleontologists to be a type of "armored" worm. Part of a (*Dalmanites*) trilobite is in the center. Middle Silurian, Reynales, New York. (Value range G)

Tentaculites sp. Middle Devonian, Czortkov, Ukraine. (Value range F)

Glossary

Bioturbation: Sediment and sedimentary rock showing evidence of burrowing by various types of organisms when it was still soft sediment. Bioturbation can be done by various types of organisms, most being worm-like organisms. Bioturbation usually is not found in rocks older than the Cambrian. This earliest period of the Paleozoic represents not only the first abundant appearance of organisms with hard parts, but also (concurrently) the first appearance of abundant bioturbation.

Flysch: Sedimentary rocks deposited on the floor of the open, deep sea ocean. Flysch deposits can be covered with a variety of trace fossils collectively known as "worm burrows." They are relatively uncommon in the Paleozoic, where most sediments (now of course sedimentary rocks) were deposited in shallow, epicontinental seaways.

Ichnology: That branch of paleontology related to the study of trace fossils such as tracks, trackways, and burrows

Lithification: The process by which a sediment becomes sedimentary rock. Sediments often show evidence of bioturbation, which may become more evident upon lithification, becoming the so called "worm tracks" frequently seen on both bedding surfaces and within beds of rocks like siltstone, sandstone, and impure limestone.

Open or Deep Ocean: Deep oceans are those marine waters, as compared with seas, which overlay continental shelves and the edges of continents. Deep oceans have their crust composed of mafic rock, in contrast to continents, which have crustal material composed of felsic (silica rich) rock. This is in reference to flysch deposits, which are sediments deposited in the deep oceans and later thrust onto continental crust by geologic processes associated with plate tectonics.

Phoronids: A phylum of small worm-like animals also known as horseshoe worms. Phoronids are lophophorates (filter feeders with a lophophore), which allies them with the brachiopods and bryozoans.

Bibliography

Hantzschel, Walter, 1975. *Trace Fossils and Problematica. Treatise on Invertebrate Paleontology, Miscellanea.* Geological Society of America and the University of Kansas.

Trace Fossils and Paleontology of the Ouachita Geosyncline, A Guide to, 1978. Society of Economic Paleontologists and Mineralogists, Tulsa Oklahoma.

Conularia crustula. Upper Pennsylvanian, Kansas City Group, Kansas City, Missouri. (Value range E for group)

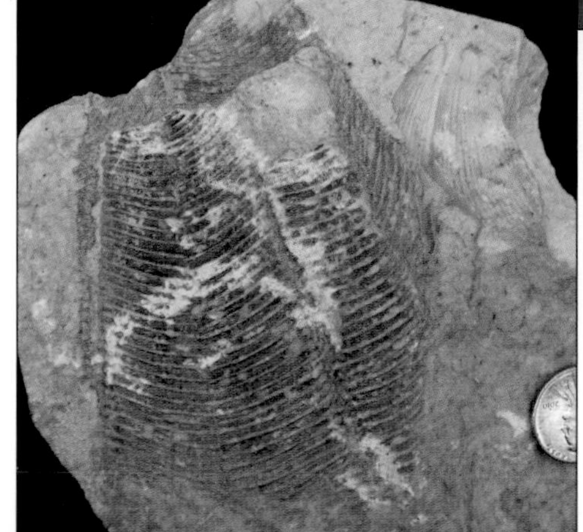

Conularia missouriensis. Burlington Limestone, Middle Mississippian. (Value range F)

Conularia crustula. Upper Pennsylvanian, Kansas City Group. Platte County, Missouri.

Brachiopods and Bryozoans

Inarticulate Brachiopods

Brachiopods (lamp shells) may be the most abundant fossil invertebrates of the Paleozoic. Inarticulate brachiopods are the earliest occurring brachiopods (and presumably the most primitive). Having a shell composed of calcium phosphate and organic matter, they are the earliest brachiopods to appear in the rock record and are peculiar in their utilization of calcium phosphate rather than a (calcium) carbonate composition in their shells. Inarticulate brachiopods even appear before the first trilobites near the beginning of the Cambrian Period. Originally classified with the mollusks, brachiopods have an internal soft part anatomy completely different from mollusks. They are more closely related to worms (phoronids) and to bryozoans (with which they are paired in this chapter).

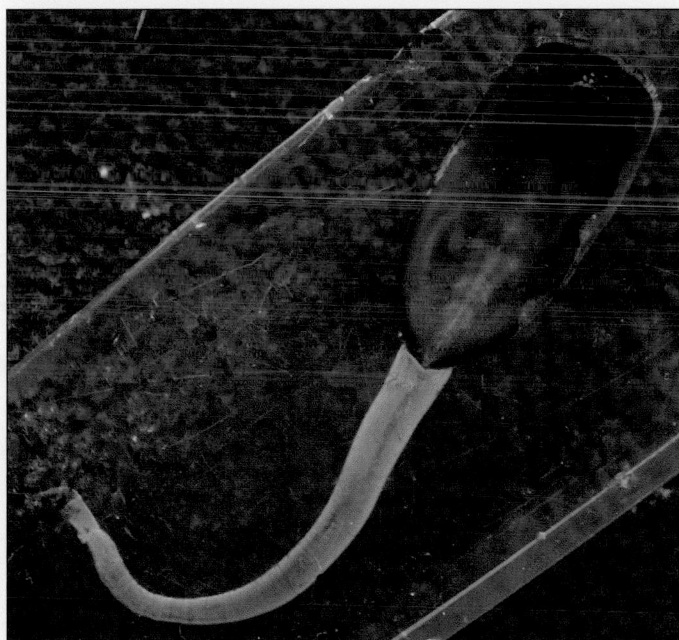

Lingula sp. A modern, inarticulate brachiopod embedded in lucite. The fleshy, worm-like stem or pedicil is almost never preserved in fossil brachiopods, otherwise many of the inarticulate brachiopods found as fossils are identical to this modern form.

Over great breadths of the sea bottom we find vast numbers of little bivalve shells of the form and size of a finger-nail, fastened by fleshy peduncles imbedded in the sand or mud; and thus anchored, collecting their food by a pair of fringed arms from the minute animals and plants which swarm in the surrounding waters. These are the *Lingulæ*, from the abundance of which some of the Primordial beds have received in England and Wales the name of Lingula flags. In America, in like manner, in some beds near St. John, New Brunswick, the valves of these shells are so abundant as to constitute at least half of the material of the bed; and alike in Europe and America, Lingula and allied forms are among the most abundant Primordial fossils. The Lingulæ are usually reckoned to belong to the great sub-kingdom of mollusks, which includes all the bivalve and univalve shell-fish, and several other groups of creatures; but an able American naturalist, Mr. Morse, has recently shown that they have many points of resemblance to the worms; and thus, perhaps, constitute one of those curious old-fashioned "comprehensive" types, as they have been called, which present

Discussion on inarticulate brachiopods by J. William Dawson. He states that "The Lingulae are usually reckoned to belong to the great sub-kingdom of mollusks, etc." This no longer is the taxonomic placement of them as well as other brachiopods. **Brachiopods now occupy their own separate phylum.**

Dawson's discourse on the inarticulate brachiopod *Lingula* continued.

THE PRIMORDIAL, OR CAMBRIAN AGE. 41

resemblances to groups of creatures, in more modern times quite distinct from each other. He has also found that the modern Lingulæ are very tenacious of life, and capable of suiting themselves to different circumstances, a fact which, perhaps, has some connection with their long persistence in geological time. They are in any case members of the group of lamp-shells, creatures specially numerous and important in the earlier geological ages.

The Lingulæ are especially interesting as examples of a type of beings continued almost from the dawn of life until now; for their shells, as they exist in the Primordial, are scarcely distinguishable from those of members of the genus which still live. While other tribes of animals have run through a great number of different forms, these little creatures remain the same. Another interesting point is a most curious chemical relation of the Lingula, with reference to the material of its shell. The shells of mollusks generally, and even of the ordinary lamp-shells, are hardened by common limestone or carbonate of lime: the rarer substance, phosphate of lime, is in general restricted to the formation of the bones of the higher animals. In the case of the latter, this relation depends apparently on the fact that the albuminous substances on which animals are chiefly nourished require for their formation the presence of phosphates in the plant. Hence the animal naturally obtains phosphate of lime or bone-earth with its food, and its system is related to this chemi-

3*

cal fact in such wise that phosphate of lime is a most appropriate and suitable material for its teeth and bones. Now, in the case of the lower animals of the sea, their food, not being of the nature of the richer land plants, but consisting mainly of minute algæ and of animals which prey on these, furnishes, not phosphate of lime, but carbonate. An exception to this occurs in the case of certain animals of low grade, sponges, etc., which, feeding on minute plants with siliceous cell-walls, assimilate the flinty matter and form a siliceous skeleton. But this is an exception of downward tendency, in which these animals approach to plants of low grade. The exception in the case of Lingulæ is in the other direction. It gives to these humble creatures the same material for their hard parts which is usually restricted to animals of much higher rank. The purpose of this arrangement, whether in relation to the cause of the deviation from the ordinary rule or its utility to the animal itself, remains unknown. It has, however, been ascertained by Dr. Hunt, who first observed the fact in the case of the Primordial Lingulæ, that their modern successors coincide with them, and differ from their contemporaries among the mollusks in the same particular. This may seem a trifling matter, but it shows in this early period the origination of the difference still existing in the materials of which animals construct their skeletons, and also the wonderful persistence of the Lingulæ, through all the geological ages, in the material of their shells.

Lingula discussion continued.

Lingula sp. A 300 million year old (Upper Pennsylvanian) *Lingula*. Note that there is essentially no difference between this and the previously shown modern specimen (except for the modern Lingula's "stem" or pedicil, which is rarely preserved on fossils). Wabunsee Shale, Nodaway River and I-29 excavations. (Value range F)

Lingula sp. Another shale slab covered with specimens of this inarticulate brachiopod. Upper Pennsylvanian, Wabunsee Shale, I-29 excavations at Nodaway River, Missouri. (Value range F)

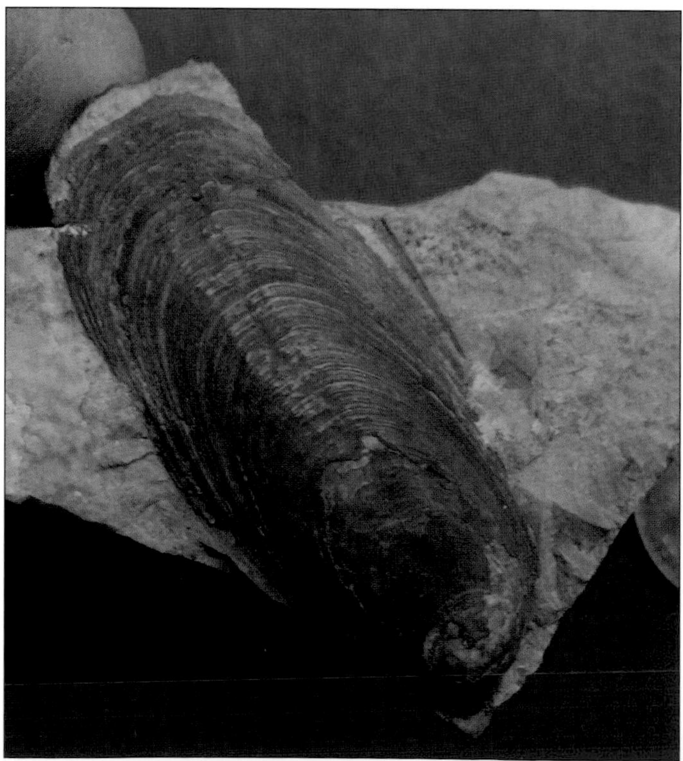

A 400 million year old *Lingula*. Fossil Lingula can be identical to those living today. Lingula has been virtually unchanged in 500 million years. Bromide Formation, Middle Ordovician, Arbuckle Mountains, Oklahoma.

Orbiculoidea missouriensis. Severely flattened inarticulate brachiopods are commonly found associated with black shale of the Pennsylvanian Period. This specimen came from shale above the Herrin No. 6 coal, Freeburg, Illinois. (Value range G)

Orbiculoidea missouriensis. Specimens of this widespread (in the US Midwest) brachiopod preserved in grey shale, dorsal valves at the right. Upper Pennsylvanian, Kansas City, Missouri area. (Value range G)

Orbiculoidea missouriensis. (Shumard.) The ventral valves in the center of this slab have been severely flattened, the way in which most specimens of *Orbiculoidea* are preserved. Specimens at the bottom with the white rims (original phosphate shell material) are dorsal valves. These valves show the shell apex, which is preserved in a black, silty limestone. Middle Pennsylvanian, Sparta, Illinois. (Value range G)

Lingula sp. The impression of a single, inarticulate brachiopod in shale. Inarticulate brachiopods are found with some frequency in shale. They could (and can) tolerate very muddy conditions, which were (and are) unfavorable for most other marine invertebrates.

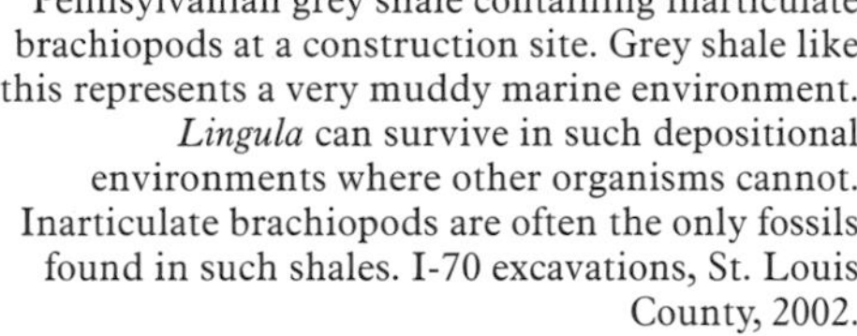

Pennsylvanian grey shale containing inarticulate brachiopods at a construction site. Grey shale like this represents a very muddy marine environment. *Lingula* can survive in such depositional environments where other organisms cannot. Inarticulate brachiopods are often the only fossils found in such shales. I-70 excavations, St. Louis County, 2002.

Lingulepis walcotti. Lingula-type inarticulate brachiopods can exist in large numbers. Here is a Cambrian limestone from Minnesota made almost entirely of them. The species is named after Charles D. Walcott, the late nineteenth-early twentieth century paleontologist who discovered the Burgess Shale. (Value range F)

Lingulepis sp. Flattened specimens of this inarticulate brachiopod. The white material is the original calcium phosphate shell of the brachiopod animal. Inarticulate brachiopods have their shells composed of calcium phosphate (phosphate of lime) while other brachiopods have shells composed of calcium carbonate. Lodi Formation, Lodi, Wisconsin. (Value range G)

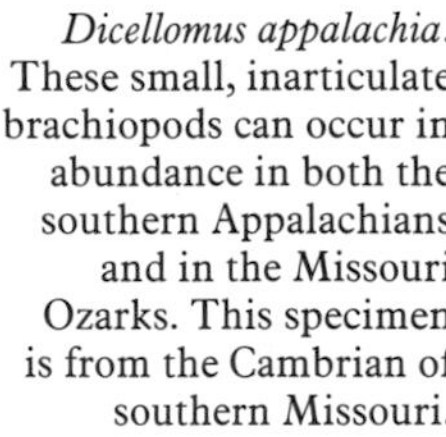

Dicellomus appalachia. These small, inarticulate brachiopods can occur in abundance in both the southern Appalachians and in the Missouri Ozarks. This specimen is from the Cambrian of southern Missouri.

Brand of gasoline (now defunct) that was sold near the outcrop yielding *Dicellomus appalachia*, shown in the previous photo.

Vehicle parked near the brachiopod bearing outcrop, which probably used the Ozark Gas brand (now defunct).

Flattened specimens of *Dicellomus appalachia* in buff shale. Rumors circulated that the above gasoline was produced from Cambrian hydrocarbons derived from the same dark grey shale that preserved these brachiopods. Rumors have also circulated that only vehicles like that in the previous photo would run on this gasoline.

Dicellomus politus. A small, inarticulate brachiopod that often occurs in large numbers on slabs of sandstone in the upper Mississippi Valley of Minnesota and Wisconsin. Upper Cambrian of Wisconsin. (Value range F)

Articulate Brachiopods

These are probably the most commonly seen Paleozoic fossils. The biomass of brachiopods during the Paleozoic was such that some Paleozoic strata can be composed almost entirely of their shells. Articulate brachiopods, unlike the inarticulate forms, have the two valves opening and closing with a hinge.

Collecting articulate brachiopods on limestone slabs covered with them. **Articulate brachiopods** were some of the most prolific invertebrates during the Paleozoic Era. Paleozoic limestones often can be found crowded with their shells. Today, by contrast (although they still live today), brachiopods are a minor element in shallow water, marine faunas.

Rhynchotrema capax. Silicified specimens of this Upper Ordovician brachiopod. Beds of volcanic ash (metabentonite), exposed at the outcrop shown in the previous photo (and present at the outcrop from whence this slab came), probably were the source of the silica that replaced these brachiopod shells. Fernvale Formation, Upper Ordovician, Jefferson County, Missouri. (Value range F)

Macgeea proteus. Upper Devonian, Hay River Formation. North of Enterprise, NWT Canada. (Value range G)

Spinatrypa arctica. Hay River Formation, Upper Devonian, North of Enterprise, NWT Canada. (Value range H)

Atrypa independensis. Hay River Formation, Upper Devonian, west bank of Hay River, Upper Devonian, NWT Canada. (Value range G)

Calvinaria variabilis. Hay River Formation, Upper Devonian, Hay River NWT, Canada. (Value range G)

Platystrophia ponderosa. These lovely brachiopods occur in great quantity in Upper Ordovician beds near Cincinnati, Ohio, and south into Kentucky. Some of the beds shown in the previous photos also are full of *Platystrophia*. (Value range G for all)

Nervostrophia vestita. Hay River Formation, Upper Devonian, Hay River, NWT. (Value range G)

Close-up of the brachiopod-rich strata shown below.

Road cut in central Kentucky dug into Upper Ordovician shaly limestone, which is chocked full of brachiopods.

Schizophoria multistriata. Internal molds of these brachiopods preserved in quartzite. Isolated occurrences of Middle and Late Paleozoic strata occur scattered over the Ozarks. These represent sediments (outliers) that, at one time, covered the area, but today are almost entirely eroded away. These brachiopods occur associated with small outliers (remnants) of Devonian strata, which occur near Owensville, Missouri. (Value range F for all)

Rafinesquina trentonensis with numerous other fossils, including crinoid debris. Anticosti Island, Quebec. (Value range G)

Dinorthis transversa. Ribbed brachiopods on this highly fossiliferous slab from the Upper Ordovician of Anticosti Island, Quebec. (Value range G)

Eoorthis remnicha. An articulate brachiopod occuring locally in abundance in the Upper Cambrian. Articulate brachiopods usually are not too common in Cambrian rocks, certainly not in the abundance that they are found in younger Paleozoic strata. Davis Formation, Reynolds County, Missouri. (Value range G)

Rafinesquina trentonensis. Many specimens on a slab from the Middle Ordovician of Anticosti Island, Quebec, Canada. (Value range G)

Eoorthis remnicha. Impressions of these articulate brachiopods in Upper Cambrian Dolomite, Reynolds County, Missouri. (Value range F)

Eoorthis remnicha. Another nice group of these fan shaped, Cambrian brachiopods. (Value range F, Cambrian inarticulate brachiopods are relatively rare)

Hebertella sinuata. Upper Ordovician, Richmond, Indiana. (Value range G)

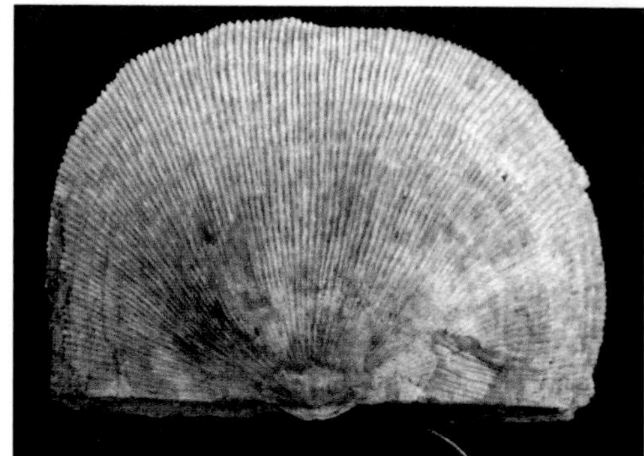

Derbyia cymbula. Fort Riley Limestone, Lower Permian. Cedar Point, Chase County, Kansas. (Value range G)

Syntrophina campbelli (Walcott). A chert slab covered with impressions of this Upper Cambrian and Lowermost Ordovician brachiopod. Gasconade Formation, Lower Ordovician, Womack, Missouri. (Value range F)

Atrypia independensis. Dorsal valve. Devonian, Hay River, NWT Canada. (Value range G)

Syntrophina campbelli. Another chert slab crowded with these early-most Ordovician articulate brachiopods. Gasconade Formation, Womack, Missouri.

Atrypia independensis. Ventral valve. Cedar Valley Limestone, Iowa City, Iowa. (Value range G)

Strophodonta sp. Middle Devonian, Callaway Limestone (Snyder Creek Shale), Callaway County, Missouri. (Value range G)

Cyrtospirifer sp. Hay River Formation, NWT Canada. A Devonian Spirifera. (Value range G)

Leptaena analoga. A wide ranging brachiopod (Silurian through Mississippian) in the Paleozoic Era. This is a chert specimen from the Mississippian of Missouri. (Keokuk Formation.) (Value range G)

Paraspirifer bownockeri. Silica Shale, Middle Devonian, Sylvania, Ohio. (Value range G)

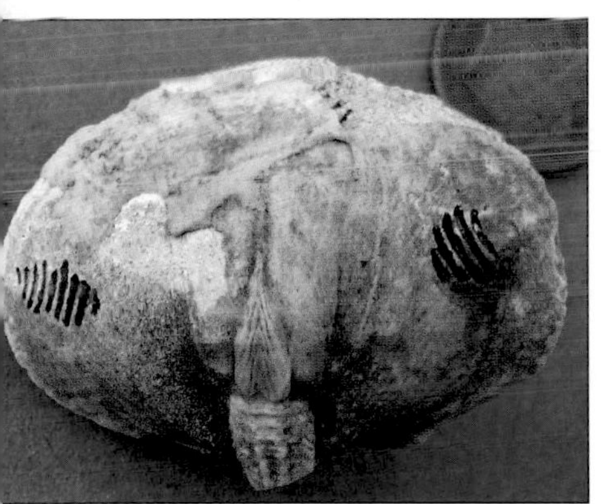

Schizophoria sp. A chert steinkern of this widespread genus. The spiralia can be seen at both right and left sides of the brachiopod. Keokuk Formation (Chert), Cedar Creek, Callaway County, Missouri. (Value range G)

Paraspirifer bownockeri. Silica Shale, Middle Devonian, Sylvania, Ohio.

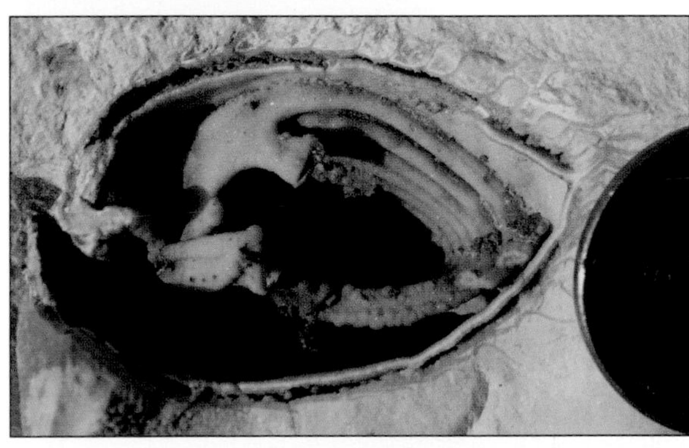

Schizophoria sp. Cross section of silicified specimen showing spiralia preserved in chert. Keokuk Formation, Callaway County, Missouri.

Brachyspirifer audaculus. A large Devonian spirifer. Cedar Valley Limestone, Iowa City, Iowa. (Value range G)

Spirifer sp. An internal chert mold of this relative common and widespread brachiopod. Mississippian, Black Hills, South Dakota. (Value range H)

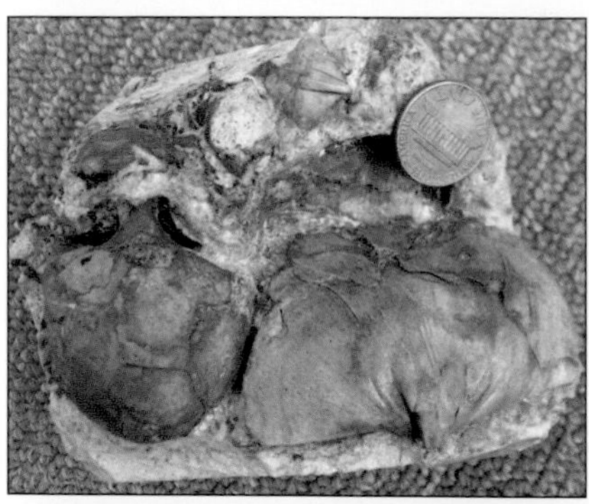

Chert mold of the internal structure of *Spirifera* associated with a crinoid calyx (left) of the genus *Platycrinites.* Osagian cherts, northern Ozarks, Missouri. (Value range G)

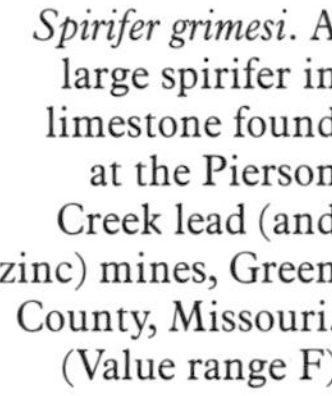

Spirifer grimesi. A large spirifer in limestone found at the Pierson Creek lead (and zinc) mines, Green County, Missouri. (Value range F)

Spirifer sp. Shows the spiralia magnificently preserved. The spiralia, an organ unique to the brachiopods, can contain some minerals. When it does, under the right conditions, it can be totally preserved with silica, as has happened with these specimens. All of these were found in Mississippian cherts of the Ozarks, the two specimens on the left being found with chert gravel in a creek. The specimen at the top is an impression of the spiralia. All of these specimens were associate with Osagian cherts. (Value range D for group)

Spirifer grimesi. A large spirifer in Osagian (Burlington) chert and limestone. Burlington Limestone, Lincoln County, Missouri. (Value range F)

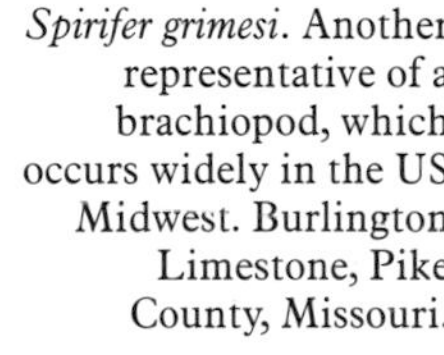

Spirifer grimesi. Another representative of a brachiopod, which occurs widely in the US Midwest. Burlington Limestone, Pike County, Missouri.

The same specimens as in the previous photo, but with a quartz coated spiralia at the left associated with the brachiopod genus *Composita*. Here the spirals of the spiralia have been broken and scattered. Unusual preservation like this represents one of the fascinating phenomena of chert fossils.

Spirifer grimesi. A chert cast of this large and relatively common Mississippian brachiopod. This specimen has been preserved in flint (a hard form of chert). It was found associated with flint used by Native Americans for making arrowheads. (Value range F)

Neospirifer cameratus. Middle Pennsylvanian, Urich, Missouri. A well preserved common brachiopod in the Middle Pennsylvanian of the US Midwest. (Value range F)

Neospirifer sp. Lower Permian, Council Grove, Morris County, Kansas. Both valves are showing on this spiriferid brachiopod. (Value range F)

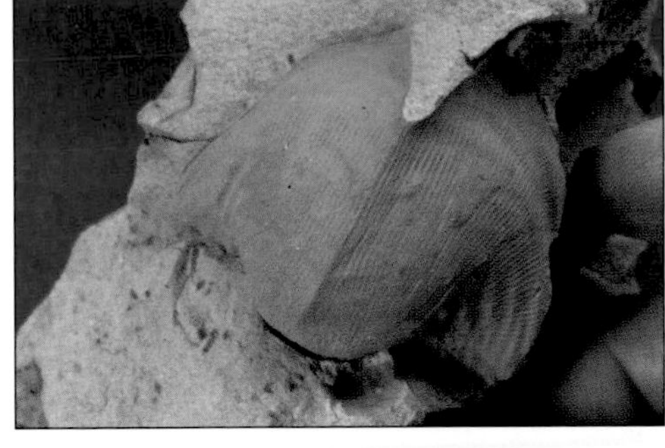

Linoproductus oklahoma. Lower Permian sandstone, Osage County, Oklahoma. (Value range F)

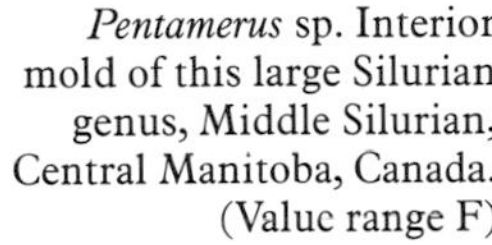

Pentamerus sp. Interior mold of this large Silurian genus, Middle Silurian, Central Manitoba, Canada. (Valuc range F)

Echinoconchus semipunctatus. A large productid characteristic of the mid-Pennsylvanian of the US Midwest. Pennsylvanian, St. Louis County, Missouri. (Value range F)

Composita subtilita. Pennsylvanian, Grand River, Missouri. (Value range G)

Paucispinifera sp. Leonard Formation, Permian, Marathon, Texas. One of a number of productids which are silicified and thus can be extracted from the limestone in which they occur by acid etching (Value range G)

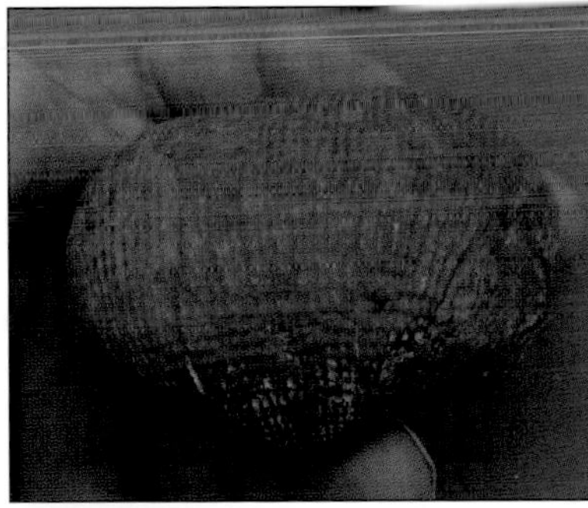

Dictyclostus americanus. Upper Pennsylvanian, Grand River, Missouri. A large productid characteristic of the late Paleozoic. (Value range G)

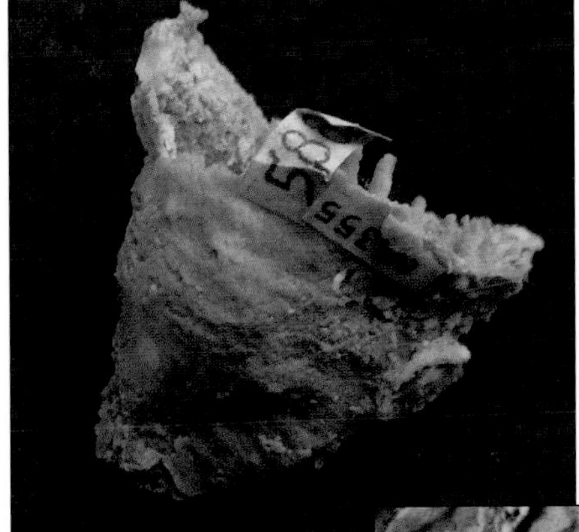

Prorichtofenia sp. Word Limestone, Leonard Formation, Permian, Marathon, Texas. A silicified (etched from limestone) reef building brachiopod, which forms reef-like structures in the Permian of west Texas, New Mexico, and northern Mexico.

Linoproductus ovatus. Cluster of this widespread Carboniferous genus. *Linoproductus* as well as other productids commonly are gregarious. Middle Mississippian, Salem Formation, St. Louis County, Missouri. (Value range G)

Leptodus americanus. Another silicified reef forming brachiopod. Word Limestone, Leonard Formation, late Permian, Marathon, Texas. (Value range F)

Bryozoans

Bryozoans, like brachiopods, are lophophorates (animals having a lophophore)—both phyla are closely related to each other. Bryozoans always occur in colonies, marine bryozoan animals precipitating an exoskeleton composed of calcium carbonate. Bryozoan colonies can be a major component of some Paleozoic limestones. Like brachiopods, bryozoans were conspicuous and dominant elements of Paleozoic marine life. Also, like brachiopods, bryozoans today are minor elements of living marine faunas. Bryozoans during the Paleozoic Era underwent a great deal of speciation, but to distinguish many taxa from each other requires microscopic examination. Prior to the late nineteenth century, bryozoan taxonomy was rather simple. Microscopic examination made them much more diverse (and complicated). One of the early workers on these "moss-animals" was Hiram Prout of St. Louis and the St. Louis Academy of Science. Dr. Prout used bryozoan colony impressions locally found in abundance in cherts of the Mississippian, St. Louis Limestone found in the St. Louis, Missouri, area.

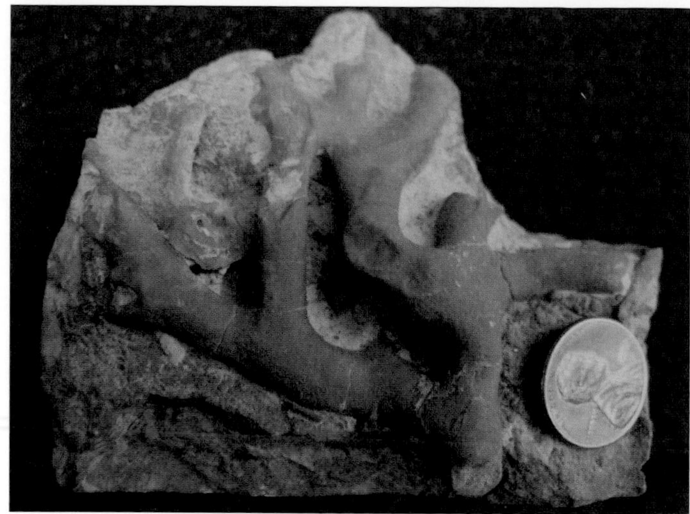

Batostoma sp. A branching bryozoan characteristic of the Middle and Upper Ordovician. A number of genera of these robust, branching bryozoans occur in the Ordovician. Genera of this type include *Prasopora*, *Rhinidictya*, *Homotrypa* as well as other genera. They can, however, only be distinguished with certainty by microscopic examination. Upper Ordovician, Murfreesboro, Tennessee. (Value range F, specimen attractive and distinct)

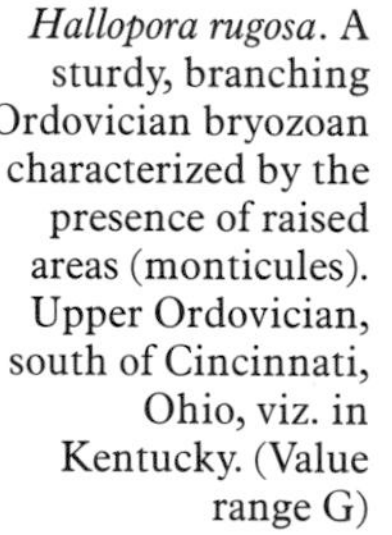

Hallopora rugosa. A sturdy, branching Ordovician bryozoan characterized by the presence of raised areas (monticules). Upper Ordovician, south of Cincinnati, Ohio, viz. in Kentucky. (Value range G)

Nicholsonella sp. ("Nothing Fossils.") One of the first bryozoans, *Nicholsonella* has also been placed by some paleontologists with the stromatoporoids and corals by other paleontologists. Its confusing taxonomy has earned its name as a "nothing fossil." *Nicholsonella* is restricted to the late Lower Ordovician, the majority of specimens coming from the Smithville Formation of northern Arkansas. These come from reef-like associations with stromatolites. (Value range F)

Arthropora simplex. A branching bryozoan. Plattin Limestone, Black Riverian, Jefferson County, Missouri. (Value range G)

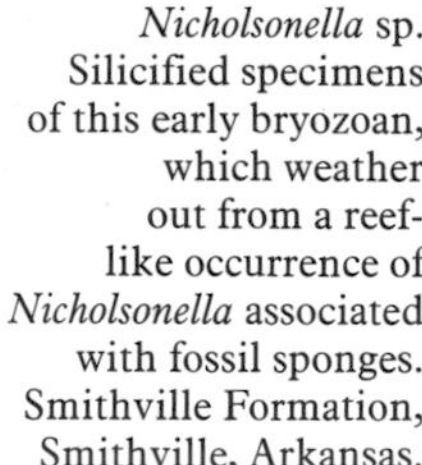

Nicholsonella sp. Silicified specimens of this early bryozoan, which weather out from a reef-like occurrence of *Nicholsonella* associated with fossil sponges. Smithville Formation, Smithville, Arkansas.

Coscinium sp. A robust bryozoan that grew around some sort of support. Warsaw Formation, Middle Mississippian, Arnold, Missouri. (Value range G)

Coscinium latum. The same genus as in the previous photo, but here formed in a branching pattern. Warsaw Formation, Cuvier River, Moscow Mills, Missouri. (Value range F—distinct colony)

Fenestrellina sp. An impression (no original-material preserved) of the zooecium of a fenestrellate bryozoan in siltstone. Warsaw Formation, Middle Mississippian, Fenton, Missouri. (Value range H)

Fenestrellina sp. This is a frond of the common fenestrellate bryozoan. These moss animals were, at times, so abundant as to make up whole layers of limestone with their zoaria. This is an impression in chert of the fenestrellate zoaria. Cherts weathering from the St. Louis Limestone in the St. Louis area frequently can be found carrying well preserved and distinct impressions of a variety of bryozoans. In the mid-nineteenth century, these were a topic of scientific interest and Dr. Hiram Prout of the St. Louis Academy of Science described and illustrated a number of them in the 1850s. Later, near the end of the nineteenth century, utilizing a microscope, most bryozoans were found to be structurally and taxonomically more complicated than previously thought so that earlier Paleozoic taxa were invalidated (placed in synonymy). (Value range H)

Fenestrellina emaciate. Impression of this fenestrellate bryozoan having large zoaria. Keokuk Formation, Cedar Creek, Callaway County, Missouri. (Value range G)

Fenestrellina sp. Portions of this common Mississippian bryozoan preserved as impressions in chert. St. Louis Limestone, St. Louis, Missouri. (Value range H)

Fenestrellina cf. *elegans*. Impression in chert of this delicate fenestrellate bryozoan. Keokuk Formation, Middle Mississippian, Cedar Creek, Callaway County, Missouri. (Value range G)

Fenestrellina sp. Very clear and distinct zoaria preserved in siltstone. The genus name fenestrellina comes from fenstra, that is "window." Individual zooecia do resemble small windows. Salem Formation, Middle Mississippian, Arnold, Missouri. (Value range G)

Polypora shumardi Prout. Similar to *fenestrellina*, but with a keel between adjacent zoaria. The genus was named by Hiram Prout of St. Louis in the mid-nineteenth century. Dr. Prout was a St. Louis physician who, like L. P. Yandell of Louisville, Kentucky, had a strong interest in the nascent field of paleontology. He did fundamental work on bryozoan taxonomy before it came under the influence of "splitters" who utilized microscopic observations to totally revise bryozoan taxa. He was also a founding member of the St. Louis Academy of Science, which in the nineteenth century was on the cutting edge of North American scientific discovery, especially regarding natural phenomena that existed to the west of St. Louis. St. Louis at that time really was the "Gateway to the West!" The St. Louis Academy of Science still exists today, but focuses primarily on the health care and biotechnology fields.

Fenestrellina sp. A small frond from Mississippian Limestone found at the Frank Alberta slide site. (Value range G)

Fenestrellina sp. Close-up of previously shown specimen.

Fenestrellina sp. This chert slab, and similar slabs, bear fossils of distinct fronds of this bryozoan. Such slabs occur along the banks of the Mississippi River at low water level about one mile downstream from downtown St. Louis (below the arch). Similar slabs probably were the type specimens used by Dr. H. Prout in his bryozoan descriptions of the late 1850s. It's from similar slabs that the bryozoan genus *Fenestrellina* and *Polypora* were (probably) based. (Value range G)

Rubble pile of cherty Mississippian limestone from the 1903 Frank Alberta rock slide. Large numbers of limestone boulders occur where the Trans-Canadian Highway traverses southern Alberta. These came from a rock slide that occurred in 1903. The limestone is massive and relatively unfossiliferous; however, if one looks in the jumble of rocks, specimens like the example shown here may occasionally be found. Anywhere a large amount of limestone like this occurs and has weathered sufficiently, fossils might be seen.

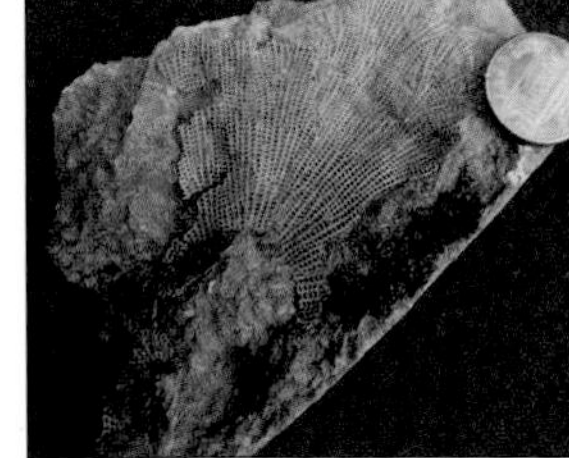

Fenestrellina tenax. A frond of this common Upper Mississippian bryozoan. Glen Dean Formation, Chester, Illinois. (Value range G+, distinct bryozoan frond)

Fenestrellina tenax. Another frond of a well preserved and distinct fenestrellate bryozoan. (Value range F)

Boulders of Mississippian limestone north (uphill) from the Frank slide.

Cherty Mississippian limestone at the Frank slide on the Trans-Canadian Highway, southern Alberta.

Lyropora quinecuncialis (Hall). A fenestrellate bryozoan which resembles a lyre, the fenestrated portion (like the strings of a lyre) strung between a robust calcareous support. Glen Dean Limestone, Perry County, Missouri. (Value range F)

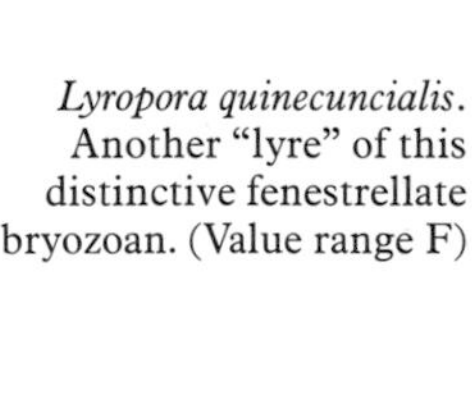

Lyropora quinecuncialis. Another "lyre" of this distinctive fenestrellate bryozoan. (Value range F)

An **encrusting bryozoan** with regions lacking zoaria; these regions are known as maculae. These massive bryozoans, which can be limestone formers, are interesting to encounter in natural outcrops but don't lend themselves to a collection. Glen Dean Limestone, Chester Series, Perry County, Missouri.

A more distinctive **encrusting bryozoan** showing well formed maculae. Glen Dean Limestone, Chester Series, Star Landing, Perry County, Missouri. (Value range G)

A Plethora of Archimedes

Archimedes "corkscrews" can locally be common fossils in Mississippian age rocks, especially in Mississippian (Lower Carboniferous) limestone of the Midwestern United States. *Archimedes* is hypothesized to have involved a symbiotic relationship between bryozoans and a calcareous red algae, the red algae being responsible for the distinctive spiral axis.

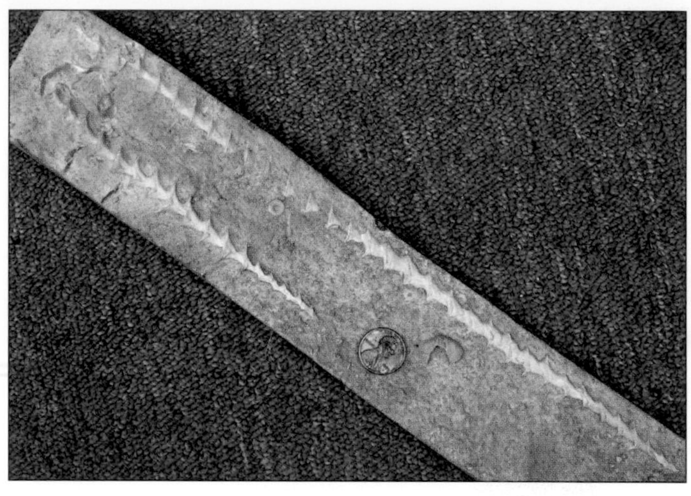

Two parallel slender spiral supports of *Archimedes wortheni*. Warsaw Formation, Arnold, Missouri. (Value range F)

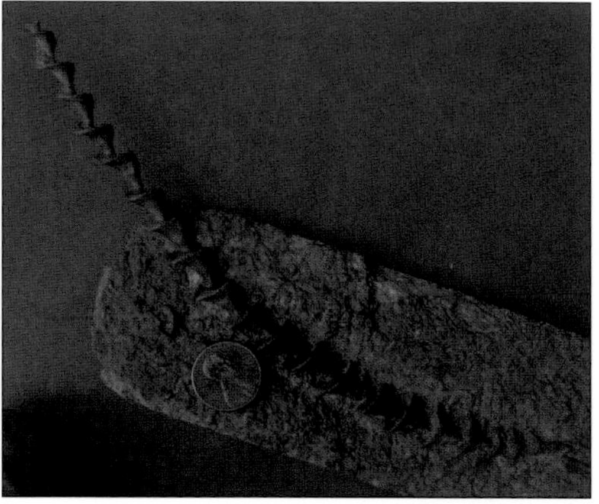

Archimedes wortheni Hall. This bryozoan has a spiral axis which supports fenestrellate fronds. *Archimedes* is characteristic of Mississippian strata of the US Midwest. It has been suggested that *Archimedes* represents a symbiosis of bryozoa with its spiral supporting axis formed by a calcareous red algae. The algae may have been symbiotic to the bryozoan, which is represented by the fenestrellate portion of the organism (not shown on this specimen). Warsaw Formation, Lincoln County, Missouri. (Value range F)

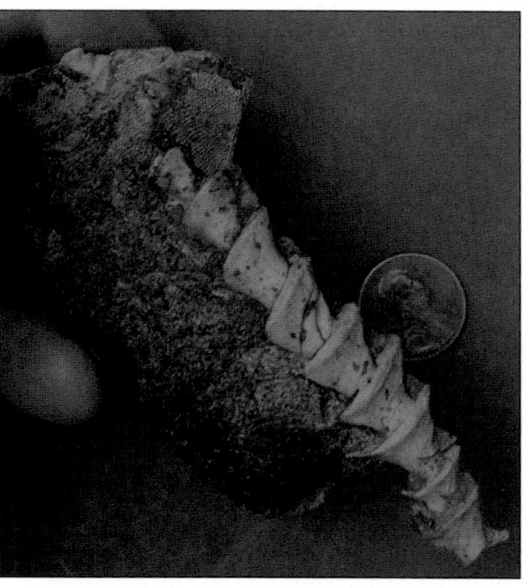

A robust form of *Archimedes wortheni*. Some of the attached fenestrellate fronds are seen attached to the spiral axis. Warsaw Formation, Lincoln County, Missouri.

A robust central axis of *Archimedes*. Older colonies of this peculiar life form grew massive and had a more robust spiral axis. Compare this specimen with that of the previous photo. Warsaw Formation, Lincoln County, Missouri. (Value range F)

Archimedes wortheni. A chert impression of the central axis showing the extending bryozoan fronds. Fossils such as this can incur the curiosity of its finder, as did this specimen found as a cobble in a creek by a farmer. Callaway County, Missouri.

Archimedes communis. The spiral axis of this species can weather out in large numbers from thin shale beds associated with limestone of Upper Mississippian (Chesterian) age. These came from rocks exposed along the Mississippi River during low water. (Value range F)

Archimedes communis. A smaller and more slender species of *Archimedes* which is restricted to the Upper Mississippian of the US Midwest. (Value range F)

Archimedes sp. with fenestrellate bryozoan fronds supported by robust pillars. *Archimedes* in the Upper Mississippian Pitkin Limestone of northwestern Arkansas is peculiar in having these supports. The radiating fronds can be seen on the weathered surface of this specimen. Upper Mississippian, Pitkin Limestone, Leslie, Arkansas. (Value range F)

Outcrop of late Mississippian strata containing *Archimedes* near Leslie, Arkansas. The distinctly layered (cyclic) strata in the lower portion of the cutting is the Fayetteville Shale, a current source of interest as it can contain great amounts of natural gas.

Evactinopora sexradiata. The star-shaped support of a fenestrellate bryozoan. *Evactinopora*, like *Archimedes*, is restricted to the US Midwest. Also like *Archimedes*, the calcareous support may represent a form of symbiosis between a marine algae and a bryozoan. Specimens of *Evactinopora* are often thought to be a small fossil starfish. The number of arms varies from four to eight. The most common number being six. Fern Glen Formation, Jefferson County, Missouri. (Value range F)

Archimedes intermedius. A spiral axis of this Upper Mississippian species preserved in a hard, black limestone from the previously shown outcrop. Pitkin Limestone, Chester Series, Leslie, Arkansas.

Two closely spaced specimens of this bryozoan, often confused with starfish. Fern Glen Formation, Middle Mississippian.

Evactinopora sexradiata. A seven-armed specimen preserved in chert found as a creek pebble. Fern Glen Formation, Jefferson County, Missouri. (Value range F)

Evactinopora grandis. A six-rayed specimen of this bryozoan. Note the zooacium containing mineralized tissue extending off of the arms. Burlington Limestone, Hannibal, Missouri. (Value range E)

Evactinopora grandis Meek and Worthen. A large species of *Evactinopora* occuring in the lower part of the crinoidal Burlington Limestone. Note how the limestone matrix between the five arms is composed of crinoid fragments. Like *E. sexradiata* shown previously, *E. grandis* can have a variable number of arms. Burlington Limestone, Springfield, Green County, Missouri. (Value range F).

Evactinopora grandis. A four-rayed specimen. Burlington Formation, Middle Mississippian. (Value range G)

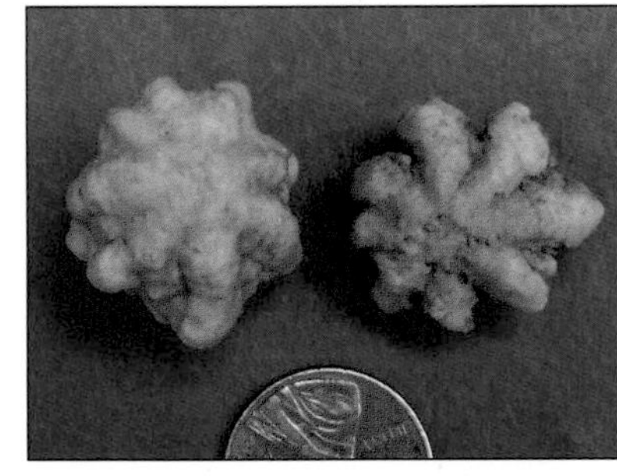

Geodized *Evactinopora*. Fossils can form the nucleus of geodes and direct their formation retaining (in a vague way) the shape of the original fossil. Quartz somehow replaces and enlarges the original fossil to produce a geode. (Value range G)

Evactinopora grandis Meek and Worthen. A large five-rayed specimen of this interesting bryozoan. Middle Mississippian Burlington Limestone occurrence just above the Hannibal Shale, Hannibal, Missouri. (Value range F)

Glossary

Lophophore: A food-catching organ consisting of a circular fold of the body wall that encircles the mouth and bears numerous small tentacles. A lophophore is found in the brachiopods, bryozoans, and phoronid worms—all of which are referred to as lophophorates by invertebrate zoologists.

Symbiotic relationship: An ecological strategy in which two (or more) totally different organisms live together in a mutually beneficial relationship. In reference to the bryozoan *Archimedes,* it is believed to be a symbiosis between a bryozoan and a calcareous red algae.

Mollusks

Fossils of the various types of shells representative of this large phylum of animals are some of the most common, yet often highly collectible, fossils of the Paleozoic Era. Mollusks are soft bodied animals usually enclosed within a calcareous shell, which preserves well in sedimentary rock, especially in limestone. Some mollusks, like gastropods (snails), pelecypods (clams) and cephalopods, are well known animals, while others like monoplacophorans, chitons, and scaphopods are less so. Some molluscan classes are also extinct; they are known only from fossils, many of which are found in strata of the Cambrian Period.

A group of hypseloconid monoplacophorans on a late Cambrian sea floor in what is now southern Missouri. Large, well preserved monoplacophorans (monoplacs) are not common fossils and are relatively unknown to collectors. *Artwork by Virginia M. Stinchcomb*

Monoplacophorans

Almost extinct today, "monoplacs" are a type of primitive mollusk showing evidence of body segmentation (an anatomical feature normally not associated with mollusks). What are now relegated to the class monoplacophora were first known as fossils, but prior to the 1960s were considered to be primitive and/or odd gastropods. Paleontologists prior to the 1970s were reluctant to establish new classes based upon fossils. The fossil record was considered as being too poor to contribute to such "high level" biologic classifications or taxonomy. Rather, these (and other) odd fossil mollusks were taxonomically "shoehorned" into living classes, in this case into the class gastropoda (snails). Monoplacophorans are especially characteristic of the Cambrian Period and the early part of the Lower Ordovican. This was because they became abundant animals in the seas when they underwent an "explosive" radiation in diversity. Monoplacophorans represent part of the Cambrian radiation event, but they underwent their radiation in both diversity and abundance late in the Cambrian, unlike the trilobites, archeocyathids, and eocrinoids, which diversified earlier in the period.

Monoplacophoran locality, 1956. This barite pit south of St. Louis still produces specimens, though now grown up with cedar trees. The monoplacs occur in the Cambrian age stromatolitic chert, along with a variety of interesting mineral specimens. The previous artwork depicts this locality as it looked 500 million years ago during the late Cambrian.

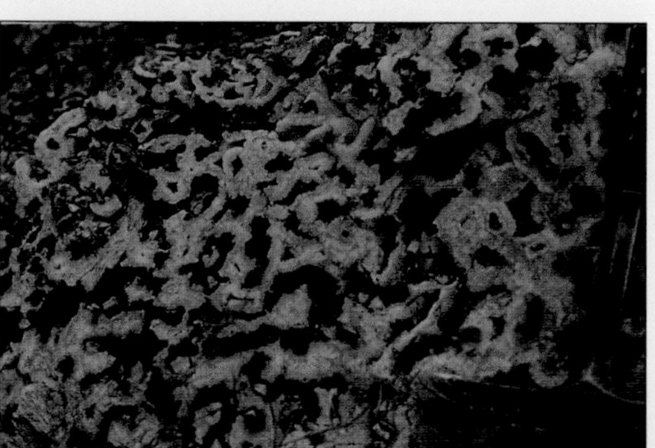

Stromatolitic chert at the barite pit locality. Monoplacophorans are found here, occurring between stromatolite "fingers" now represented by holes in the chert.

In the early 1950s, living cap-shaped mollusks were dredged from a deep sea trench. These mollusks were found to have a soft part anatomy distinct from other mollusks. From these "living fossils," with their partial segmentation, the class Monoplacophora was established by zoologists. With this, it was realized by paleontologists that various odd cap-shaped fossil shells bearing multiple muscle scars (indicating partial segmentation) were **fossil monoplacophorans**. Recognition of this new molluscan class breached some of the taxonomic conservatism of paleontology so that the discipline became more disposed to the erection of high level taxa (phyla and classes) based upon fossils. Paleontologists then started looking at other odd and peculiar fossils to determine if these might also represent previously unknown body plans and hence be extinct classes of various phyla. In other words, the recognition of the monoplacophorans as an extinct molluscan class, crossed a mental threshold which previously had limited the establishment of extinct classes based upon fossils. The class monoplacophora has since been greatly expanded and what are considered by some workers as other extinct molluscan classes have now been split off from the monoplacophorans.

Hypseloconid monoplacophorans (and snail-like *Scaevogyra*) from previously shown outcrops.

Group of hypseloconid monoplacophorans (monoplacs) in stromatolitic chert from the previous locality in southern Missouri. (Value range E)

Group of hypseloconid monoplacophorans preserved in the position close to that in which they lived, that is between stromatolite "fingers" now represented by circular holes.

Group of hypseloconid monoplacophorans (and *Scaevogyra*) positioned around digitate stromatolites (now represented by holes in the chert). (Value range D)

Another view of the above specimen. A hole left by a stromatolite "finger" is at the upper left.

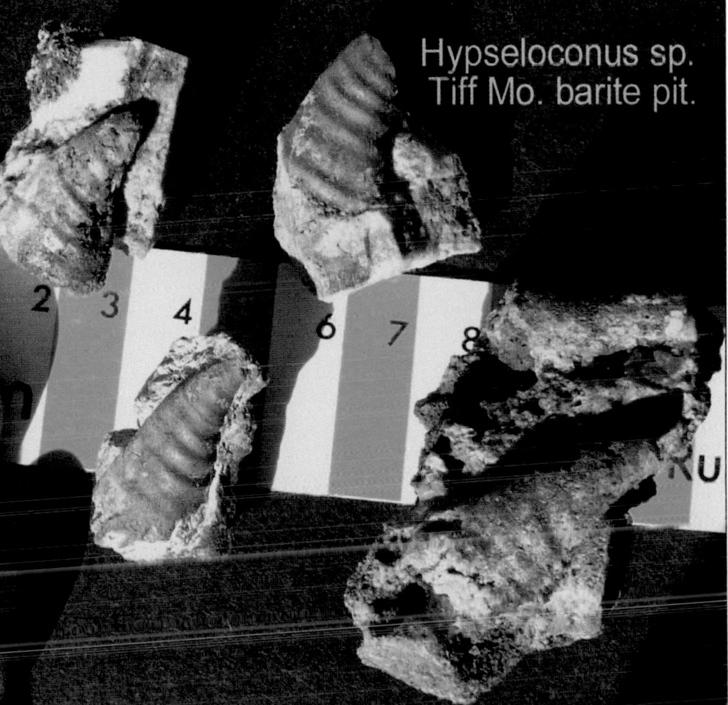

Gayneoconus echolsi. An ornamented, elongate monoplacophoran from the Tiff, Missouri, barite pit shown in a previous photo. Original descriptions by the author of this ornamented monoplac included the mention of incidents associated with recorded orchestral music from *Gayne* Ballet where specimens of the form were first observed and collected (Jour. Paleontology V. 76, No. 6). Likewise under multiplated mollusks later in this chapter, mention is made of a "convoluted field relationship," also involving this musical work by the Georgian (Soviet) composer Aram Khachaturian. What this "convoluted relationship" was is as follows: The author as an early teen, acquired a number of albums of symphonic recordings on 78 RPM records in the early 1950s. 78's were becoming obsolete at this time and those acquired were almost entirely of Soviet composers. Liking the music on the records, he took them and a WWII portable record player to a boy scout summer camp near Irondale, Washington County, Missouri (located appropriately in Cambrian fossil-rich territory). One of the scout troops committee members who was also a guard at McDonnell Aircraft Co. in St. Louis stayed at the camp with his asthma-prone son. This committee member, upon seeing both the records and their album covers (with hammer and sickle flags), became noticeably upset, insisting that some sort of "investigation" be consummated to ascertain why such mind-infecting, Soviet propaganda was being brought to Camp Irondale. Presumably this infraction had already affected *me* and by the playing of these records would also (somehow) subliminally and adversely affect other boys at the camp.
It turned out that Camp Irondale also had Cambrian molluscan fossils in its rocks, which (later) I found to be undescribed forms, which yours truly eventually described in the J. P. Not wanting to miss an opportunity to relate this personal "cold war" incident, I named the fossils originally recognized and found at the camp after this incident and its offending and fearful recordings—especially those of A. Khachaturian, which I especially like.

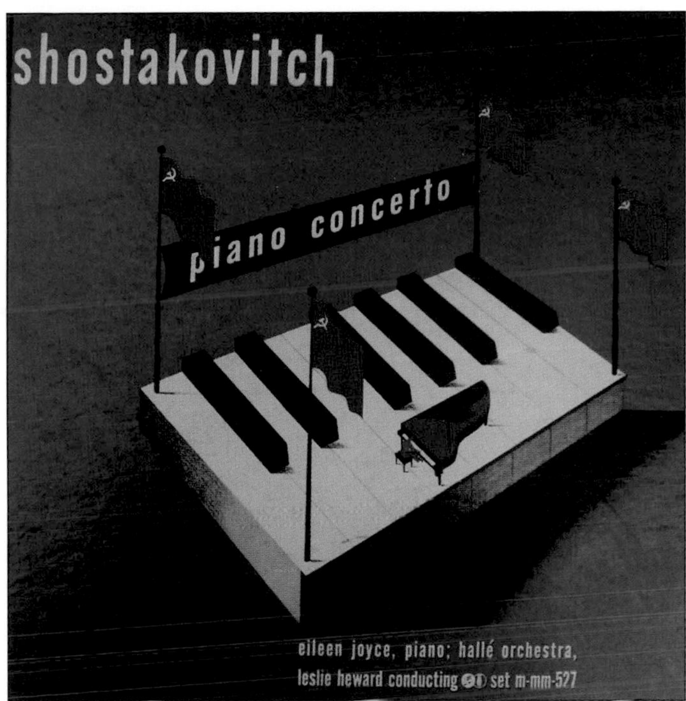

Soviet flags on the record album cover of Shostokovitch work brought to Camp Irondale, which presumably, when played, would subliminally and insidiously turn 1950s American youth into "loyal followers of Marx, Lenin, and Stalin."

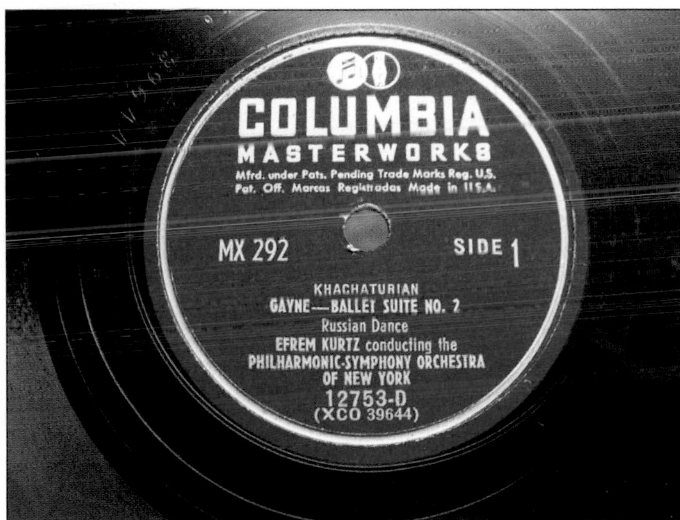

Aram Khachaturian's *Gayne* Ballet, which included the popular Sabre Dance and the nomenclatural basis for *Gayneoconus* sp. *Gayne* Ballet included Hero Colonel Kazanoff of the Red Army Border Patrol who was "bedecked with medals" or in latin *Phalleratus* = wearing medallions (see multiplated mollusks).

Hammer-and-sickle rooster label of Khachaturian's work (*Masquerade Suite*), which invoked additional red-scare fears at Camp Irondale and also was a part of this "convoluted field relationship."

Massive Upper Cambrian Eminence Dolomite outcrops along the Meramec River, northeastern Ozarks. The Eminence Formation in dolomite outcrops such as this carries no fossils. When dolomite like this becomes deeply weathered, fossils do appear in chert, which accumulates as the dolomite weathers. The Eminence Formation is upper-most Cambrian in age.

Shelbyoceras robustum. A large, well preserved monoplacophoran once considered a cephalopod. *Shelbyoceras* has chambers at its apex like a cephalopod; however, these chambers usually shatter when a specimen is broken from the rock (they are very fragile). It is not a cephalopod as it lacks a siphuncle. With the appearance of a siphuncle, these curved monoplacs became ellesmeroid (primitive) cephalopods. (Value range D)

Cambrioconus missourensis. A large monoplacophoran with distinct growth lines. Monoplacophorans appear to have reached their zenith of diversification during the late (Upper) Cambrian. This specimen is from the Upper Cambrian Eminence Formation of Missouri.

Monoplacophoran bearing sandstone near Taylor's Falls, Minnesota. Monoplacophorans described from this area along the St. Croix River in eastern Minnesota were originally considered as being primitive gastropods (snails). Like many cap and cone shaped mollusks of the Ozark region, these fossils were later found to be monoplacophorans.

Hypseloconus bessemerense. This specimen was originally considered to be a cephalopod of the genus *Shelbyoceras*, hence the ending *ceras*. Many elongate monoplacophorans found in Cambrian strata during the early twentieth century were thought to be early and primitive cephalopods. The genus and species name *Shelbyoceras bessemerense* was given to this specimen (the type specimen of the genus and species). Later it was realized that these fossils are **not** cephalopods at all (they lack a siphuncle although some have septa), but rather they were related to modern representatives of mollusks established as the class Monoplacophora, a molluscan class established from living specimens dredged from the deep ocean in the early 1950s.

Proplina cornutiformis. A group of spoon-shaped monoplacophorans, all of which came from the same area of the Missouri Ozarks. These occur in strata almost on the Cambrian-Ordovician boundary.

Bipulvina croftse Yochelson. A spoon-shaped monoplacophoran similar to the previous examples, but which shows ornamentation and muscle scars. However, these markings don't show up very well in the red-orange chert. (Value range G, single specimen)

Peculiar Gastropod-like Fossils (Paragastropods)

A number of snail-like fossils occur in Cambrian rocks, but for one reason or another they are suspect as being true or undoubted gastropods. They are known as *paragastropods*.

Plagiella sp. These small, coiled shells are found in Cambrian rocks. They can coil either in a right (clockwise) or left (counterclockwise) direction. (Value range G)

On the left is a gastropod (it coils in a right handed, clockwise direction). On the right is the Cambrian snail-like fossil *Scaevogyra* (a paragastropod), which coils in a counter-clockwise direction. A number of these peculiar, gastropod-like fossils occur in Cambrian strata; most of them suspect as to being actual gastropods. There appear to have been a number of animal "body plans" (either phyla or classes) which became evolutionary "dead ends" either at the end or during the Cambrian Period, while other body plans present in the Cambrian survived and became the dominant phyla of today.

A group of *Scaevogyra swezeyi*. A group of these puzzling snail-like mollusks (paragastropods) found in a remote area on the Ozark Trail of southern Missouri.

Scaevogyra swezeyi. Snail-like Cambrian fossils from the locality shown described previously in the second photo of this chapter. (Value range E for group)

Matherella sp. High spired gastropod-like mollusk related to *Scaevogyra* but different, from Cambrian strata of the Ozark Uplift of Missouri. (Value range F)

Rhacopea grandis. A widespread gastropod characteristic of the earliest Ordovician in North America. (Value range F)

Gastropods

Gastropods are snails (usually) have a coiled shell and a body which is unsegmented and torted. Gastropods represent a class of mollusks that have left a rich and diverse fossil record.

Lecanospira compacta. Chert slab covered with impressions of the ventral part of these left handed gastropods. Roubidoux Formation, Lower Ordovician, Berryman, Washington County, Missouri. (Value range E)

Maclurites bigsbyi and a straight cephalopod. Lander Sandstone, Big Horn Mountains, Wyoming. This large, left handed gastropod is common in the Middle and Upper Ordovician. Unlike Cambrian left-handed forms, *Maclurites* is considered to be a true gastropod. (Value range F)

Helicotoma ungulata. A widely occurring early gastropod (archeogastropod) from just above the Cambrian-Ordovician boundary. (Value range F)

Maclurites manitobaensis. These large, left handed gastropods come from "Arctic" Ordovician strata of Manitoba, Canada. This is an Ordovician fauna that lived close to the Ordovician equator; many of its fossils being quite large, presumably for this reason. (Value range G, single specimen)

Maclurites bigsbyi. Plateville Group, Mifflin Limestone, Lee County, Illinois. (Value range G)

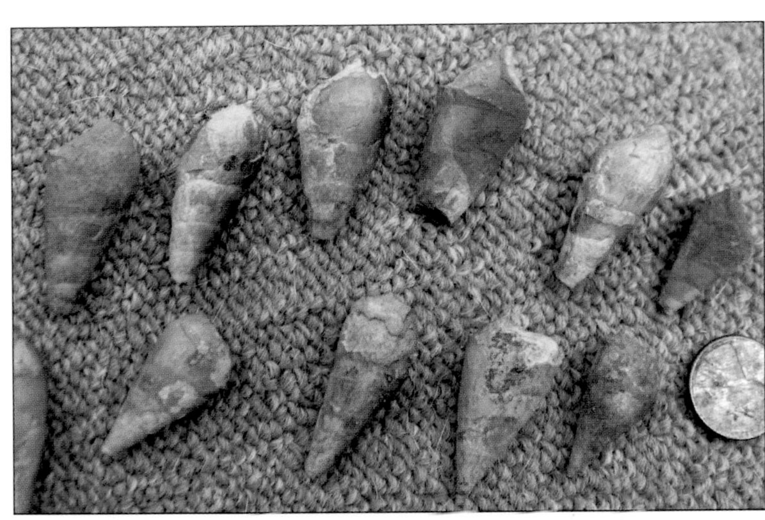

Meekospira peracuta. Wayland Shale, Graham Group. Upper Pennsylvanian, Gunsight, Stephens County, Texas. (Value range G for group)

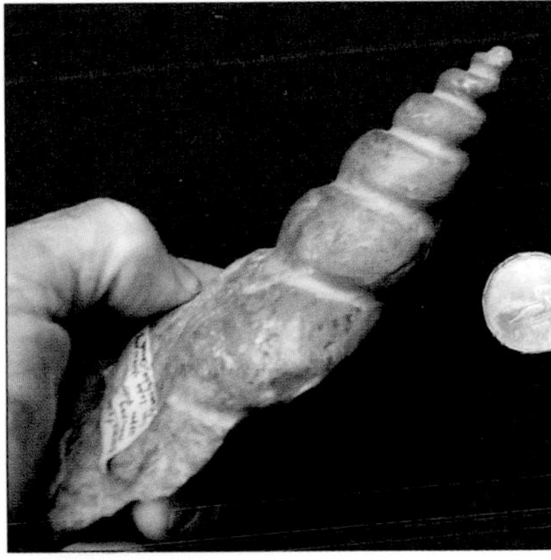

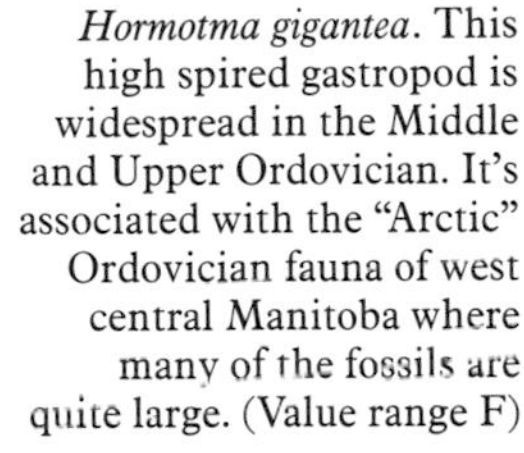

Hormotma gigantea. This high spired gastropod is widespread in the Middle and Upper Ordovician. It's associated with the "Arctic" Ordovician fauna of west central Manitoba where many of the fossils are quite large. (Value range F)

Loxoplocus (Lophospira) milleri. This is a common gastropod in Middle Ordovician rocks of the mid-United States. (Value range G for slab)

(in matrix)
Gastropod Cat. No
Name Loxoplocus (Lophospira) milleri
Locality Fruitland, MO, Cape Girardeau Co.
Donor Bruce Stinchcomb
Remarks Plattin Limestone
Middle Ordovician
Date 12·31·86 Acc. No 86·50
St. Louis Museum of Science and Natural History

Trepospira depressa. Gastropods characteristic of the Pennsylvanian Period. Wayland Shale, Graham Group, Upper Pennsylvanian, Gunsight, Stephens County, Texas. (Value range G for group)

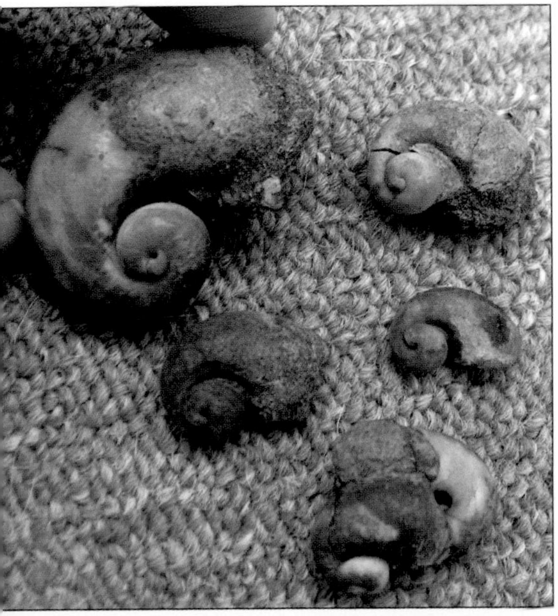

Strophostylus sp. Internal molds of this rapidly expanding gastropod. From the Kansas City Group, Kansas City, Missouri. (Value range G for group)

Euryzone arata. Cedar Valley Limestone, Middle Devonian, Iowa City, Iowa. (Value range G)

Amphiscapha reedsi. Middle Pennsylvanian, Grand River, Missouri. A widespread Pennsylvanian gastropod in the US Midwest. (Value range G for group)

Euomphalus (Straparolus) latus. Large gastropods from Mississippian outliers near Rolla, Missouri. Mollusk-rich cherts, which are remnants of strata that once covered large portions of the Ozark Uplift locally, can yield nice fossils. These occurrences were preserved by being deposited in sinkholes or solution depressions formed in underlying Lower Ordovician strata. This is one of the larger mollusks of the Mississippian outliers. Other outliers (or remnants) of strata in the Ozarks can be Devonian, Pennsylvanian, and even Cretaceous in age, the later of which has yielded Missouri's only known dinosaur. These outliers were first discovered, collected, and studied in the 1920s by geologists at what was, at the time, the Missouri School of Mines. The author uses their designation for the genus *Euomphalus*, a genus which *Index Fossils of North America* places in synonymy under *Straparolus*. (Value range E for group)

Straparolus latus. Burlington Limestone, Boliver, Missouri. (Value range G)

Euomphalus (Straparolus) latus. Bottom (ventral) view of specimen from north of Rolla, Missouri, Osagian outlier. Note distinct growth lines.

Straparolus (Euomphalus) sp. Impression in a chert pebble. Fossils like this can be found in stream pebbles or elsewhere where Paleozoic rocks occur. This one was found by an agate hunter. Middle Mississippian, Black Hills, South Dakota. (Value range H)

Euomphalus (Straparolus) latus. Well-preserved specimen (bottom view) in residual chert, Rolla, Missouri. (Value range F)

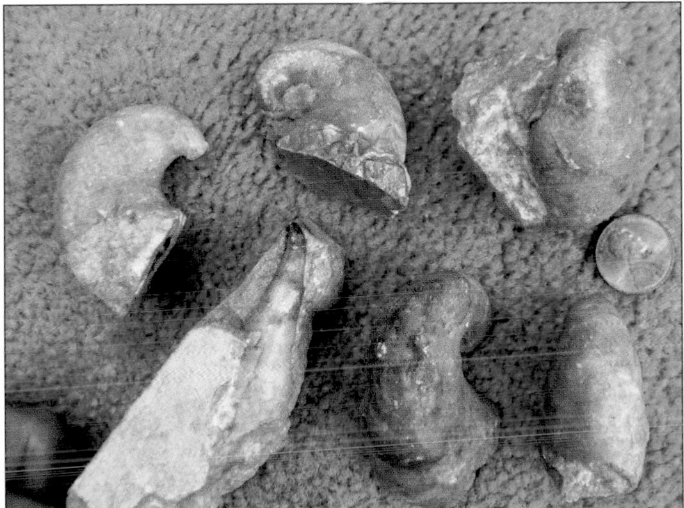

Platyceras sp. *Platyceras* is a Paleozoic cap-shaped gastropod often confused with monoplacophorans. They vary in shape and some forms are found attached to crinoids and other echinoderms. Grand Tower Limestone, Lower Devonian, Ozora, Missouri. (Value range G, single specimen)

Bellerophonts

These mollusks are characteristic of and representative of the Paleozoic Era. Some bellerophonts appear early in the Cambrian and are considered primitive mollusks, possibly monoplacophorans. Others (the majority) appear later in the Paleozoic Era and appear to be derived from gastropods. A few bellerophonts survived the Paleozoic-Mesozoic extinction event and continued into the Triassic Period of the Mesozoic Era). Unlike the shells of other gastropods (including those living today), which are torted (having a distinct top and a bottom), the shells of **bellerophonts are coiled in a plane**.

Bellerophonts can be easily confused with coiled cephalopods, which also coil in a plane. Cephalopods have chambers and other shell characteristics, which bellerophonts lack. Good bellerophontid gastropods are also less frequently seen than are planispiral cephalopods, especially considering the ammonoid cephalopods. Some bellerophont gastropods also have been considered to be a type of monoplacophoran, a class of mollusks more primitive than gastropods. Bellerophonts are found most frequently as internal molds so that surface ornamentation (which usually distinguishes species) is absent. The best that can be done in this case is to label the fossil as *Bellerophon* sp.

Bellerophont sp. Internal molds of these planispiral gastropods. Bellerophonts are often found clustered together in a manner similar to that found with monoplacophorans. All of these specimens came from a single Pennsylvanian age boulder near Cuba, New Mexico. (Value range F for group)

Bellerophont sp. One of the last of the Bellerophonts. From the Permian Phosphoria Formation of southern Idaho. Bellerophonts are one of the Paleozoic organisms found in Triassic strata, one of the few major Paleozoic life forms (other than conodonts) to survive the Paleozoic-Mesozoic extinction event and then go extinct before the Mesozoic extinction event. (Value range G)

Bellerophon missourensis Shumard. Internal molds of a narrow species from Upper Mississippian (Chesterian) strata, Chester, Illinois. (Value range G)

Bellerophon sp. Internal molds, St. Louis Limestone, St. Louis, Missouri.

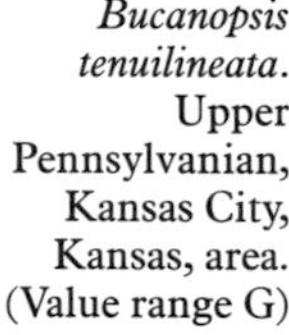

Bucanopsis tenuilineata. Upper Pennsylvanian, Kansas City, Kansas, area. (Value range G)

Euphemites nodocarinatus (Hall). Specimen of bellerophontid showing some color patterns. Middle Pennsylvanian, St. Louis, Missouri. (Value range G)

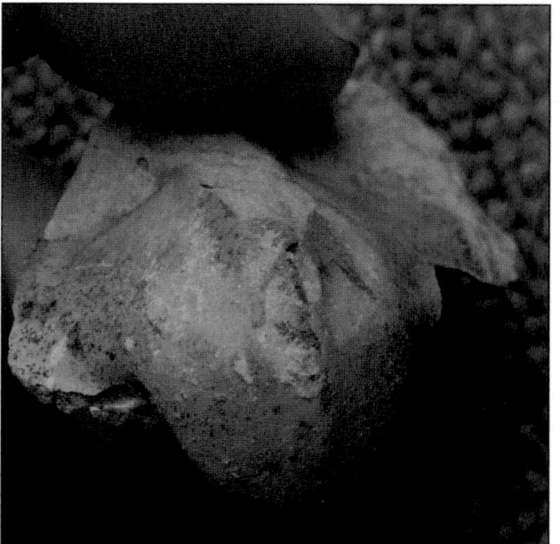

Tetranota wisconsinensis. Middle Ordovician, Platteville Group, Mifflin Formation, Ogle County, northern Illinois. (Value range G)

Bellerophon sp. Internal mold of a fairly large specimen of this planispiral gastropod. St. Louis Limestone, St. Louis, Missouri. (Value range G)

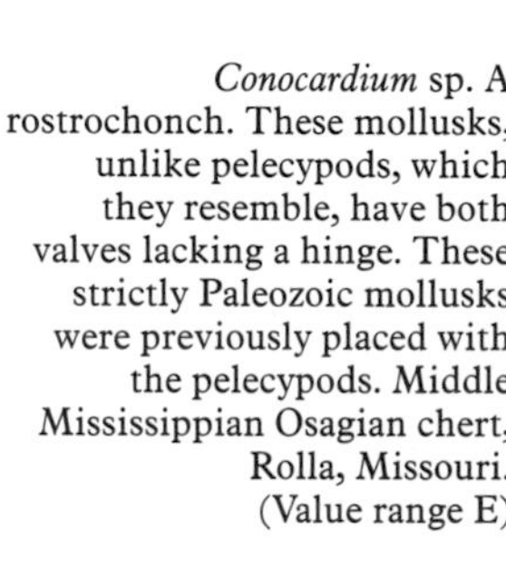

Conocardium sp. A rostrochonch. These mollusks, unlike pelecypods, which they resemble, have both valves lacking a hinge. These strictly Paleozoic mollusks were previously placed with the pelecypods. Middle Mississippian Osagian chert, Rolla, Missouri. (Value range E)

Rostrochonchs

Rostrochonchs are considered to be an extinct class of Paleozoic mollusks. They have two valves like a clam, but the valves, unlike a clam, are **not** hinged.

Two additional specimens of these interesting and unusual mollusks.

Conocardium (a rostrochonch) at bottom right, brachiopod impression (*Rhynchopora*), left. Osagian chert, Middle Mississippian, Callaway County, Missouri. (Value range F)

Pelecypods (Clams and Related Mollusks)

Mylina subaquadrata. These pelecypods come from Pennsylvanian strata of the St. Louis, Missouri, area. Pelecypods are relatively rare fossils in Paleozoic rocks, especially when compared with their abundance in post Paleozoic strata. (Value range F for group, not commonly seen so well preserved)

These pelecypods, like gastropods, are major elements of the phylum mollusca. In the Paleozoic, pelecypods were not especially abundant, their abundance came with the Mesozoic, Cenozoic, and modern molluscan faunas. Pelecypods also make excellent chowder! But, in the Paleozoic, to gather a sufficient number of clams to create a large pot of chowder would have been quite difficult.

Close-up of *Mylina*, a very pretty clam with a very pretty name!

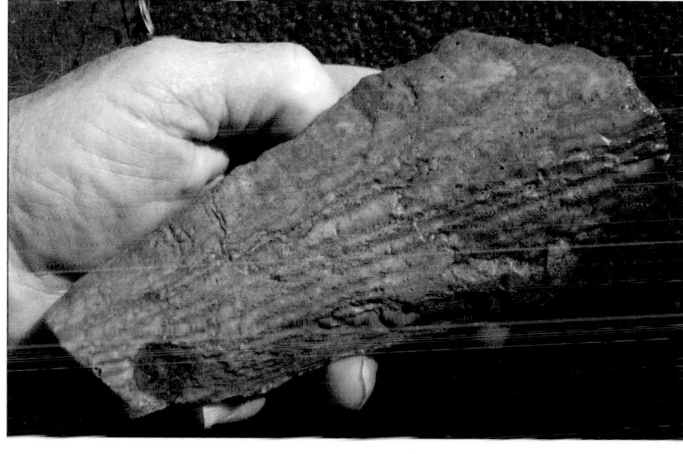

Aviculopinna americana. The genus *Pinna* (also known as razor clams or sea pens) were dominant pelecypods during the Mesozoic Era. This is a Paleozoic ancestor of these peculiar pelecypods. Specimen preserved as a chert cast from the Burlington Formation, Dade County, Missouri. (Value range F—unusual)

Aviculopinna americanna. A small specimen of a Paleozoic sea pen or razor clam. St. Louis Limestone (chert), Arnold, Missouri. (Value range G)

Aviculopectin sp. This is the Paleozoic equivalent of *Pectin* (the scallop of fish markets and gourmets). Mississippian (Osagian) chert, Springfield, Missouri. (Value range F, relatively rare)

Allorisma sp. A very fine clam from the late Paleozoic. St. Louis Limestone, Arnold, Missouri. (Value range G)

Cephalopods

The Cambrian Period, with its radiation event, saw the first great radiation of body plans in the animal kingdom. Many forms at that time were peculiar and went extinct either during or at the end of the Period. The Ordovician Period saw the appearance of animal classes and phyla which would diversify and become dominant life forms which still live today, life forms like the pelecypods, corals, bryozoans, and even the vertebrates. This first appearance of taxa still living today is known as the Great Ordovician Biodiversification Event (GOBE)—cephalopods are part of it.

Cephalopods are the most advanced and sophisticated of mollusks! The living octopus, pearly nautilus, and the squid represent living examples of the class, a class that also has a long and extensive fossil record. Paleozoic cephalopods consist primarily of the animals straight, curved or coiled shells, shells which sometimes can be quite large and have a series of septa and a siphuncle by which the animal remains in contact with its now abandoned (but previously occupied) living chambers. Three groups of shelled cephalopods lived in Paleozoic seas. The **ellesmeroids** (the most primitive cephalopods, often resembling an elongate monoplacophoran), the **nautaloids** consisting of a variety of straight and curved shells, and the **ammonoids**. This last order represents a group with slightly convoluted septa which evolved into the rich diversity of ammonites characteristic of the Mesozoic Era. The suborder goniatites represents one of the most attractive of Paleozoic ammonoids. Goniatites are found in strata of the mid- and late Paleozoic and go extinct with the Permian extinction event.

Ventral (bottom) view of an octopus, a modern cephalopod. The octopus has a visual system similar to that of vertebrates—yet it's in an entirely different phylum, the mollusks. It also has a highly developed nervous system similar in complexity to that of many vertebrates.

Modern squids: These mollusks are also cephalopods. Note the tentacles and large eye.

Ellesmeroid cephalopods—the first cephalopods! Reconstruction of two ellesmeroid cephalopods living associated with stromatolite reefs. There is disagreement as to whether these early cephalopods had tentacles as shown here. Later and modern cephalopods did (and do) have tentacles; however, when these appeared in geologic time is unclear as fossil cephalopods actually showing them are very rare. *Artwork by Virginia M. Stinchcomb*

Tentacles on a Late Paleozoic fossil cephalopod. The number of tentacles on living cephalopods vary. Shelled cephalopods may have had a larger number, as does the modern pearly nautilus. This cephalopod, from the marine facies (Essex fauna) of the Mazon Creek Konservat-Lagerstatten (or paleontological "window"), with its eight tentacles, was probably an early relative of the octopus.

Cephalopods and Ellesmeroid Cephalopods

Ellesmeroid cephalopods represent the most primitive and unspecialized members of the Class Cephalopoda. They appear at the very end of the Cambrian Period (or immediately after it, depending upon where the Cambrian-Ordovician boundary is drawn). Ellesmeroids resemble elongate (tergomyiad) monoplacophorans from which they almost certainly were derived. Characterized by a slightly curved shell containing closely spaced septa, ellesmeroids are relatively uncommon fossils in most strata. However, when they occur in strata at, or near the Cambrian-Ordovician boundary, they can occur in abundance. The Ozark region of Missouri has yielded a rich fauna of these primitive cephalopods, some of which are presented here.

Dakeoceras subcurvatum Ulrich and Foerste. A group of these early ellesmeroids. The Van Buren Formation (or the Van Buren Member of the Gasconade Formation) occurs at the Cambrian-Ordovician boundary. Some paleontologists consider it Cambrian in age (Vendrasco, Pojeta, and Darrough), while others consider it as representing the very beginning of the Ordovician Period. Ellesmeroid cephalopods, considered "officially" as being Cambrian in age like the much heralded ones found near El Paso, Texas, are probably from this same horizon. Correlations of strata at the Cambrian-Ordovician boundary are tenuous in North America and even more tenuous when correlations are made with strata in other parts of the globe. It is the author's opinion that the rich fauna of ellesmeroids found in the Ozarks represent the oldest cephalopods and that those reported to be older actually are of the same age, their Cambrian age coming from differences of opinion regarding the correlation of strata. (Value range G for single specimen, **these are rare fossils**)

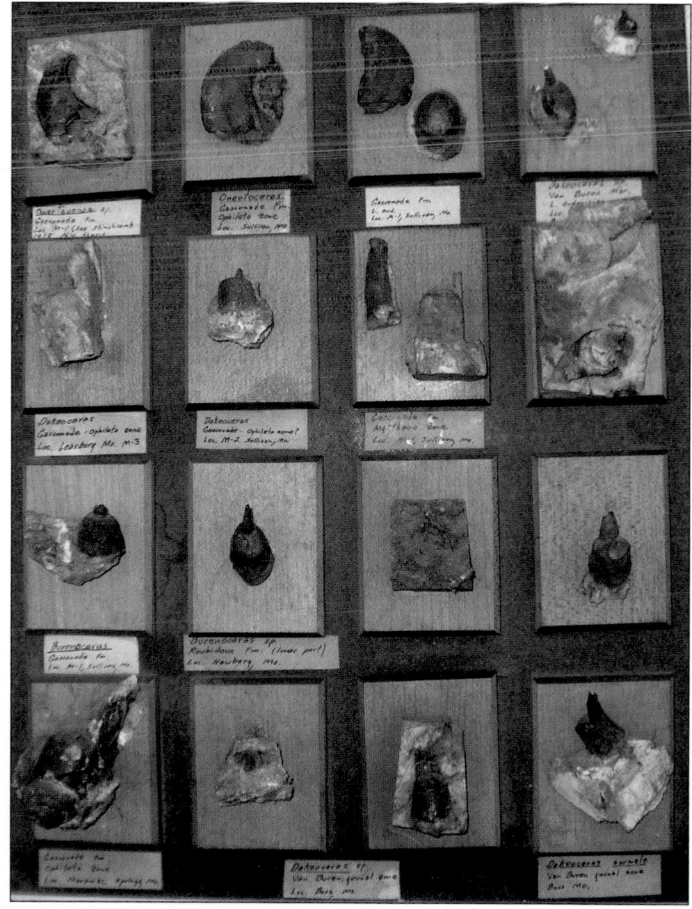

Dakeoceras sp. and *Burenoceras* sp. A board mount of specimens of these very early cephalopods from the Van Buren Formation, eastern Missouri Ozarks (Washington County).

Levisoceras sp. Gasconade Formation, Lowermost Ordovician, Washington County, Missouri. (Value range F, well preserved, rare fossil)

Cassinoceras sp. A large ellesmeroid cephalopod from the Gasconade Formation of the Missouri Ozarks. Note the cone-shaped siphuncle. Gasconade Formation, Big Piney, Missouri.

Clarkoceras sp. A large specimen of this genus with a large siphuncle. Gasconade Formation, Washington County, Missouri. (Value range F)

Oneotoceras locullosum (Hall). Gasconade Formation, Southwest of Potosi, Missouri. Washington County, Missouri. (Value range F)

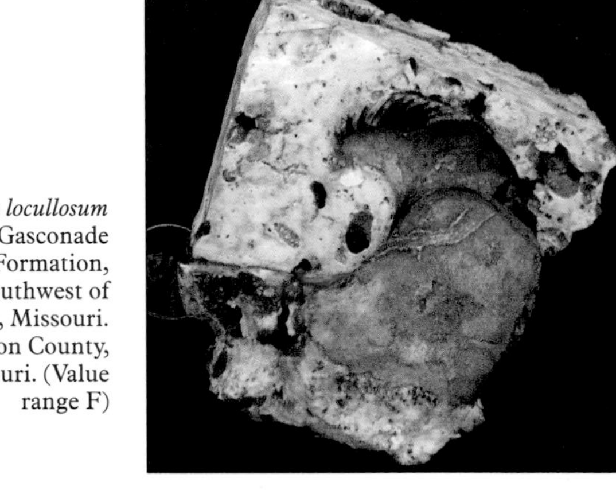

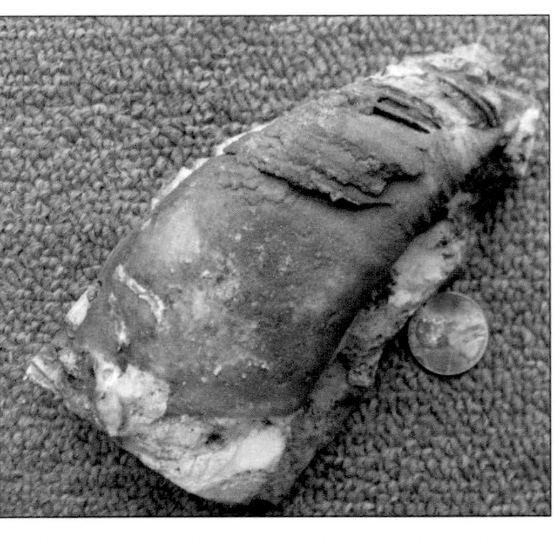

Clarkoceras sp. Specimen with siphuncle (X-rated) preserved with some chamber walls. Gasconade Formation, Washington County, Missouri. (Value range F)

A Gallery of Paleozoic Cephalopods

Nautaloid cephalopods were diverse, often large and prolific mollusks in Paleozoic seas. After the Paleozoic Era, only the coiled nautaloids survived; all straight forms (like those shown here) becoming extinct in this "Greatest of all Extinction Events."

Clarkoceras sp. Specimen with phragmacone preserved with another small specimen, Gasconade Formation, Washington County, Missouri.

"Orthoceras" (*Michelinoceras* sp.). A large, straight cephalopod in a Middle Ordovician limestone exposed on a bench in a road cut. The bench is cut into the Plattin Limestone on the west side of I-55 near Barnhart, Jefferson County, Missouri. These were some of the largest animals to live in the early Paleozoic.

Same specimen as above. Photo taken at a different time and angle.

Actinoceras sp. An abraded surface of this Ordovician cephalopod. *Actinoceras* has a siphuncle filled with calcareous deposits, which made the phragmacone (end of the shell with chambers) heavier and less buoyant. Galena Formation, Middle Ordovician, Cannon City, Minnesota. (Value range F)

Actinoceras bigsbyi. Sliced section showing large siphuncle made up of calcareous deposits. Plattin Limestone, Jefferson County, Missouri. (Value range F)

Huronia bigsbyi. The siphuncle of this cephalopod genus is most characteristic—it resembles the rattle of a rattlesnake. Ordovician, northern Alabama. (Value range F)

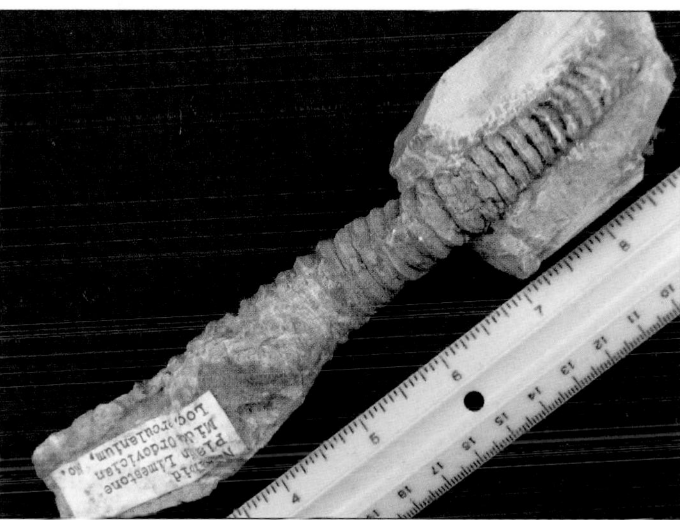

Spyroceras sp. A straight nautaloid with annulations. Middle Ordovician, Jefferson County, Missouri. (Value range G)

Spyroceras bilinnneatum (Hall). This is a straight cephalopod with distinct annulations. Plattin Limestone, Middle Ordovician, eastern Missouri. (Value range F)

Spyroceras sp. Middle Ordovician, Northern Alabama. (Value range G)

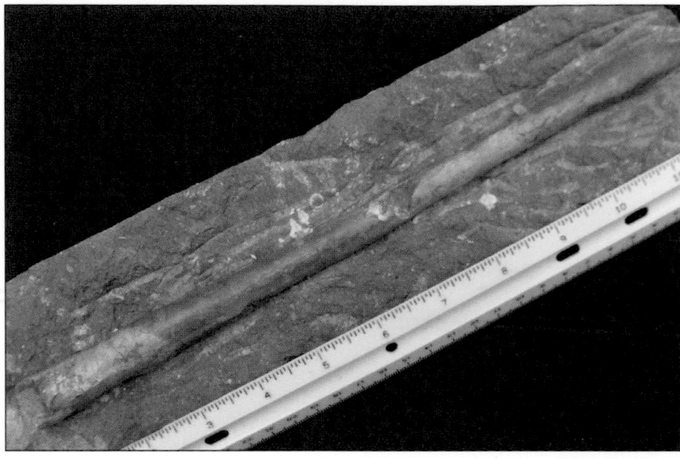

"*Orthoceras*." A straight cephalopod with a bulb or inflation at the end or posterior. Maquoketa Formation, Upper Ordovician, Volga River, Iowa. (Value range F)

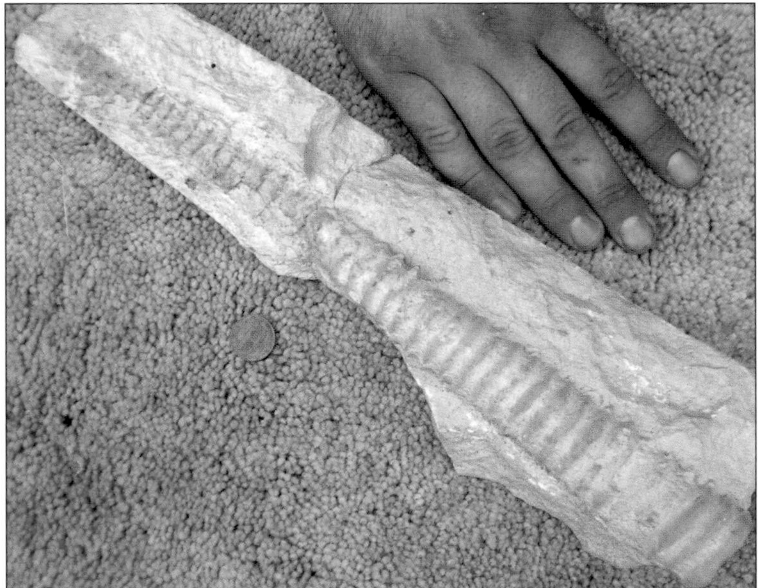

Spyroceras (Orthoceras) vertabrale. Middle Silurian, Grafton, Illinois. (Value range F)

Michelinoceras sp. A frequently occurring Middle Ordovician straight cephalopod. Kimmswick Limestone, Ralls County, northeastern Missouri.

Pseudorthoceras knoxense. A group of these slightly curved nautaloids, which have widespread occurrence in the US Midwest. Middle Pennsylvanian, Limestone of the Henrietta Group, Ferguson, Missouri, St. Louis County. (Value range F for group)

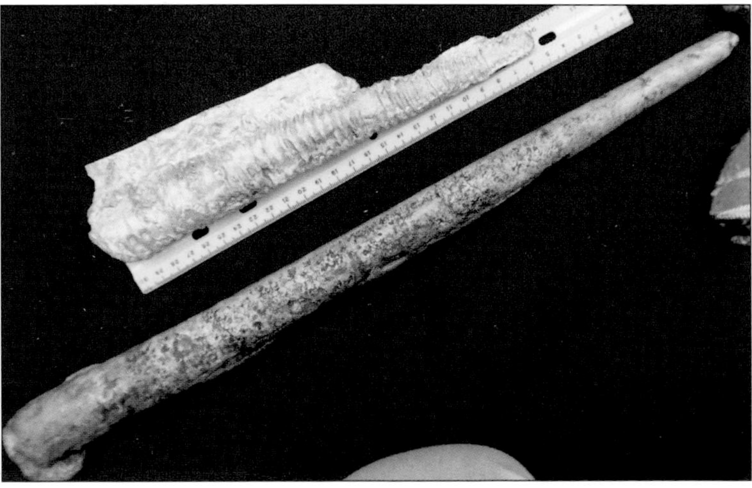

Spyroceras (top), *Michelinoceras* (bottom). *Michelinoceras* (Orthoceras) is an example of a straight cephalopod lacking ornamentation—just a tapering stick. Both are from the Middle Ordovician of Missouri.

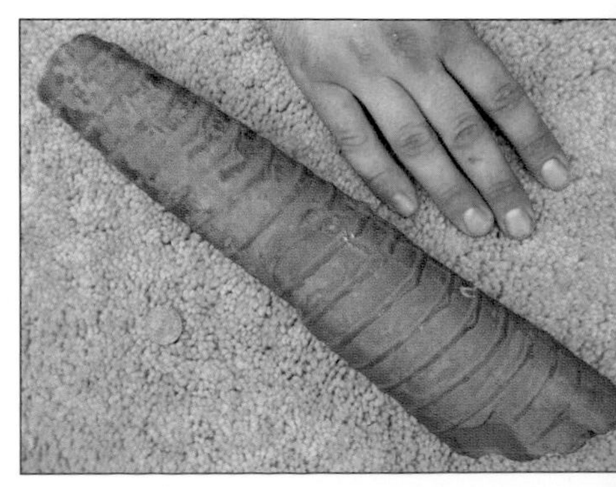

Siphuncle of a giant straight cephalopod, which is the sediment filled inner structure extending the length of the chambered portion of a cephalopod. Platteville Formation, Turkey River, northeastern Iowa. (Value range F)

Geisonoceras (Orthoceras) sp. Straight cephalopods from lower Devonian limestone of Morocco have been widely distributed not only as inexpensive fossils but also as hard, black limestone ("marble") full of these cephalopods. This cephalopod-filled "marble" is carved into bowls, table tops, sinks, and even marble toilets. (Value range F for slab)

Large slab from the Lower Devonian of Morocco with a variety of both **straight** and **coiled** nautaloid cephalopods. Numerous slabs like this with the cephalopods exposed and polished have become widely available and distributed primarily through the Tucson Mineral, Rock, and Fossil show. (Value range D)

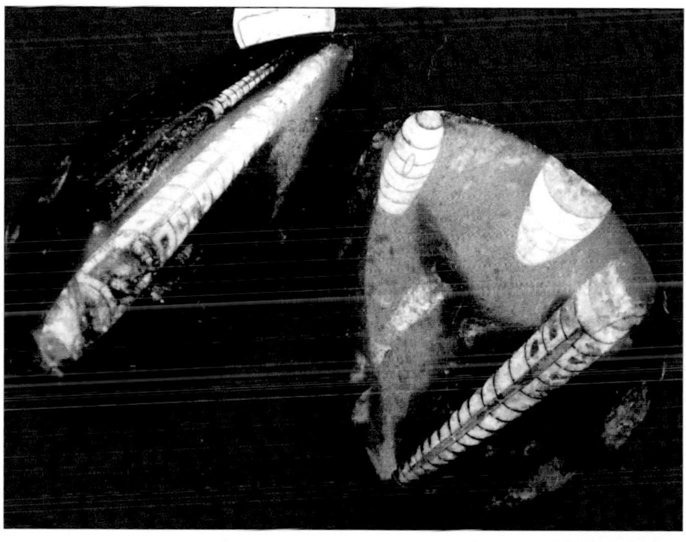

Another group of *Geisonoceras* (Orthoceras) sp. from the Lower Devonian of Morocco. (Value range G for group)

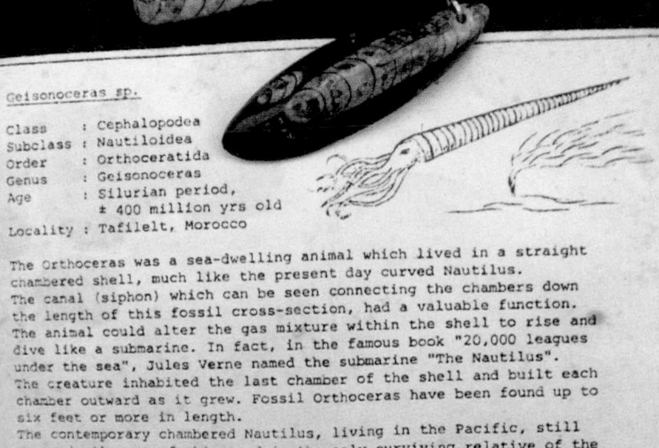

Explanatory card often accompanying Moroccan ("Orthoceras") cephalopods.

Arctic Fauna and Its Large Mollusks

Ordovician strata occurring in the northern portion of North America, specifically north of what is known as the transcontinental arch, are of interest in many ways because:

- Fossils in this strata often are especially large;
- Fossils in this strata are sometimes considerably different from those to the "south."

Ordovician beds containing this fauna crop out in Manitoba, including along Hudson's Bay and in the Hudson's Bay lowland south of the bay. These Upper Ordovician strata also crop out just west of the Canadian Shield in Manitoba and in Saskatchewan. They also are well exposed in the Big Horn Mountains of Wyoming, where the Big Horn Dolomite and the Lander Sandstone at its base carries many Arctic Ordovician fossils. Sometimes the large fossils of this fauna can be seen on cut surfaces of building stone used in Canada known as Tyndall Stone—white limestone cut and widely used. Tyndall Stone is quarried near Winnipeg, Manitoba, and is used in a similar way as is the Mississippian age Bedford Limestone of the United States. (Bedford Stone, which is quarried near the towns of Bedford and Oolitic, Indiana, also contains fossils, but they are small, unlike the large ones in the Tyndall Stone of Canada).

Arctic Ordovician strata cropping out in the Big Horn Mountains, Wyoming. Most of the area of Arctic Ordovician is in Canada, especially Manitoba, the Hudson's Bay region of Ontario, Saskatchewan, and northern Canada. (Ellesmeroid Cephalopods are named after Ellesmere Island of northern Canada). Upper Ordovician outcrops like these in Wyoming's Big Horn Mountains, however, were deposited in the same seaway as were those in Canada.

Big Horn Dolomite (or limestone), Big Horn Mountains, northern Wyoming.

Big Horn Dolomite, northern Wyoming. Being uplifted to form part of the Rocky Mountains during the Laramide orogeny, these Upper Ordovician limestones outcrop in spectacular exposures in the Rocky Mountains, those outcrops in Manitoba, Ontario (Hudson's Bay Region), and Saskatchewan are less spectacular.

Arctic Ordovician faunas occur in the northern portion of North America, often associated with relative low relief topography like this in central Manitoba.

Paleozoic rocks bearing the Arctic Ordovician Fauna crop out around Hudson's Bay into which many streams flow such as those in this area south of Hudson's Bay.

Hudson's Bay watershed near the western Ontario-Manitoba border.

Slabby limestone exposed in drainage ditches dug during road construction and which can expose these arctic fossils. If not covered by glacial drift gravel, bedrock is often close to the surface in the north but its surface may be a weathered one ground down by the continental ice sheet or the surface may be covered with lichens. When road construction digs into the glaciated surface of these Paleozoic limestones, fossils may become exposed on the recently exposed slabs.

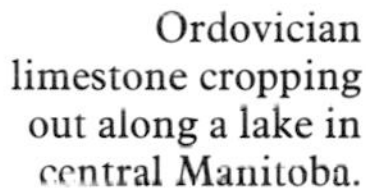

Ordovician limestone cropping out along a lake in central Manitoba.

Tyndall Limestone, Garson Manitoba. Outcrops of Arctic Upper Ordovician strata in Canada are exposed along streams, along the southern shore of Hudson's Bay or exposed in quarries like those which produce this building stone near Winnipeg, Manitoba.

Large slabs of Upper Ordovician limestone used in preparation of cut Tyndall building stone. Red River Group, Garson, Manitoba.

Cutting limestone blocks used in preparation of building stone similar to Manitoba's Tyndall Stone. The limestone being quarried here is Indiana's "Bedford" stone, widely used in the states in the same manner as Canada's Tyndall stone.

Large block of quarried limestone being lifted from dimension stone quarry. When the block is sawed, cross-sections of fossils like the following may be seen.

Stockpiles of blocks of Indiana Bedford Stone. Operations involving limestone block quarrying in the states is larger, as might be expected, than is Canada's operations.

Kochoceras sp. A large, flat nautaloid in a slab of Tyndall Limestone, Garson, Manitoba. These large, flat cephalopods are suggested to have lived on the sea floor like flat fish or flounders. It has been suggested that they may have been ambush predators living partially buried like living flounders. Note the specimen of *Receptaculites oweni* to the right.

Close-up of large, flat *Kochoceras* nautaloid, Garson, Manitoba.

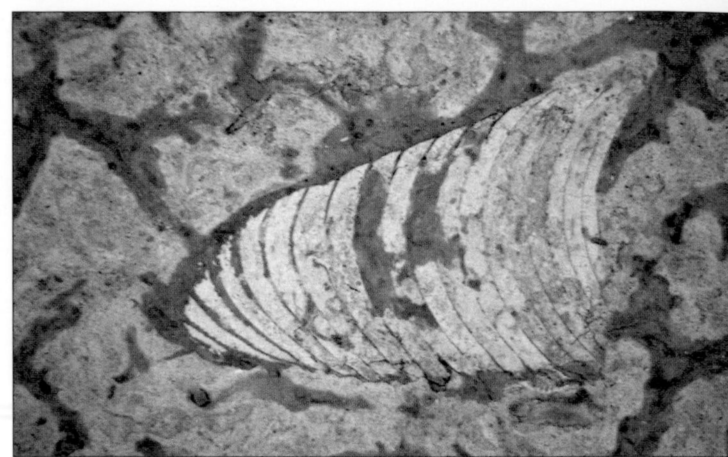

Beloitoceras sp. Angular cross section of a portion of a cephalopod phragmacone on a cut surface of Tyndall Stone. This photo is taken from a slab set into the wall of a building.

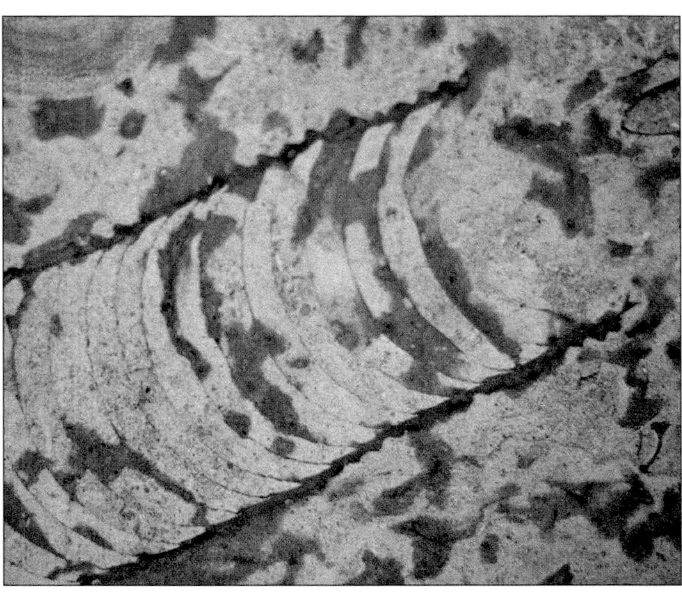

Lamboceras sp. Cross section of another specimen of this Red River Group cephalopod with its closely-spaced chamber walls. Tyndall Stone, Garson, Manitoba.

Lamboceras sp. Close-up of the above sliced cephalopod occurring in a building wall, Winnipeg, Manitoba.

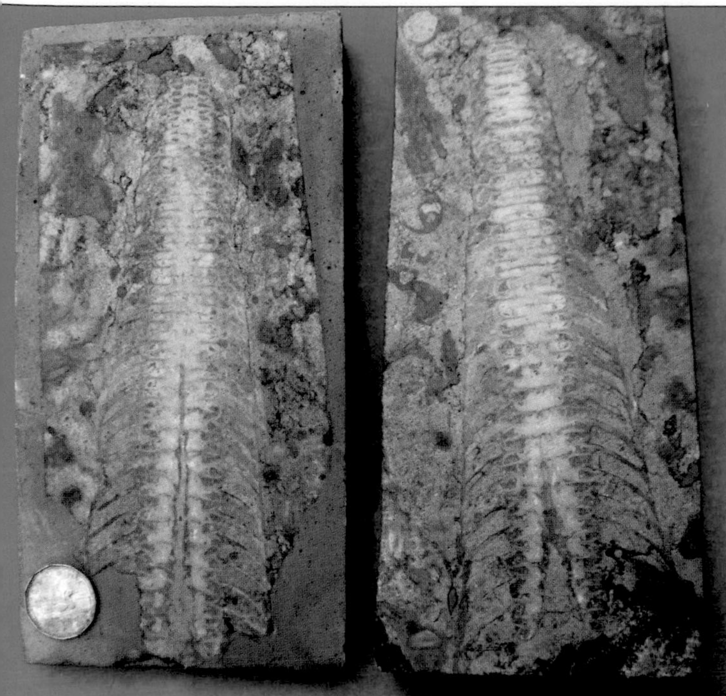

Armenoceras sp. Sliced section of this *Actinoceras*-like cephalopod characteristic of the Arctic Upper Ordovician fauna. Garson, Manitoba. (Value range F)

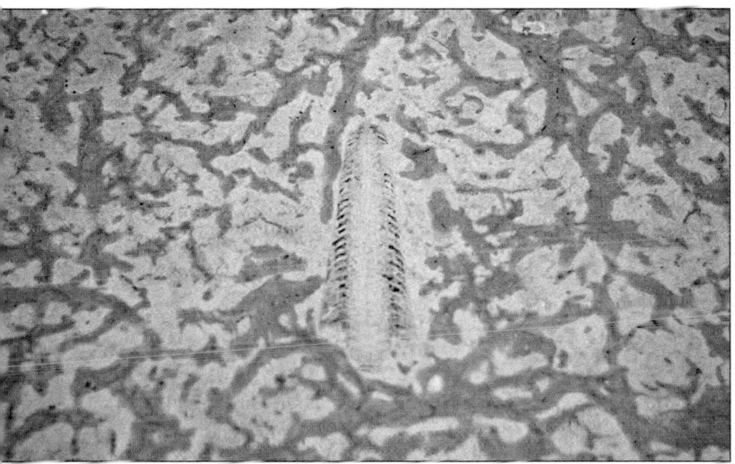

Armenoceras sp. or *Actinoceras* sp. Sectioned specimen in a stone wall of a building, Winnipeg, Manitoba. The cephalopod is surrounded by sediment filled burrows (burrowed carbonate mud), a sedimentational phenomena especially characteristic of Middle and Upper Ordovician limestones.

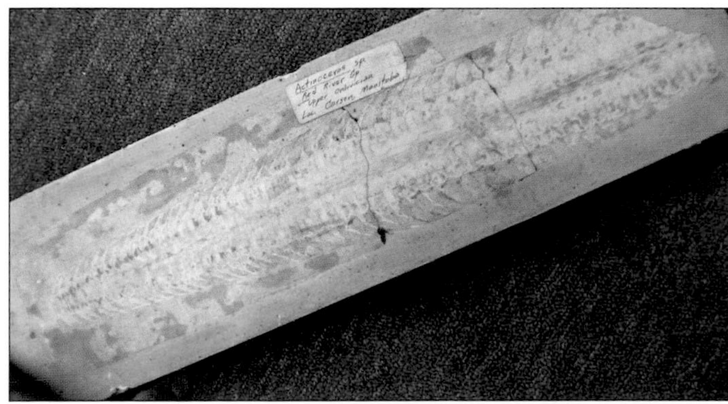

Armenoceras sp. A sectioned specimen of this *Actinoceras*-like mid- and late Ordovician cephalopod. Red River Group, Garson, Manitoba. (Value range F)

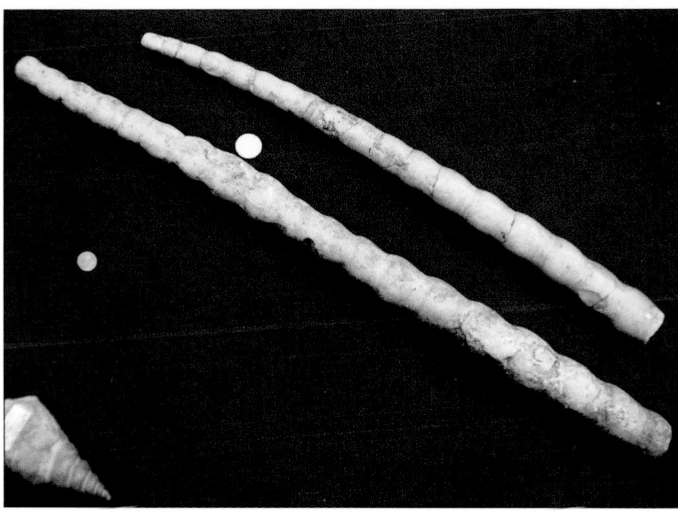

Narthecoceras sp. A large siphuncular weight from Tyndall Limestone, Garson, Manitoba. These siphuncular deposits presumably prevented the apical end of these large cephalopods from being upended, ventral (end) downward. They resemble the horns of unicorns. (Value range E)

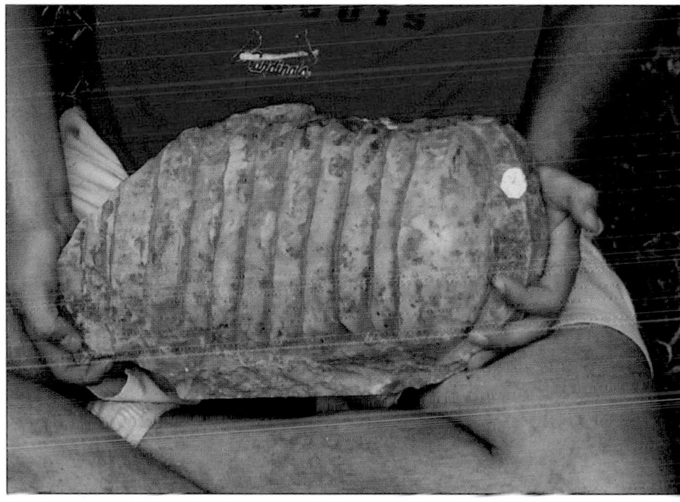

Portion of a super-large straight cephalopod, central Manitoba. This Upper Ordovician mollusk may have been almost 30 feet in length. Large size is a characteristic of many Arctic Ordovician fossils. (Value range F)

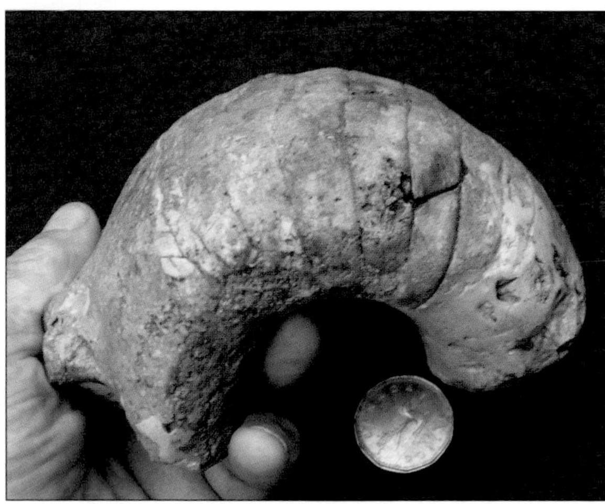

Ryticeras sp. A large (partially) coiled Silurian nautaloid from west central Manitoba. Silurian and Devonian nautaloids are also large in the northern portions of North America. (Value range F)

Ryticeras sp. Partially coiled nautaloids (Crytocones). Silurian, west central Manitoba. (Value range F)

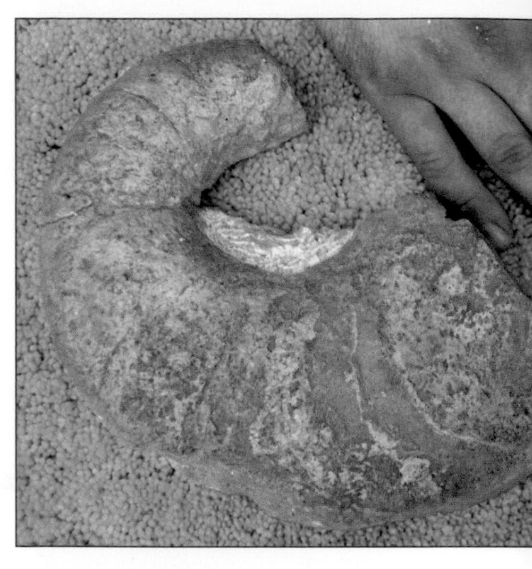

Crytoceras sp. Middle Silurian, Joliet Formation, Grafton, Illinois. (Value range F)

Ryticeras sp. Callaway Limestone, Middle Devonian, Callaway County, Missouri. (Value range F)

Sometimes the large fossils of this Arctic-Ordovician fauna are found in glacial erratics, which were carried southward by Pleistocene glaciers. Such erratics occur in western Minnesota, Iowa, and in North and South Dakota. These fossils are intriguing, not only for their large size but also because the animals found as fossils lived close to the Ordovician equator. The equator of the Ordovician Period cut across North America when, what is now the southern portion of the continent, was located in the southern hemisphere. The large size of many of the fossils may be because of the low latitudes where they lived, there being lots of plankton available (or other photosynthetic marine life). This plankton provided sufficient nutrients to support a large population of invertebrates—invertebrates which included lots of cephalopods.

Metacoceras sangamonnense. Winterset Limestone, Upper Pennsylvanian, Kansas City, Missouri. A widely occurring coiled nautaloid in the US Midwest. (Value range F)

Coiled Nataloid Cephalopods

These are coiled cephalopods, which can be similar to living nautilus. The body of the animal has a number of tentacles and is housed in a coiled shell containing many air filled chambers. Like the nautilus, these cephalopods could probably control their buoyancy by injecting or removing gas from the chambers through the connecting siphuncle, a hollow calcareous tube running through the shell's chambers.

Metacoceras cavatiforme. Topeka Limestone, Upper Pennsylvanian, Topeka, Kansas. (Value range F)

Naedyceras? A coiled nautaloid. Lower Devonian of Morocco. Numerous Devonian cephalopods occur (on the fossil market) which are in a dark shade of hard limestone occurring in the Atlas Mountains of that north African country. Some of these are coiled nautaloids like this, others are goniatites. All have been ground out of this hard limestone and polished to show the sutures so that few surface features are present. This makes it hard or impossible to determine their exact taxonomic position, especially as to species. (Value range F)

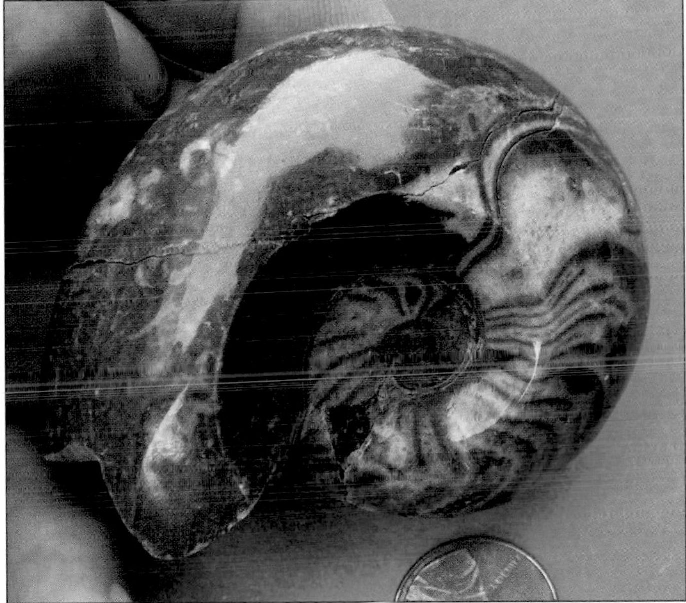

Polished coiled nautaloid, Lower Devonian of Morocco. Some of the Devonian cephalopods from Morocco, like this specimen, have been ground down to the point where it is difficult or impossible to even determine the genus. They do make attractive specimens for display to show a coiled nautaloid with its calcite filled chambers (Value range F)

Amminoids (Goniatites)

These are coiled cephalopods like the nautilus, but the chambers of the shell are separated by chamber walls which are scalloped or fluted. The scalloped chamber wall on interior molds of the shell produce sutures which, as these vary through geologic time, can be used in establishing goniatite genera and species. A large number of Lower Devonian goniatites have come onto the fossil collecting market recently from the Anti-Atlas Mountains of Morocco. Many of these are highly polished and show the goniatite sutures to full advantage, making them very attractive specimens. Often these Devonian goniatites have been confused with Jurassic (Mesozoic Era) ammonites, which also come from Morocco. These Jurassic ammonites have a more complex suture pattern and usually are preserved in a lighter colored limestone.

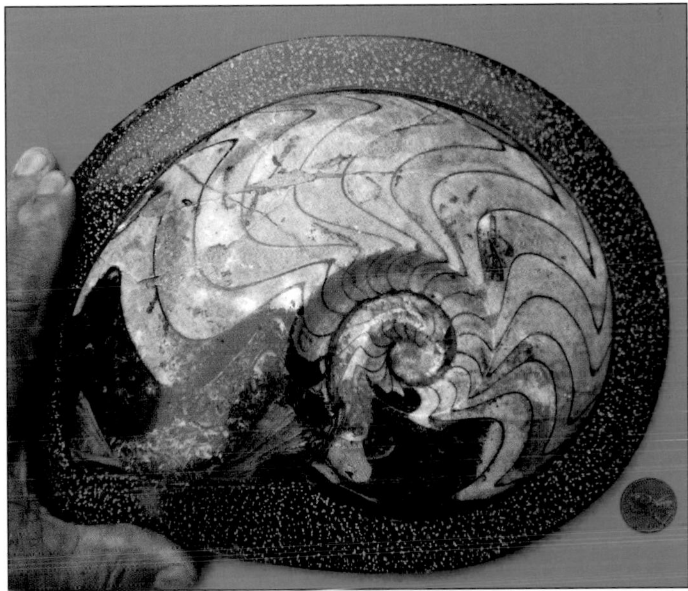

Manticoceras sp. A Moroccan goniatite in black limestone. Lower Devonian. Cephalopods from Morocco are quite similar to those of the Devonian of New York, Pennsylvania, and Virginia. This is because they all occupied the same Tethys seaway during the Devonian Period, whose sea floor sediments where distributed between eastern North America, North Africa, and Europe. (Value range F)

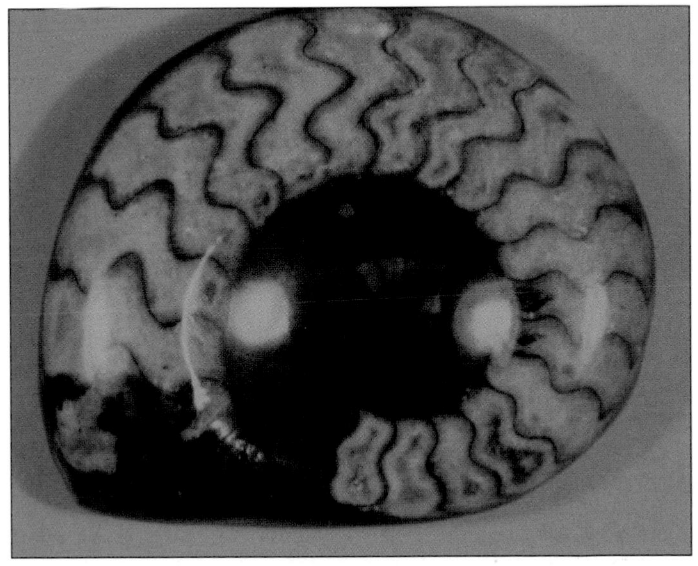

Manticoceras sp. A goniatite with the chamber walls contrasting with calcite filled abandoned chambers. Lower Devonian, Morocco. Specimen is five inches in width. (Value range F)

Agoniatites sp. Septa on this involute goniatite genus are less jagged then are those of the previous photo. Lower Devonian, Atlas Mountains, Morocco. (Value range F)

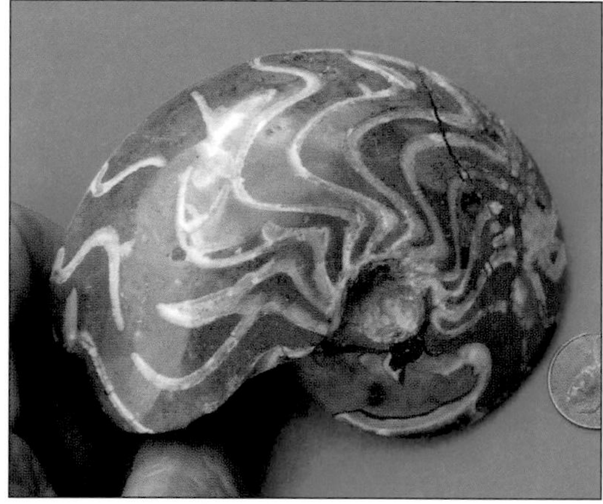

Agoniatites sp. Lower Devonian, Atlas Mountains, Morocco—a goniatite! Identifying labels rarely come with these cephalopods, and when they do they often are wrong. There are no true ammonites in the Paleozoic Era, although Devonian goniatites often are labeled as ammonites. This one has the chamber walls contrasting strongly with the limestone filled chambers. (Value range F)

Back side of the above specimen. Chambers on this side of the fossil are filled with crystalline calcite.

Agoniatites sp. Another large goniatite from the Lower Devonian of Morocco. (Value range F)

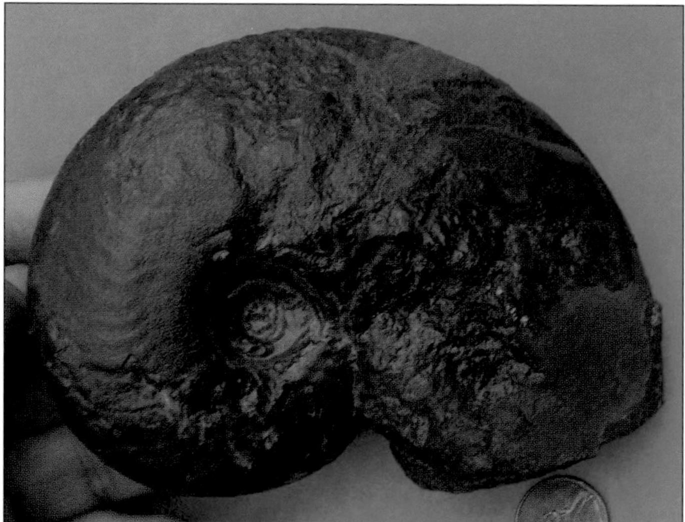

Agoniatites vanuxemi (Hall). Cherry Valley Limestone, Middle Devonian, New York. This goniatite is very much like those from the Lower Devonian of Morocco, even to the black limestone in which it occurs. During the Devonian, sediments of the same seaway that existed in North Africa (Morocco) also covered portions of what would later become northeastern North America. All of this happened before the Atlantic Ocean opened, which it did during the Mesozoic Era. (Value range F)

Multi-plated Mollusks

The thrill of original discovery is one of the attractions of paleontology! The potential fossil record in rocks of the earth's crust is vast and only a small portion of what exists today has actually been sampled. Fossils can be preserved under a variety of conditions, sometimes the finding of "new-to-science" occurrences is serendipitous, but still requiring, as is the case with most quality fossils, considerable drive and effort. With the matter of fossil discovery, it's cogent to consider that the first fossil faunas discovered in North America were those of large, obvious fossil bones, specifically the skulls, teeth, and bones of mastodons and mammoths.

These fossils were becoming objects of interest in the mid-1700s and the subject of investigations by such notables as Benjamin Franklin and Thomas Jefferson. Both of these individuals thrived on the thrill of discovery, a phenomena which, when you are the first to discover something and bring it to light by publication, especially something potentially scientifically significant, can give the discoverer quite a "high." Franklin and Jefferson lay at one end of a spectrum of paleontological discovery. This discovery became more intense in the nineteenth century, when fossils of the Paleozoic and Mesozoic rocks of North America came under investigation. Such paleontologic notables as David Owen, William J. Dawson, James Hall, Joseph Leidy, E. D. Cope, and O. Marsh, to name a few, were driven by this quest-for-discovery. All of them experienced the mental elation which it brings. Late nineteenth and early twentieth century paleontologists-geologists like C. D. Walcott, Charles Butts, and E. O. Ulrich likewise experienced this elation. However, ease of acquisition of new-to-science fossils for them was not as easy as it was for the earlier workers.

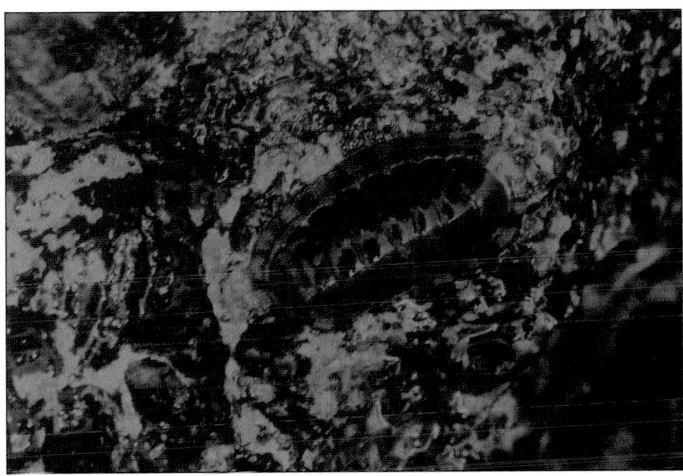

Modern chiton. Chitons are the only multi-valved (or plated) mollusks living today. They have eight valves or plates. Late Cambrian and early Ordovician multiplated mollusks may also have had eight plates (or valves) and hence would be early (stem group) chitons.

Robustum sp. The larger forms shown here are *Robustum nodum*. The shorter plates are *Robustum phallerium*. *Robustum* is a multi-plated mollusk with very thick, spongy valves, the shorter valves may have been terminal plates. These valves are always found disarticulated—some rare ones exhibit muscle scars similar to those of monoplacophorans. Counts of *Robustum* valves from a single pocket which produced this group suggested a 2 : 3 ratio of short to long valves. This would give a five valved form like that illustrated. If this ratio is valid, *Robustum* would not be a chiton, which has a 2 : 6 ratio of tail to intermediate valves. The matter as to what molluscan class these valves belong to is still unsettled. (Value range E for group—rare)

Fossil chiton. Articulated chitons are rare Paleozoic fossils. This is a specimen from the "Mazon Creek" fossil beds preserved in an ironstone concretion. (Value range F)

Robustum sp. Another group of *Robustum* valves, which came from a single chert boulder. Did these all originate from the same mollusk, or were they washed into the same area by currents? (Value range F)

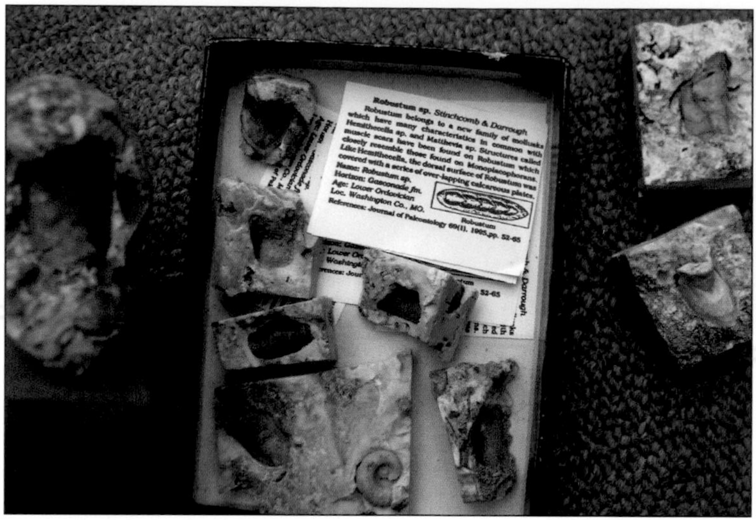

Robustum sp. Another count of specimens in the previous photo, but also including specimens from another boulder that occurred nearby.

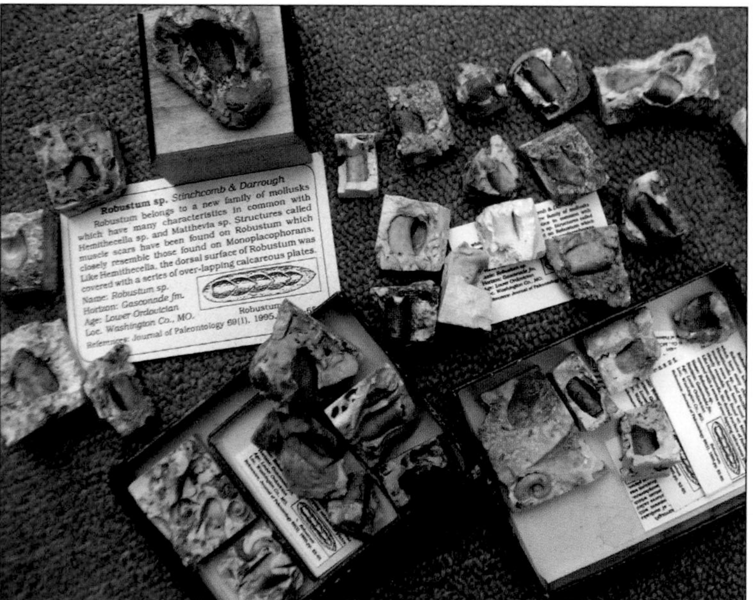

Robustum nodum. An assortment of valves of plated mollusks from Washington County, Missouri, where they appear to be especially abundant. *Robustum nodum* is associated with *R. phallerium*, the later species named after *Phalleratus*, a Latin term for wearing medallions or medals. The author made this association from "bedecked-with-medals" Colonel Kazanoff, who Soviet composer Aram Khatchaturian features in his *Gayne* Ballet—an incident previously related under the monoplacophoran *Gayneoconus* sp.

Hemithecella eminensis Stinchcomb and Darrough. A narrow or slender form (species) of Hemithecellid that originates from strata below the Cambrian-Ordovician boundary. Multiplated mollusks are dominant faunal elements in Missouri Ozark strata. Specimens are placed around one reconstruction of the genus *Hemithecella*—one with sixteen valves. These are from near Potosi, Missouri, at a locality apparently visited by C. D. Walcott around 1903.

Hemithecella eminensis. A collection of multiplated (or multi-valved) mollusk valves. Each box of specimens came from a single chert mass (or occurrence). They are always preserved as internal molds in chert. *Hemithecella* and *Robustum* are considered to be either early chitons by some paleontologists or as being representatives of an extinct molluscan class by others like Ellis Yochelson.

Hemithecella expansa. This is a plated mollusk with arrow-head shaped, pointed valves. Like *Robustum*, these can occur clustered together in a single chert cobble that formed interstitially between stromatolites. Again, no articulated specimens of this form have been found to date, but valve counts suggest a multi-valved, chiton-like mollusk with some counts suggesting fifteen or sixteen valves. (Value range F)

What seemingly might be seen as a disadvantage turned out, however, as with Walcott, to actually have been an advantage. The fossils of the Burgess Shale are not easy to see. Walcott's quest for new discoveries required him to look harder and to develop a keen eye for odd and increasingly subtle fossils. Walcott was directed to Mount Stephen and Mt. Wapta by geologists and collectors who had followed the building of Canada's transcontinental railroad in the 1880s. Here they discovered excellent trilobites in slaty shales on the talus slopes of Mt. Stephen. Walcott had a keen eye for discovering unusual fossils, having made in his home state of New York a discovery as a young man of trilobites with their legs preserved. Without this discovery, and the "eye" such a discovery requires, the subtle and vague Burgess Shale fossils would have been ignored by a lesser collector. The mid-twentieth century found more significant discoveries in North America, the Braidwood-Essex "Mazon Creek" ironstone concretions of Illinois, the Cambrian faunas of Nevada and Utah, and the Newfoundland vendozoans and Devonian land plants for starters. Toward the end of the twentieth century, scientifically significant fossil occurrences in North America seem to have diminished. Keep in mind again that what the author refers to are fossils representing significant life forms **new to science** or what in scientific terms are known as "**high level taxa,**" either kingdoms, phyla or classes. In the category of the latter, the author has discovered and described in the "literature" a variety of peculiar mollusks, some at a potentially "new" molluscan class level and others (the monoplacophorans) being considerably enriched in their diversity by yours truly. Multi-plated mollusks living today are the chitons, the coat-of-mail shells dating back to the early Paleozoic. Multi-plated molluscan fossils are especially characteristic of Ozark Cambrian strata and consist of an almost bewildering variety of forms. Some of these, without doubt, are chitons, but others are suspect, having muscle scars (potential soft part preservation preserving this critical molluscan feature) identical to monoplacophorans and quite unlike those of any living or fossil chitons.

To make a long story short, the author first realized that these odd mollusks (which he first found at a Boy Scout camp) were paleontologically unique when he read paleontological literature on the Ozarks as a teen. Finding that a number of fossils he found in Cambrian age cherts of the Ozarks were not in the literature, and thus were possibly new to science, appeared an intriguing matter. Discovery and determination that the fossils collected were scientifically unknown and the publication of scientific papers on them gave a "rush" which I'm certain was similar to that experienced by others mentioned above in this paleontologic-discovery-continuum. I'm also certain that a variety of scientifically significant fossils are yet to be found in strata of North America (and elsewhere). They are there waiting for that person with the drive (and the trained eye) to add to the diversity of the fossil record.

A sour note, however, is that during the past decade, field investigations that might turn up such fossils appear no longer appreciated by many younger paleontological workers. Their focus is now on extraction of data from previously collected fossils—fossils already described in the literature. This focus may take the form of new and novel preparation techniques, quantification of paleontologic data, like morphometrics as well as various other forms of paleontological "number crunching." While these techniques can yield new information and can be rewarding, it is serious field work that is the "bottom line" of paleontology. **Fossils**, potentially new to science, should be given as high priority today, as they were in the past, but **they are not**! Discovery has been relegated to a third class status and, even worse, persons who continue to do field work (like serious amateurs) sometimes are even being discouraged (or at best ignored) by some of the current paleontologic "professionals." This is an unfortunate situation and it is the author's concern that lots of significant fossils may be lost to science if this rift continues to exist. It's a big planet and far from all of its rocks have been examined by competent workers. Many of these "lowly" amateurs are also more adept in the field than are the "number crunching" professionals.

Problematic Molluscan Trackways

What are known as blanket sandstones occur interbedded with thicker dolomite and limestone beds on the craton of North America as well as on other continents. Some of these blanket sandstones are Cambrian and Lower Ordovician in age (that is they are about half a billion years old and thus older that the earliest known life on land). These sandstones also have some puzzling textures associated with them on their bedding surfaces, one of which is known as "old elephant skin." This and other peculiar textures and structures have been recognized and attributed to the growth of mats of algae formed on the bottom of the shallow sea-

"Blanket" Sandstone outcrop (Lamotte Sandstone) lies at the bottom of the stack of Paleozoic rocks in southern Missouri. This strata lies upon Precambrian granite, upon which the author is standing.

ways in which the blanket sandstones were deposited. These sandstones also often exhibit "fossil" ripple marks and desiccation polygons as well; the latter indicating that the surfaces were sometimes above sea level and exposed to drying or desiccation from exposure to the sun. What are especially interesting regarding these blanket sandstones are their fossil trackways. In some cases, these occur with desiccation polygons (often referred to as mud cracks) suggesting that their makers were walking on land and therefore breathing air rather than using gills. The most interesting of these ancient trackways are those made presumably by arthropods, but there are also examples seemingly made by mollusks. Some late Precambrian blanket sandstones also can contain the impressions of the weird Ediacarian organisms known as vendozoans. These are representative of one of the most puzzling chapters in the history of life recorded in the rocks of the earth.

Old elephant skin texture on the surface of an ancient blanket sandstone slab (photographed in a masonry wall). This texture probably was produced by mats of cyanobacteria (blue-green algae) growing on a sand surface and forming this texture in very shallow water. Note what appear to be filled worm burrows. These were probably made by organisms feeding upon the algal mats.

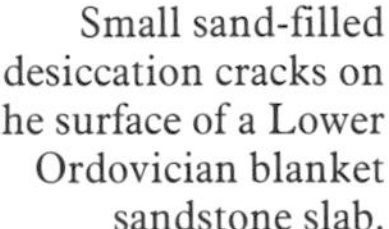

Small sand-filled desiccation cracks on the surface of a Lower Ordovician blanket sandstone slab.

Desiccation cracks associated with stromatolites, which have grown on the polygons formed from desiccation cracks. Stromatolites between the sand-filled cracks are believed to have formed in very shallow water. Stromatolites are formed by the growth of cyanobacteria (blue-green algae). These stromatolite mats desiccated during low tide and shrunk. The shrunk-mat then was covered by sand, which filled in the cracks left by shrinkage to leave this impression.

Fossil "mud cracks:" Large, desiccation tracks filled in by sand are preserved on the bedding surface of a blanket sandstone slab. What actually dried and shrunk to form the surface over which the sand was deposited to produce these so-called "mud cracks" is not clear. It is suggested to have been a mat of algae growing in very shallow water that, during low tide, was exposed to the sun and underwent drying (or desiccation). Later, this cracked and desiccated algal surface was covered with sand. Roubidoux Formation, Lowermost Ordovician, southern Missouri.

"Fossil" ripple marks on the bedding surface of an ancient blanket sandstone. Ripples like this are commonly associated with blanket sandstones. They form when sand on the bottom of a shallow body of water is moved either by waves or by currents. They are commonly seen sedimentary structures, especially in sandstones.

Ripple marks cut by another set of ripple marks at 90 degrees. Slab of Lower Ordovician (Swan Creek Sandstone) set into a masonry wall.

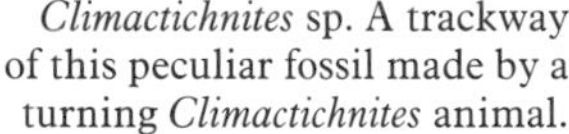

Climactichnites sp. A trackway of this peculiar fossil made by a turning *Climactichnites* animal.

Arthropod (trilobitomorph) trackway on a ripple marked slab of ancient (Cambrian) sandstone, southern Missouri.

Climactichnites sp. This trackway is about one foot in width. It is a trackway from a large mollusk! It comes from the (Cambrian?) Gunter Sandstone of the Ozark Uplift of Missouri. Note the raised ridges of sand on both sides. The animal that made these tracks has been suggested to have been an air breathing creature, an animal something like a large slug. Being a possible air breather is suggested by its association with some surfaces showing desiccation cracks.

Protichnites sp. Arthropod trackways on a ripple marked slab of Cambrian blanket sandstone. Gunter Sandstone, Williamsburg, Missouri.

Climactichnites sp. (The Cambrian motorcycle track, molluscan trackway.) This peculiar trackway (cast) resembles a motorcycle track and is restricted to the Cambrian of North America (Laurentia) where it occurs associated with blanket sandstones. Its maker is thought to have been a large, slug-like mollusk, which may have ventured out of the water onto the broad sandy beaches exposed during low tide—possibly one of the earth's first animals to do this.

A different view (with different lighting) of the previous *Climactichnites* slab.

Problematic Mollusk-like Fossils

These represent a few of numerous problematic fossils found in Paleozoic rocks, which have been suggested as being members of the phylum mollusca.

"*Climactichnites* rules." The large, presumed mollusk which made trackways, known as *Climactichnites,* ventured out onto sand flats over half a billion years ago and in doing so was one of the earth's earliest animals to venture onto land. This tee-shirt celebrates this event. *Climactichnites* also is unique to North America (Laurentia).

Cambrian sandstone slab covered with *Climactichnites*-like tracks lacking the marginal sand ridges. Mt. Simon Sandstone, Middle Cambrian, central Wisconsin.

Close-up of one of the rim-less tracks shown on previous photo.

Bergaueria or *Nemiana* sp.? These problematic fossils are found on the soles (bottoms) of ancient blanket sandstone beds. *Nemiana* is known from the late Precambrian (Ediacarian). It is one of the puzzling late Precambrian vendozoans. These specimens come from a Lower Ordovician blanket sandstone of the Ozark Uplift of Missouri. They may be mollusks, as late Precambrian forms almost identical to these have been suggested to have had a molluscan affinity. *Bergaueria* is a similar form which has been interpreted as the "resting burrows" of actinian anemones. The form occurs as part of the puzzling late Precambrian Ediacarian biotas. These, however, are Lower Ordovician in age.

Hyolithes sp. Peculiar cone shaped shells which are especially common fossils in Cambrian strata. Hyolithes are considered as mollusks by many paleontologists, others consider them as representatives of an extinct phylum (or body plan). *Hyolithes* is especially characteristic of the Cambrian, but ranges through the entire Paleozoic Era.

Hyolithes sp. This scatter of Hyolithes valves are some of the earliest of Paleozoic fossils. Lower Cambrian Addy Quartzite, Addy, Washington. (Value range F)

Tully Monster in ironstone concretion showing segmentation (not a normal molluscan attribute), snout or proboscis at the top. Below that is the transverse bar. The paddle-like tail is at the bottom.

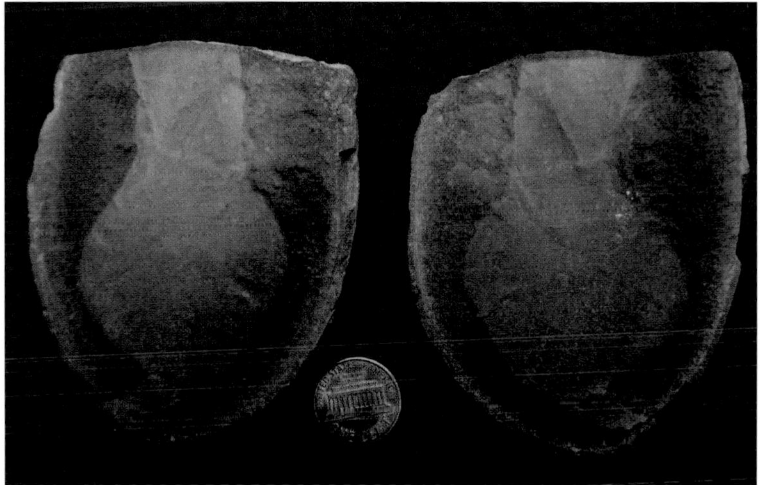

Bottom half of an ironstone concretion with paddle-like tail of Tully Monster. (Value range F)

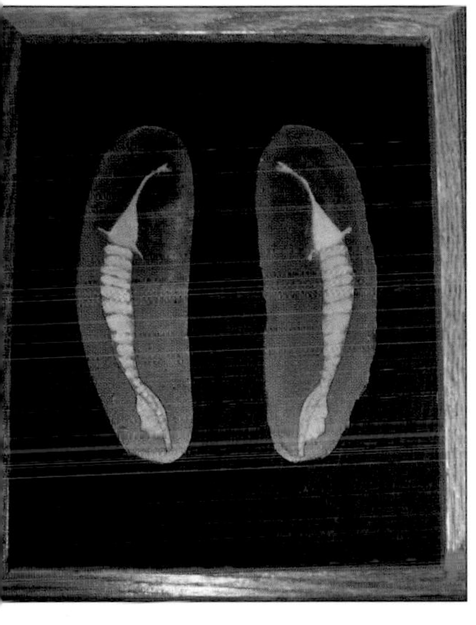

Tullimonstrum gregarium (Tully Monster) model. A problematic animal found in ironstone concretions of the "Mazon Creek," Essex fauna, tully monsters are possibly a type of extinct mollusk. Others consider it to be representative of an extinct phylum. The tully monster is the official state fossil of Illinois.

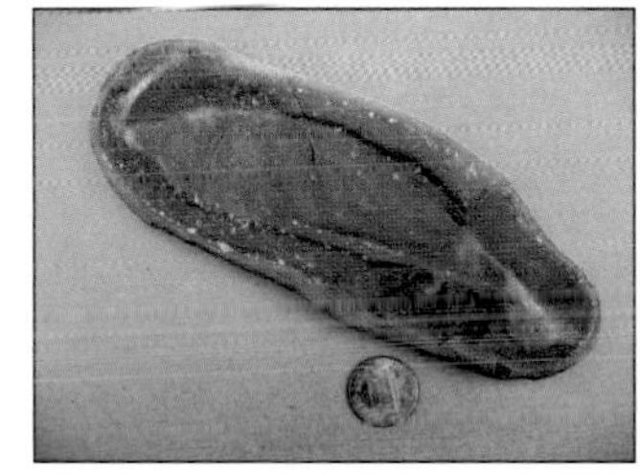

Tully Monster with paddle-like tail clumped (right), to the left is the proboscis. (Value range F for average specimen, they are desirable fossils)

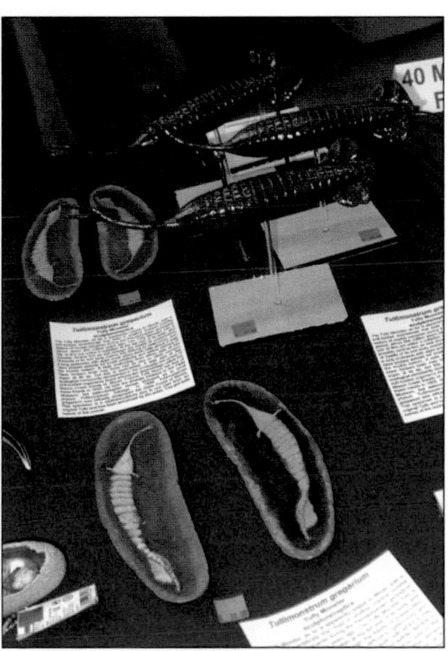

Tully Monster models with segmentation and claw or proboscis (at left on stand) and stylized reconstructions after ironstone nodules, MAPS EXPO, 2011.

Bibliography

Catalani, John, 2010. The Platteville Molluscan Fauna *in MAPS Digest—The Ordovician.* Mid American Paleontological Society.

Fedonkin, Michail A., James G. Gehling, Kathleen Grey, Guy M. Narbonnne and Patricia Vickers-Rich, 2007. *The Rise of Animals; Evolution and Diversification of the Kingdom Animala.* The John Hopkins University Press.

Frey, Robert C., 2010. Size does matter—The Giant Nautaloids of the Arctic Ordovician Fauna *in MAPS Digest, The Ordovician*. Mid American Paleontology Society.

Pojeta, John Jr., M. J. Vendrasco and Guy Darrough, 2010. Upper Cambrian chitons (Mollusca, Polyplacophora) from *Missouri, U S A. Bulletins of American Paleontology,* No. 379.

Yochelson, Ellis, 1998. *Charles Doolittle Walcott, Paleontologist.* Kent State University Press. ISBN 0-87338-599-3.

Arthropods

By far the most conspicuous and widely represented Paleozoic fossil members of this phylum are trilobites. Today crustaceans are the most obvious marine arthropods and insects the most successful on land.

Modern marine arthropods (crustaceans), ready to be placed into the soup pot. Arthropods are characterized by their jointed legs and their (often mineralized) exoskeleton.

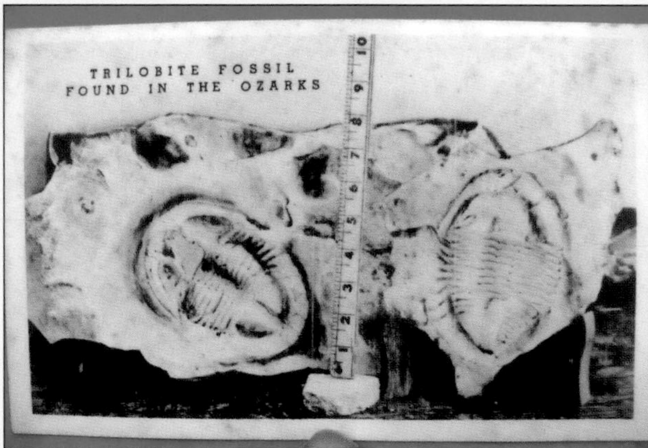

Arthropod (trilobite) postcard. Trilobites are supposedly the second most popular prehistoric animal after dinosaurs. Trilobites were the dominant arthropods, which lived in Paleozoic seas. Named for the three lobes in their midsection (thorax), as well as their distinct head (cephalon), mid or thoraxial region, and tail (pygidia), a rare trilobite is the subject of this 1950s postcard.

A RARE FIND IN THE OZARKS

The Trilobite was an ancient relative of the lobster, crayfish and horseshoe crab. He, like the honeycomb corals, lived only in shallow seas during the Paleozoic Period. This means that the very last Trilobite died at least two hundred MILLION years ago! The six inch trilobite, pictured on the other side, was found one mile from Busch, Ark., near White River by C. S. (Cobb) Gaskins. As you will notice it is in two parts and was found at different times 12 feet apart. This Trilobite is on display at Huffman's Rock Shop with other rare specimens, including a quartz crystal with an interior bubble, bending rock, fluorescent rock display and a large collection of Indian artifacts--located 10 miles west of Eureka Springs, Ark., on highway 62.

Lusterkote Litho Card by Times-Echo, Eureka Springs, Ark.

P

Explanation on back of the trilobite postcard.

Trilobites

Like other arthropods, trilobites have jointed legs and an exoskeleton. In the case of trilobites, this exoskeleton contains calcium carbonate, so trilobites are commonly well represented as fossils.

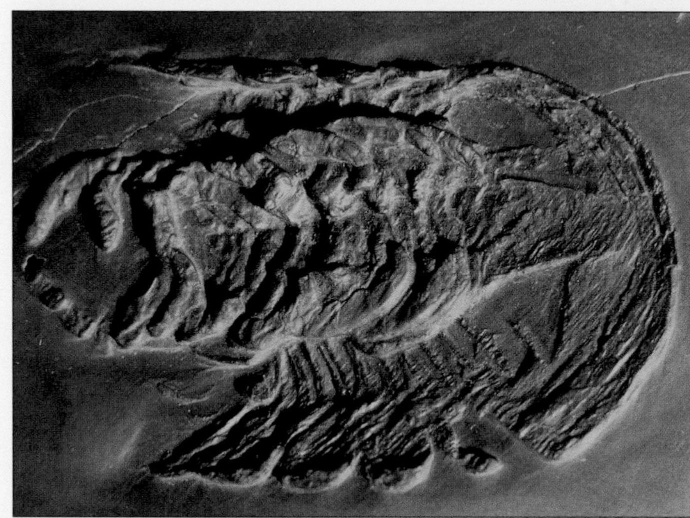

Ventral (bottom) of a trilobite showing the rarely preserved segmented legs of the animal. Bundenbach (Hunsruckschieffer) slates, Germany.

Trilobite cephalon from which extend glandular diverticles (radiating lines at the margin of glabella). These are believed to be from nerve fibers radiating from the trilobite's central nervous system. Upper Cambrian, Davis Formation.

Vertical trilobite bearing strata in the Appalachian Mountains of northern Alabama. This strata was deposited in an ocean 500+ million years ago. Forces of mountain building resulted in the strata now being placed nearly on end. Coosa River, northern Alabama

Olenellid Trilobites

Olenellids are the earliest and most primitive trilobites. They are characterized by a cephalon which lacks separate genal spines, a pygidia ("tail") with an elongate telson-like extension and a large number of thoraxial segments. Olenellids are restricted to the earliest part of the Cambrian, the Lower Cambrian.

Paedumias, an olenellid trilobite. Olenellids were the first and most primitive trilobites. They characterize the first third of the Cambrian Period, the Lower Cambrian. This specimen is from Lower Cambrian strata near Cranbrook, British Columbia. (Value range E)

Vertical trilobite bearing strata of Cambrian age. The Cambrian is sometimes called the age of trilobites, for not only was it when they first appeared but was also when they reached their greatest abundance. This strata, like that of the previous photo, has been tilted on end by the forces of mountain building.

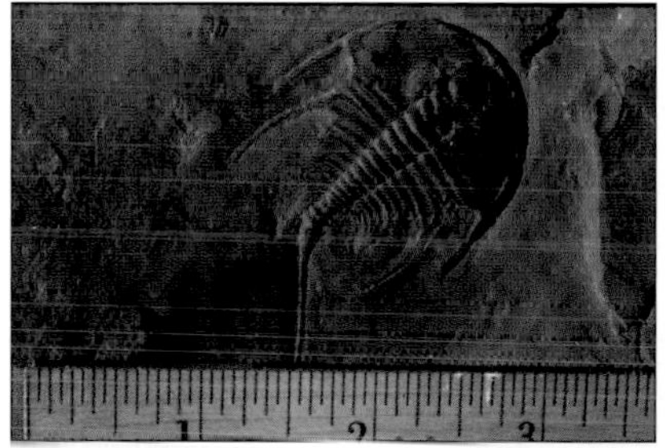

Paedumias sp. Latham Shale, Wacoba Springs, Marble Mountains, S. California. A relatively large number of these olenellid trilobites came from this locality before it was incorporated into the Mojave Desert National Monument. (Value range E)

Paedeumias transitans. York Shale (Kinzers Formation), Lititz, Pennsylvania. Lower Cambrian trilobites came from a Cambrian rock sequence, which in the nineteenth century yielded some of the animals found later in the Burgess Shale, including *Anomalocaris*, an arthropod believed to be a trilobite predator.

Another view of the same Cambrian trilobite bearing strata in northern Alabama. The more solid beds are composed of hard limestone. The rock between the limestone is shale. This shale contains fragmentary, small Cambrian trilobites.

Olenellid trilobite. Kinzers Formation, Lower Cambrian, Kinzers Pennsylvania.

Olenellus sp. York Shale, Lititz, Pennsylvania. An early trilobite preserved as an impression in slaty, Lower Cambrian shale. *Courtesy of Washington University, Dept. of Earth and Planetary Science.*

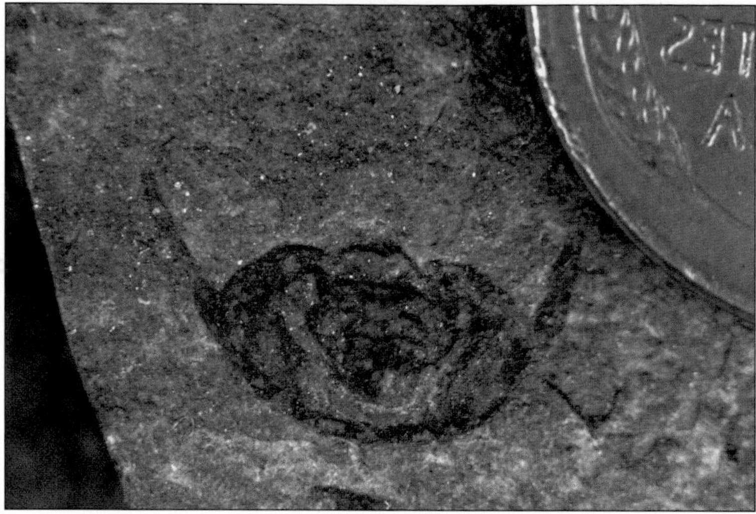

Holmia rowei Lower Cambrian, Silver Peak, Nevada. *Holmia* is an Olenellid, one of the earliest of trilobites. This is the head or cephalon of a small specimen of that genus.

Olenellus thompsoni. Georgia Slate, Georgia, Vermont. Numerous trilobites in slaty shale came from slate quarries, which worked slate of the Lower Cambrian Olenellus zone in the nineteenth century. Old collections sometimes contain specimens like this—trilobites which are rarely seen today.

An exposure of an olenellid bearing siltstone in the Rome (Montevallo) Formation, winter 1970. These dipping beds of jointed, yellow siltstone near Montevallo, Alabama, contain an abundance of excellent olenellids.

Olenellus sp. Cephalons from the previously shown locality.

Olenellus thompsoni. A superb, complete specimen of this olenellid trilobite from the previously shown outcrop near Montevallo, Alabama. (Value range C)

Cambropallis (*Andusilina*) *telesto*. These large redlichid (or Olenellid) trilobites have come from Morocco in quantity (they are quite nice). This trilobite has been stated as being from both the uppermost Lower Cambrian as well as the lowermost Middle Cambrian. The former appears most appropriate as Olenelloids, according to Charles Walcott, delineate the Lower Cambrian. It is also to be noted that all of the trilobites the author has seen are actual specimens (although some have been overly prepared). Numerous rumors have circulated that these trilobites in siltstone are fakes (reproductions). (Value range F)

Middle Cambrian Trilobites

Trilobites of the middle part of the Cambrian Period become more diverse in both genera and species than during any other time of the Paleozoic Era, so that the Cambrian is often referred to as the "Age of Trilobites."

Trilobite bearing Middle Cambrian slaty shale exposed along the Coosa River, 1965, near Centre, Alabama. Black, slabby shale from the Conasauga Formation locally yielded some of the following nice Middle Cambrian trilobites.

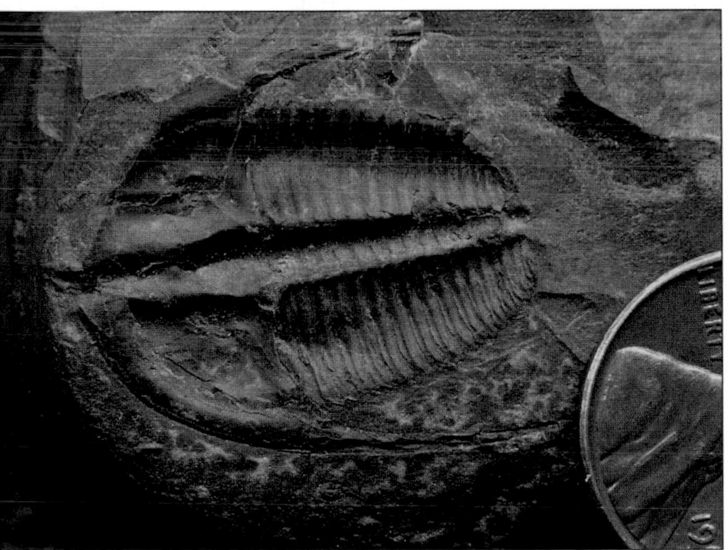

Alokistocare americanum. From the previously shown locality. Conasauga Formation, Middle Cambrian. (Value range F)

Elrathiella buttsi. Specimen in black shale. (Value range G)

Elrathiella buttsi. Specimen in phyllite from a locality along the Conasauga River in Georgia. (Value range G)

Elrathinella buttsi. Specimen in phyllite. Conasauga Formation, Conasauga River, Georgia. (Value range G)

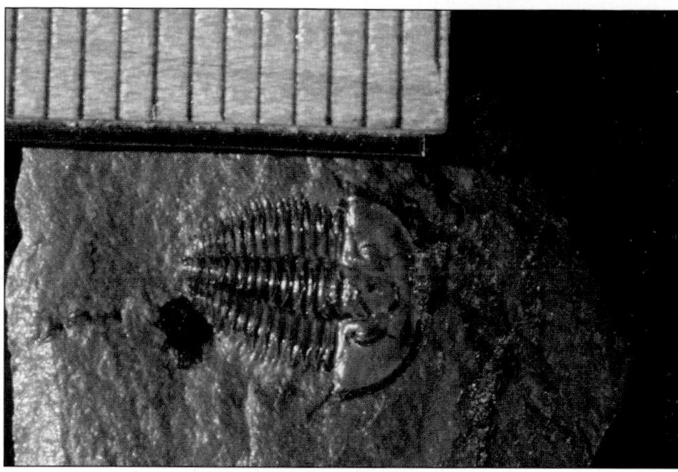

Elrathinella buttsi. Small specimen from Coosa, Georgia. (Value range G)

Elrathinella sp. Specimen without free cheeks. Conasauga Formation, Copper Bluff, Georgia. (Value range G)

Ogygopsis klotzi. Mt. Stephen Formation, Mt. Stephen, British Columbia. These trilobites, found abundantly in the talus of Mt. Stephen, led to the discovery of the Burgess Shale on nearly Mt. Wapta.

Ogygopsis klotzi. Mt. Stephen Formation, Mt. Stephen, British Columbia.

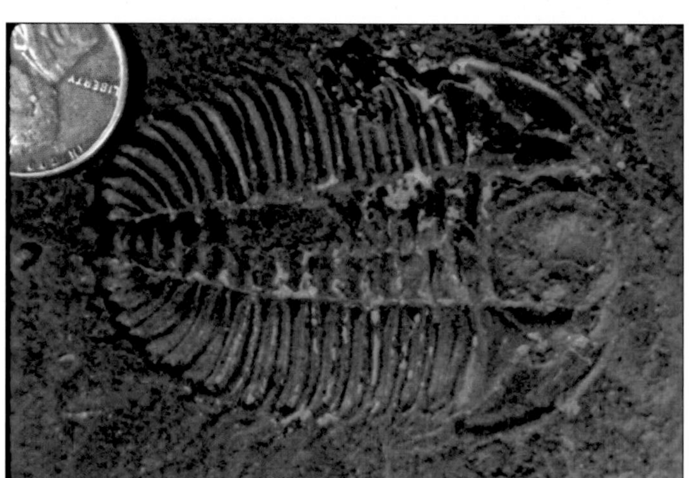

Olenoides (Neolenus) serratus. Mt. Stephen Formation, Mt. Stephen, British Columbia.

Olenoides (*Neolenus*) *serratus* with *Sidenyea inexpectans*. Burgess Shale, Mt. Wapta, British Columbia. *Courtesy of Washington University, Dept. of Earth and Planetary Sciences.*

Ellipsocephalus hoffi. Etage C, Jince Shale, Middle Cambrian, Jince, Bohemia (Czech Republic). A trilobite genus characteristic of the Atlantic or Avalonian Cambrian faunal province.

Peronopsis interstricta Wheeler Shale, Middle Cambrian, Antelope Springs, Millard County, western Utah.

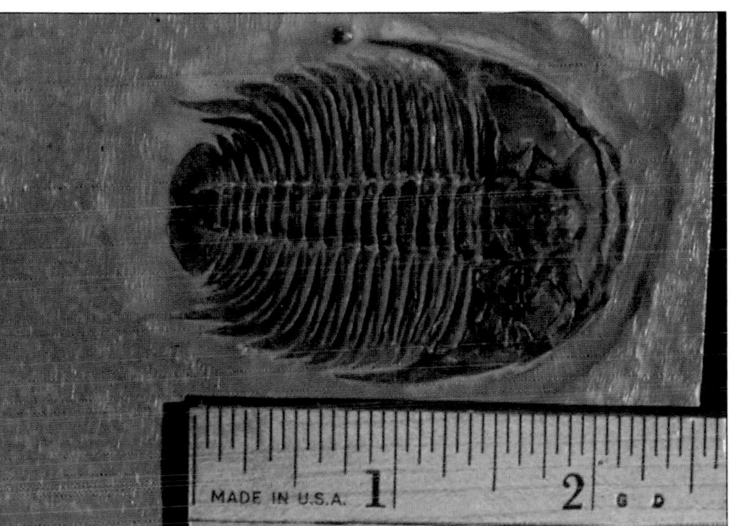

Modocia typicalis Resser. Middle Cambrian, Marjum Shale, Antelope Springs, Utah. (Value range F)

Agnostid Trilobites

The agnostids are Cambrian trilobites having only two segments. It is unknown as to which end is anterior (front) and posterior (back or rear)—the reason they are called agnostids.

Agnostus sp. Conasauga Formation, Middle Cambrian, Coosa, Georgia.

Paradoxid Trilobites

These Middle Cambrian trilobites can be quite large and thus highly collectable. Paradoxids are found in Cambrian rocks formed on the floor of the Iapatus Ocean, a seaway predating the Atlantic Ocean. When the Iapetus Ocean closed in the Silurian, some of its sediments remained to form the eastern portion of North America. Fossils (especially trilobites) of the Iapetus Ocean belong to what is referred to as the Atlantic or Avalonian Cambrian Province. It is one of about eight faunal provinces recognized in the Cambrian. Iapetus sea sediments also cover parts of Europe and North Africa—it is from the latter that the spectacular Cambrian trilobites of Morocco originate.

Acadoparadoxides briareus. Middle Cambrian, Atlas Mountains, Morocco. These are some of the largest trilobites to be found, certainly the largest ones to be readily available. They have been on the fossil market for over a decade. Many of these specimens from Morocco are highly prepared and some are casts. Some sources on the Internet state that all of them are fakes and that actual specimens are quite rare. The author believes otherwise. He collected Paradoxides at Manuels, Newfoundland, and was astonished at how packed the black shale layers were with complete or nearly complete specimens. This same situation appears to occur in Morocco, which has resulted in large excavations in the *Acadoparadoxides* bearing siltstone. Consequently Morocco has produced a large number of these fossils, which sell at relatively low prices. (Value range E)

Acadoparadoxides sp. A specimen of this widely distributed genus from Morocco, which lacks genal spines. (Value range E)

Paradoxides davidicus. A large paradoxid from Newfoundland, collected by the author. Manuels Formation, Manuels Brook, eastern Newfoundland. These fossils were found by the author to occur in amazing quantity considering they are such large trilobites. This abundance of large specimens in certain layers of Avalonian strata appears to be a characteristic of Paradoxids. (Value range E)

Paradoxides spinosus. Etage C, Skrei, Bohemia, Czech Republic. This specimen was collected from the famous Jince fossil beds early in the twentieth century. These fossil beds were first extensively described by Jacob Barrand in the nineteenth century. Specimens of this genus have more recently come from the Jince area, but their carapace is not replaced with iron oxide as were the earlier collected specimens like this one.

Paradoxides spinosus. Jince beds, Etage C, Skrei, Bohemia, Czech Republic. Preservation in hydrated iron oxide appears to be a characteristic of Paradoxids at many localities, including Morocco and Newfoundland where the author collected some specimens preserved in this manner.

Cambrian and Lower Ordovician Trilobites from Various Faunal Provinces

Various faunal provinces of the Cambrian and the related Lower Ordovician are often delineated by trilobites.

Pricyclopyge (Aeglina) prisca Barrande. Peculiar trilobite with two pits in the thorax. Lower Ordovician, Bohemia, Czech Republic. Lower Ordovician trilobites still have a Cambrian aspect about them. This trilobite belongs to the Atlantic or Avalonian faunal province.

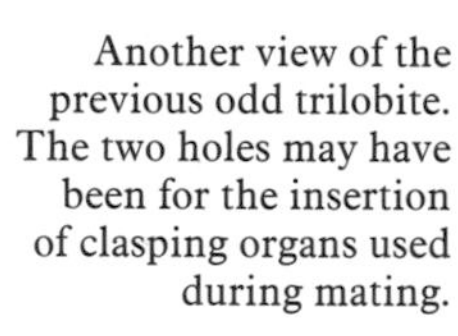

Another view of the previous odd trilobite. The two holes may have been for the insertion of clasping organs used during mating.

Spiny trilobite pygidium covering specimens of *Drepanura*. Upper Cambrian, China. These trilobites belong to one of the Cambrian faunal provinces of China.

An elongated trilobite (stretched) in slate. This is a preservational phenomena often associated with trilobites found in rocks that have undergone modification from tectonic activity. Lower Ordovician, Valongo Formation, Arouca, Portugal. (Value range E)

Stenopilus latus Ulrich. An Upper Cambrian trilobite from the Ozark Uplift of Missouri associated with stromatolites. Eminence Formation, Upper Cambrian, Potosi, Missouri. This trilobite belongs to the Laurentian or North American faunal province. (Value range E)

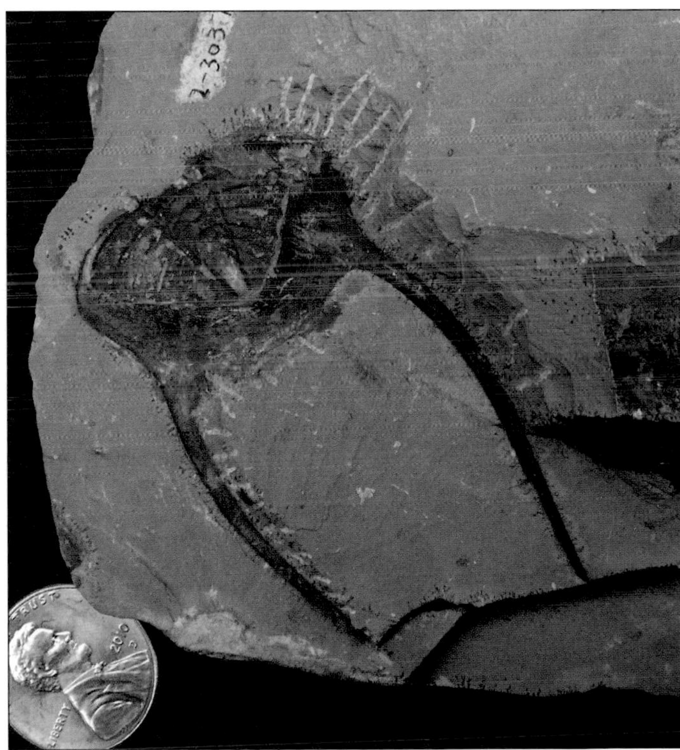

Asaphopsis sp. Pygidium ("tail") of a unique trilobite with long pygidial spines. Lower Ordovician, Hunan Province, China. A trilobite from one of the many Cambrian (and Lower Ordovician) faunal provinces of Asia.

Jeffersonia sp. The pygidia ("tail") of a Lower Ordovician trilobite from the Ozark Uplift near the Missouri-Arkansas line.

Isotelid, Illaenid and Bumastid Trilobites

These trilobites have a relatively plain cephalon and pygidia. They somewhat resemble a large pill bug. Most are characteristic of the Ordovician and Silurian periods.

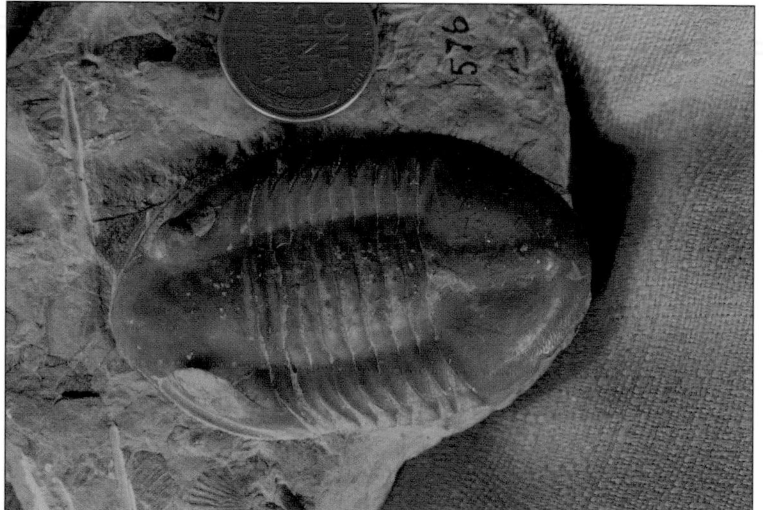

Homotelus sp. Upper Ordovician. Maysville Formation, Cincinnati, Ohio. An asaphid-like trilobite characteristic of the Middle and Upper Ordovician.

Homotelus bromidensis Esker. Bromide Formation, Middle Ordovician, Criner Hills, Oklahoma. (Value range F)

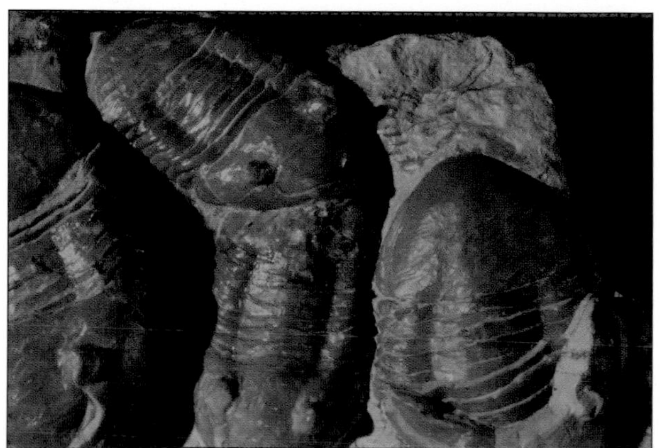

Homotelus bromidensis Esker. Group of these beautiful trilobites from the Arbuckle Mountains of Oklahoma. These were one of the specialties of Geological Enterprises of Oklahoma. Using an air abrasive machine, often for the first time ever, they cleaned and sold a number of slabs like this which established their fossil selling business. Bromide Formation, Middle Ordovician, Criner Hills, Oklahoma. (Value range E)

Homotelus bromidensis Esker. Bromide Formation, Middle Ordovician, Criner Hills, Oklahoma. A spectacular slab of these impressive trilobites, which preserve original material of the animal's carapace. (Value range C)

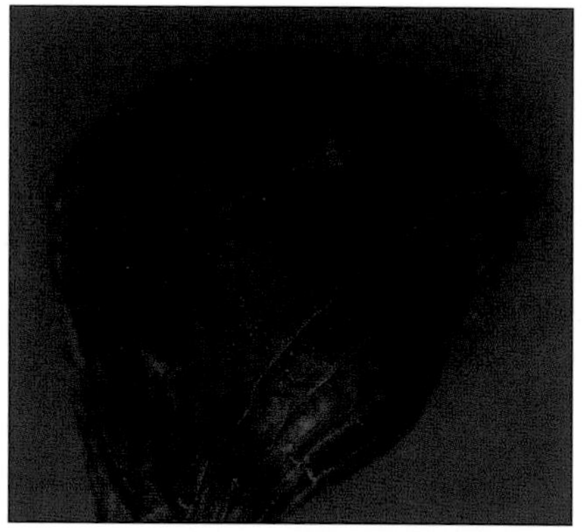

Isotelus gigas. An enrolled specimen of this widespread (and nice) Ordovician trilobite. Cincinnati Group, Cincinnati, Ohio.

Isotelus iowensis. Disarticulated specimen (probably a molt). Specimen shows the hyperstome. Decorah Formation, Salt River, Ralls County, Missouri. (Value range F)

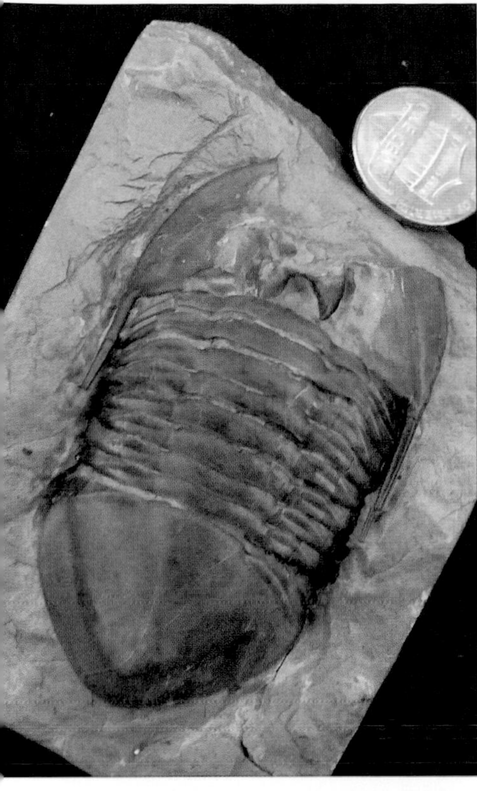

Isotelus sp. Specimen has part of the cranidium removed—it shows the position of the underlying hyperstome. Upper Ordovician, southern Ohio. (Value range F)

Collecting *Isotelus* specimens along the Turkey River, northeast Iowa. Slabby beds of the Upper Ordovician Maquoketa Formation crop out extensively along this river. These fossil beds were first noted by David D. Owen when small boats (canoes) plied the river in the late 1830s during the process of mapping geology in preparation for Iowa statehood. Canoes are still the best method to access this and many other fossil bearing beds occurring along streams.

Hyperstomes of *Isotelus*. This part of the trilobite has been hypothesized to have been used in digging in order to obtain algal detritus used as food. The trilobite hyperstome rarely shows evidence of any abrasion and abrasion would be expected if the animal routinely dug into sediment or algal mats for food on the sea bottom. Perhaps in molting, the hyperstome was replaced frequently enough to avoid obvious abrasion. Decorah Formation, Middle Ordovician, Ralls County, Missouri.

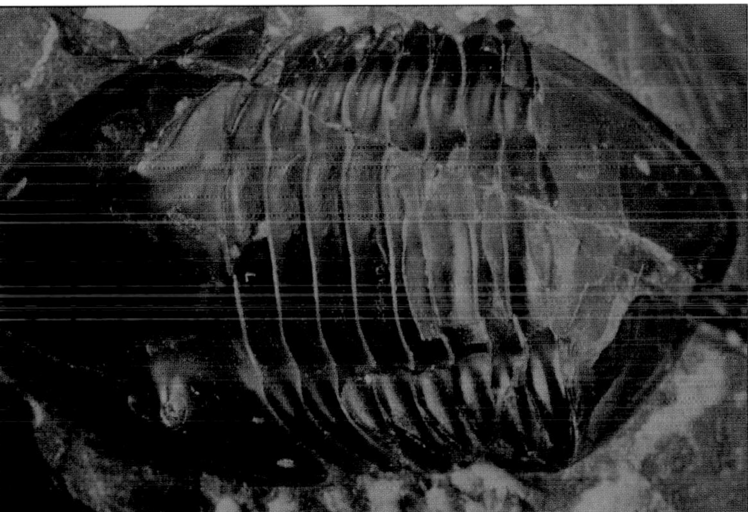

Isotelus gigas. Trenton Limestone, Middle Ordovician, Trenton Falls, New York.

Homotelus sp. Trenton Limestone, Middle Ordovician, Trenton Falls, New York. (Value range E)

Anataphrus (Isotelus) vigilans. Small, enrolled isotelids. Maquoketa Formation, Upper Ordovician, Fayette County, Iowa. (Value range F, single specimen)

Illaenopsis sp. Two specimens of this asaphid preserved in a soft, grey siltstone. Hunan Province.

Illaenopsis sp. Ordovician asaphid trilobites from China have frequently been sold on the fossil market as *Ductina vietnamica* and stated as being from the Devonian Period. This trilobite is an asaphid, a family of trilobites characteristic of the Ordovician Period and **not** found in the Devonian. Hunan Province, China. (Value range G)

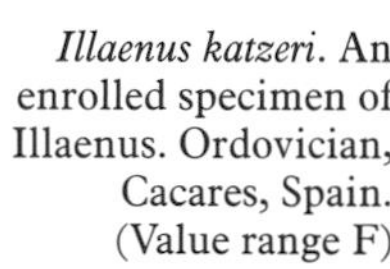

Illaenus katzeri. An enrolled specimen of Illaenus. Ordovician, Cacares, Spain. (Value range F)

Group of *Illaenopsis* sp. from the **Ordovician** of China. Hunan Province.

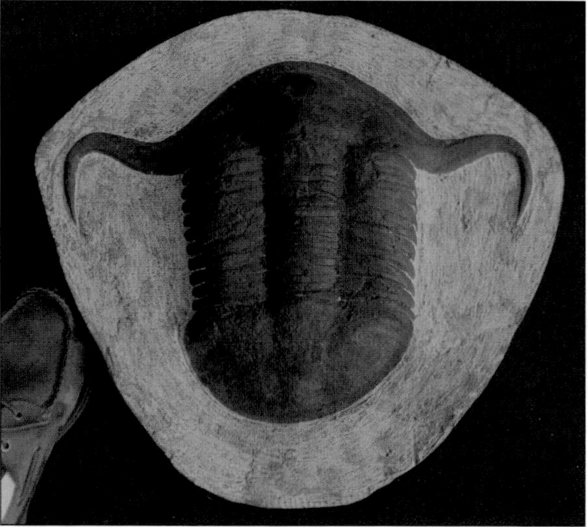

These large trilobites showed up at Tucson in 2005; this specimen is a resin cast, which becomes fairly obvious if examined closely. Many other Moroccan trilobites are also casts, but are more difficult to distinguish as such. (Value range E, as cast)

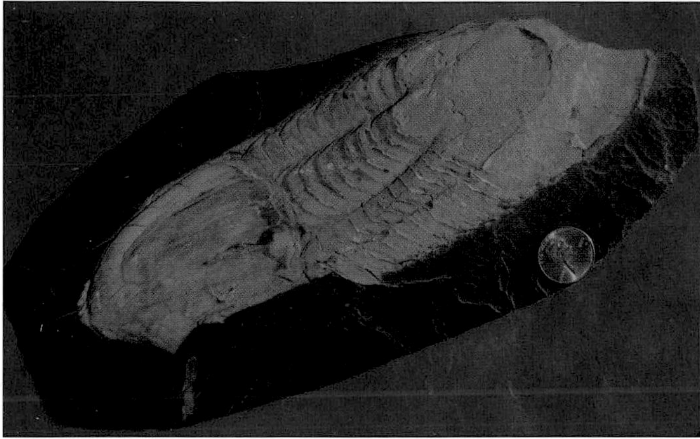

Illaenus sp. A severely flattened and deformed specimen in slate. Middle Ordovician, France.

Eyeless and Pelagic Ordovician and Silurian Trilobites

Most of these trilobites are small and, other than *Ampyxina,* usually are found in black shales, often associated with graptolites. These trilobites are generally believed to have been pelagic or floating forms that lived in the open ocean.

Ampyxina bellutula. A small, eyeless trilobite from the Upper Ordovician Maquoketa Formation of northeastern Missouri. This genus has been widely collected from northeastern Missouri and many specimens have gone into collections. (Value range F, single specimen)

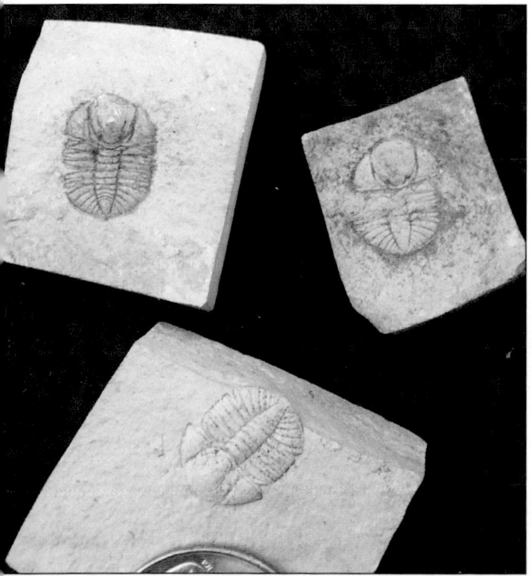

Ampyxina bellutula. Well preserved specimens in dolomitic siltstone, Pike County, Missouri. (Value range G, single specimen)

Ampyxina bellutula. Slab containing numerous specimens of this eyeless trilobite from northeastern Missouri. (Value range E)

Cnemidopyge nudus. A trilobite associated with graptolite bearing shale. Middle Ordovician, Wales.

Trinucleus fimbriatus. sp. Ordovician, Wales. (Value range E)

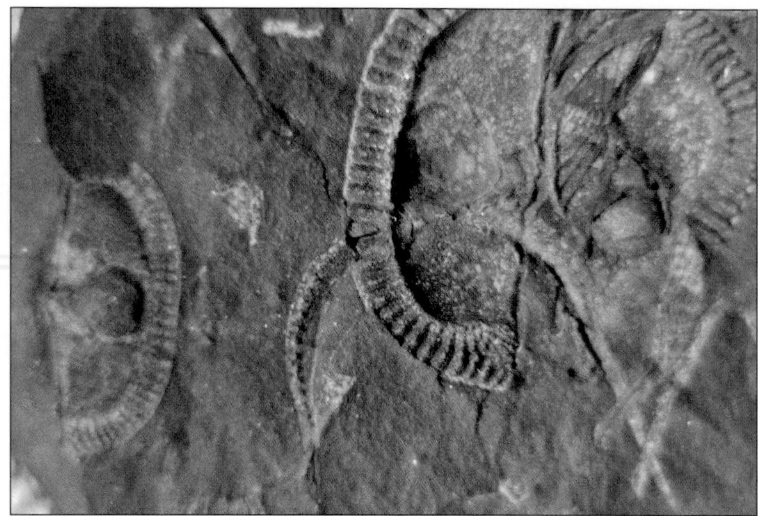

Trinucleus cf. *fimbriatus*. A group of cephalons showing the crenulated margin characteristic of this genus, a presumed pelagic trilobite. (Value range G)

Miraspis mira Barrande. A pelagic (or floating) trilobite associated with sediments deposited under deep sea conditions. Silurian, Bohemia. (Value range E)

Eoharpes sp. Bromide Formation, Middle Ordovician, Criner Hills, Oklahoma. (Value range E)

Spiny Ordovician Trilobites

These often highly ornamented trilobites are believed to have been pelagic or floating forms. As a consequence, they have a worldwide distribution. They also are popular with collectors.

Eomonorachus sp. Decorah Formation, Ralls County, Missouri. A trilobite often found associated with the genus *Cerarus* of the following photos. (Value range F)

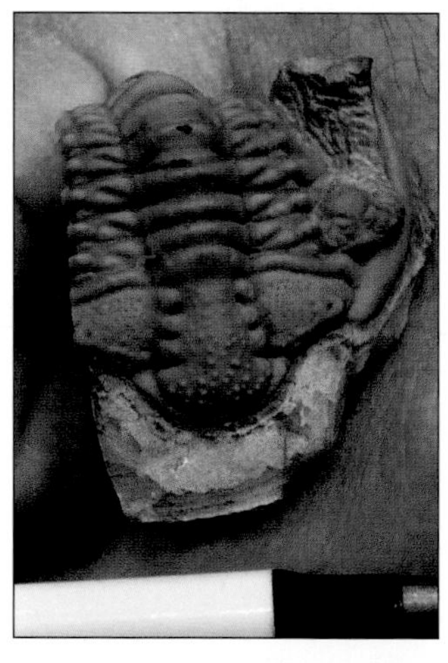

Cerarus pleurexanthemus. Specimen has been worked out of hard limestone, Decorah Formation, Cape Girardeau, Missouri. Specimen worked out of solid limestone by Gerald Kloc.

Cerarus pleurexanthemus. Specimen "plastered" to a hard ground surface. Decorah Formation, Middle Ordovician. (Value range E)

Cerarus pleurexanthemus. Repaired specimen from Decorah Formation, Missouri.

Cerarus pleurexanthemus unprepared *Cerarus* cephalons. Trilobites, as with other fossils, unless cleaned (prepared), show little of what is really there. (Value range H, unprepared)

Cerarus pleurexanthemus. Slab with three specimens. Decorah Formation, Pike County, Missouri.

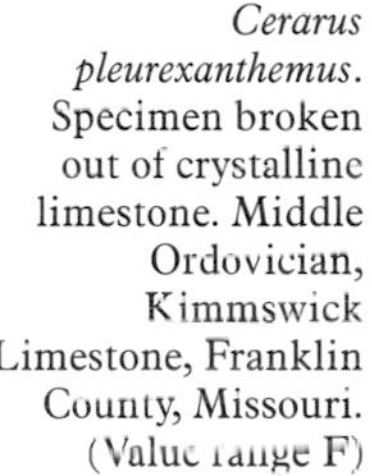

Cerarus pleurexanthemus. Specimen broken out of crystalline limestone. Middle Ordovician, Kimmswick Limestone, Franklin County, Missouri. (Value range F)

Cerarus pleurexanthemus. Close-up of complete specimen shown in previous photo. (Value range E)

Cheirurus welleri. Joliet Dolomite, Middle Silurian, Grafton, Illinois. (Value range F, single specimen)

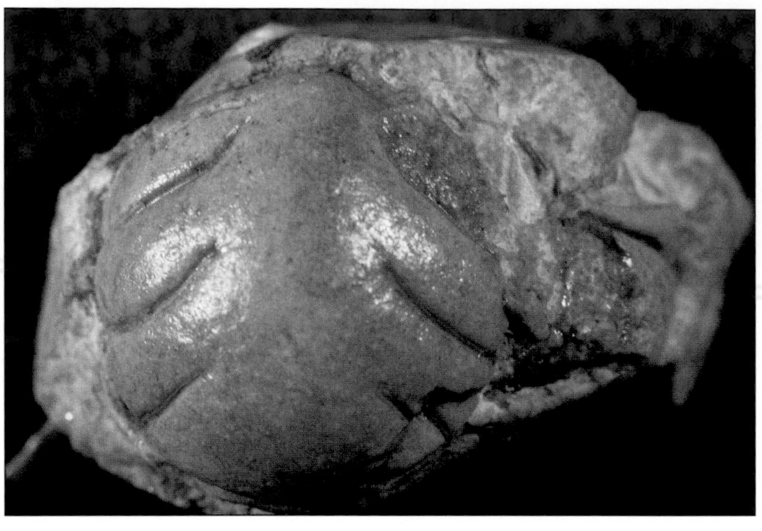

Pandospinapyga projecta Esker. An unusual Middle Ordovician Cheirurid trilobite. Kimmswick Limestone, Glen Park, Missouri.

Calymene sp. With original carapace material. Bainbridge Formation, Silurian. Southeastern Missouri. These trilobites were worked out of hard limestone of the Middle Silurian Bainbridge Formation of Missouri. Some layers of the Bainbridge contain numerous trilobites, but these can be almost impossible to work out of the hard rock. With sophisticated tools like pneumatic chisels and an air abrasive machine they have been exposed, as illustrated by these specimens.

Calymenid Trilobites

Calymenid trilobites (*Calymene* and related genera) are some of the most frequently seen and found trilobites. Their thick and sturdy exoskeleton was less prone to fragment upon molting than were those of most other trilobites so that they are commonly found complete.

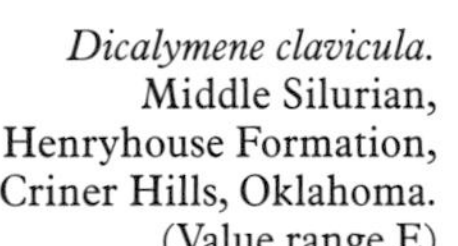

Dicalymene clavicula. Middle Silurian, Henryhouse Formation, Criner Hills, Oklahoma. (Value range E)

Gerald J. Kloc at MAPS EXPO. The previous shown specimen (as well as others) were worked out of this very hard rock by Mr. Kloc. To do this takes the proper equipment as well as considerable skill, patience, and time. Mr. Kloc is coauthor of the outstanding 2002 work, *Trilobites of New York*.

Calymene sp. Bainbridge Formation, Silurian. Southeastern Missouri.

Group of *Sthenarocalymene* (*Calymene*) *celebra*. Joliet Dolomite, Grafton, Illinois. These trilobites occur in Silurian strata brought up by the eastern edge of the Lincoln Fold (Cap aux Gris Structure) north of St. Louis, Missouri. These trilobites have also come out in quantity from the Joliet Dolomite southwest of Chicago, Illinois, and from southern Wisconsin. (Value range G, single specimen, more for groups)

The Grafton trilobite site—1965.

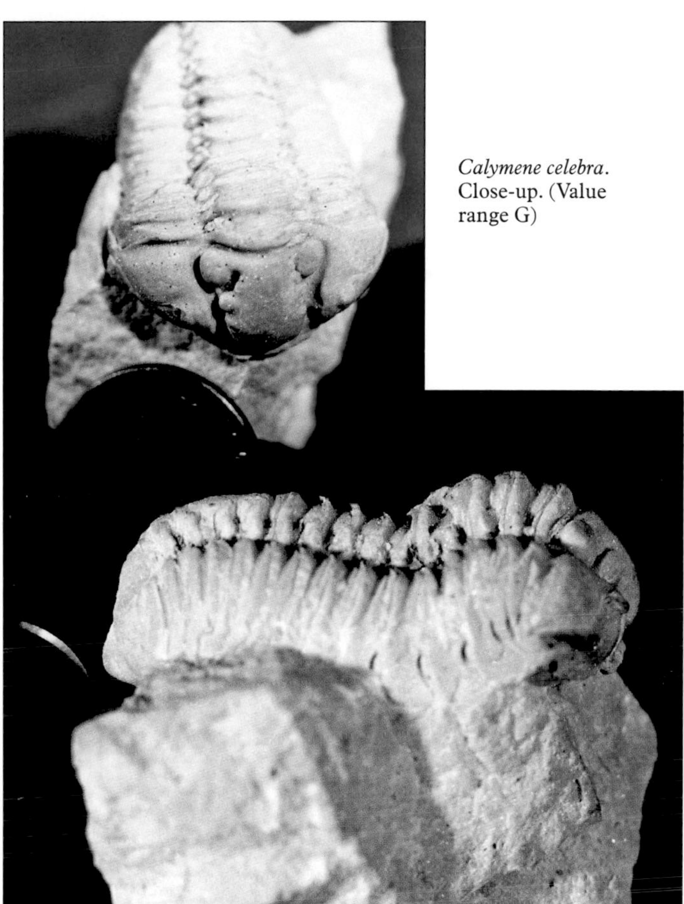

Calymene celebra. Close-up. (Value range G)

Calymene celebra (side view).

Sthenarocalymene (*Calymene*) *celebra*. Joliet Dolomite, Grafton, Illinois. (Value range E)

Group of enrolled *Calymene* specimens. Joliet Dolomite, Grafton, Illinois. (Value range E for group)

Phacopid Trilobites

Phacopid trilobites, like calymenids, were sturdy ones in reference to their exoskeleton. They were especially widespread and characteristic of the Devonian Period.

Phacops rana. Part and counterpart. Silica Shale, Sylvania, Ohio. (Value range E for pair)

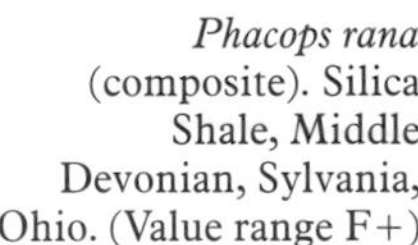

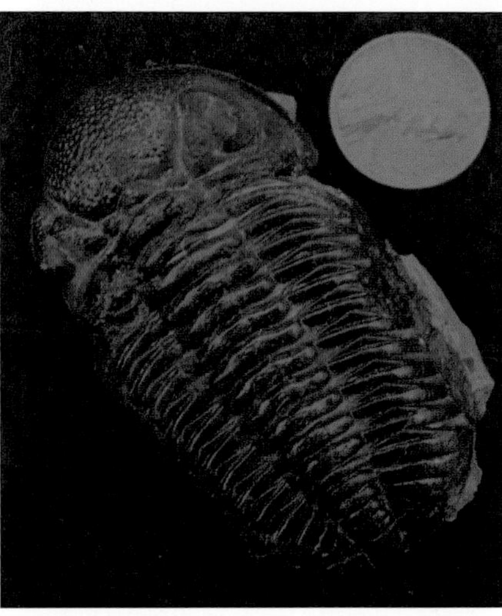

Phacops rana (composite). Silica Shale, Middle Devonian, Sylvania, Ohio. (Value range F+)

Digging for *Phacops rana*, in the Silica Shale, Sylvania, Ohio, 1975.

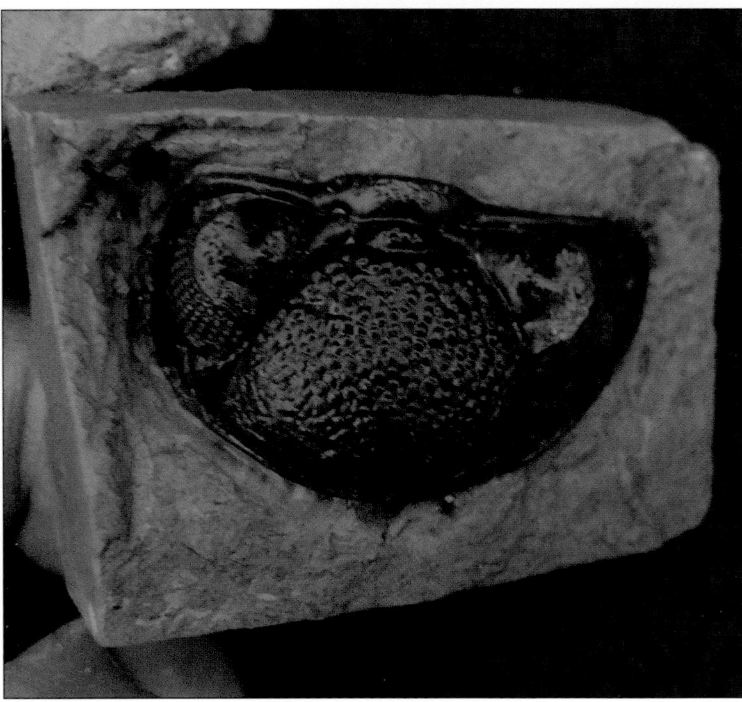

Phacops rana. Cephalon or "head" of this "frog faced" trilobite. Silica Shale, Sylvania, Ohio. (Value range F)

Phacopina devonica Ulrich. A phacopid trilobite in a concretion from the Devonian of the southern hemisphere. Middle Devonian, Viscachani Formation, La Paz, Bolivia. (Value range F)

Phacops rana. This individual had recently molted and thus had a very thinly calcified exoskeleton. The exoskeleton, being very thin, is unlike the previously shown specimens. Silica Shale, Sylvania, Ohio. (Value range F)

Reedops sp. Lower Devonian, Speed, Indiana. This trilobite occurs with corals like those at "Falls of the Ohio" near Louisville, Kentucky. Most of the trilobites like this have come from quarries north of Louisville near Speed, Indiana. (Value range G)

Reedops sp. Beechwood River, Tennessee. (Value range G, single specimen)

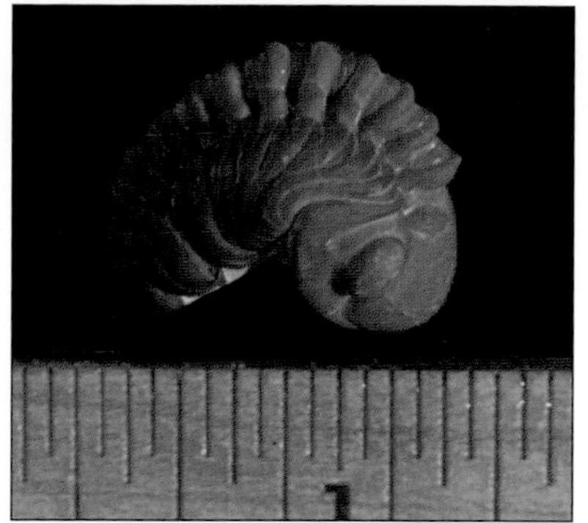

Reedops deckeri. Haragan Formation, Lower Devonian, Clarita, Coal County, Oklahoma. (Value range E)

More Diversity in Ordovician Trilobites

Trilobites of the genus *Bumastus*, *Asaphis*, and *Isotelus* resemble (somewhat) large pill bugs. They are especially characteristic of the Ordovician Period.

Odontocephalus aegeria. Onondaga Group, Middle Devonian, Perry County, Pennsylvania. (Value range F, single specimen)

Amphilichus subpunctatus. Bromide Formation, Criner Hills, Oklahoma. (Value range E)

(right) *Phacops* sp., (left) *Crotocephalus* sp. Lower Devonian, Morocco. (Value range E for group)

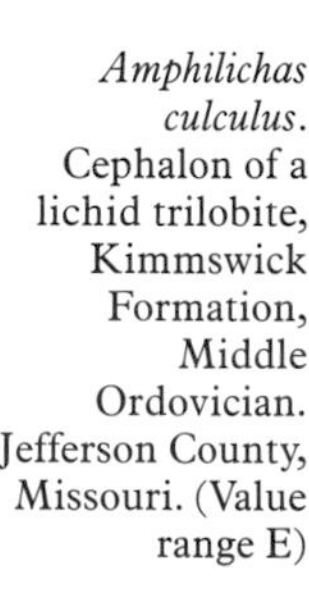

Amphilichas culculus. Cephalon of a lichid trilobite, Kimmswick Formation, Middle Ordovician. Jefferson County, Missouri. (Value range E)

Scutellum sp. Kimmswick Limestone, Middle Ordovician, Jefferson County, Missouri. (Value range E)

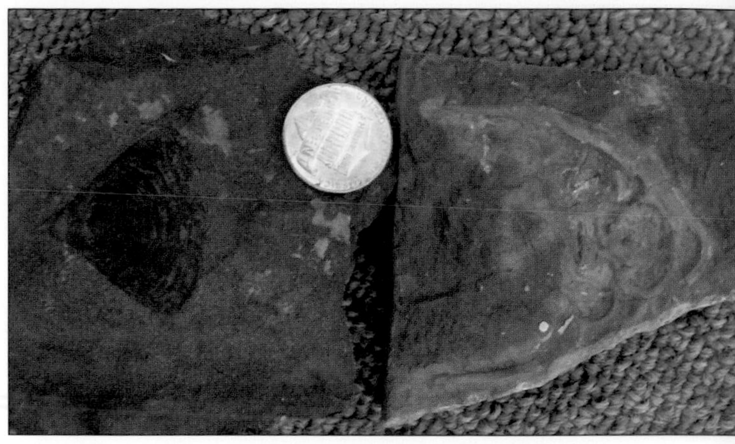

Dalmanites sp. Cephalon (reversed) and pygidia (left). Bainbridge Formation, Upper Silurian, southeastern Missouri. (Value range F for group)

Hypodicranotus missourensis. A small trilobite, almost unique to Missouri and Illinois. (Left-elongate pygidia), (right-cephalon). Kimmswick Limestone, Middle Ordovician. Jefferson County, Missouri.

Dalmanites sp. (cephalon). Bainbridge Formation, Upper Silurian, southeastern Missouri. These have been worked out of hard red limestone by Gerald Kroc.

Dalmanites sp. Pygidia (with spine, which is rarely preserved). Bainbridge Formation, southeastern Missouri. Specimen prepared by Gerald Kroc.

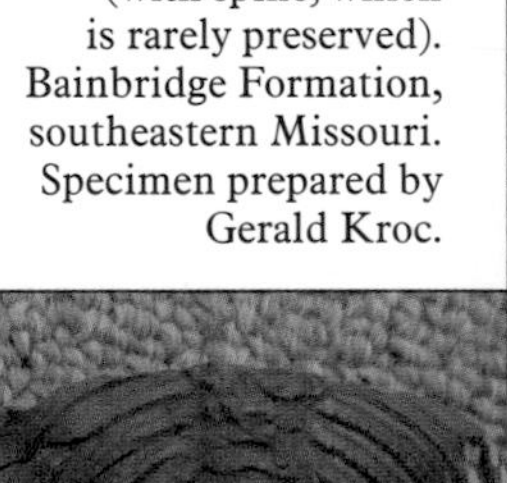

Dalmanitid Trilobites

Dalmanites and related genera are representative of and can be worldwide index fossils for rocks of the Silurian Period.

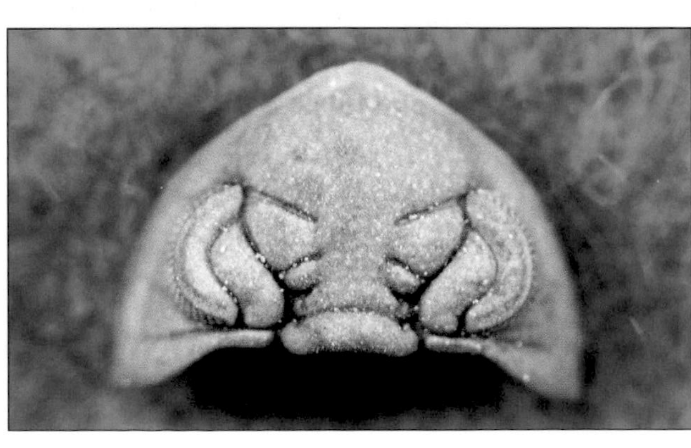

Calliops sp. Edinburgh Limestone, Virginia. Trilobites from this formation have been replaced with silica so that they can be etched from the limestone through the use of acid. (Value range F)

Odontaspis sp. Pygidium. Silurian, Bohemia, Czech Republic.

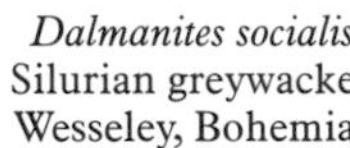

Dalmanites socialis. Silurian greywacke, Wesseley, Bohemia.

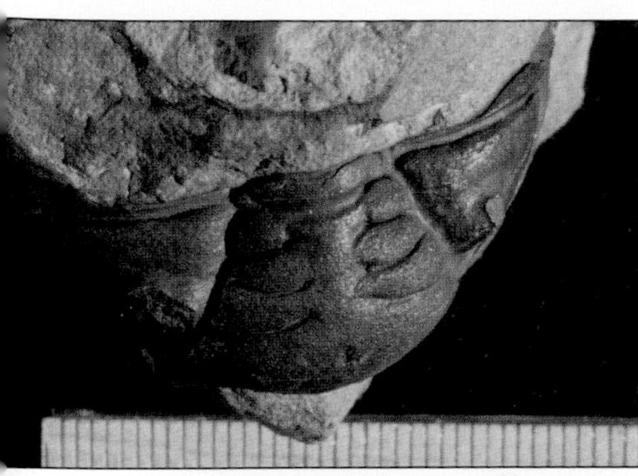

Dalmanites socialis. Cephalon, Upper Silurian, Wesseley, Bohemia.

Kettneraspis (Leonaspis) williamsi. Haragan Formation, Lower Devonian, Clarita, Coal County, Oklahoma. (Value range G)

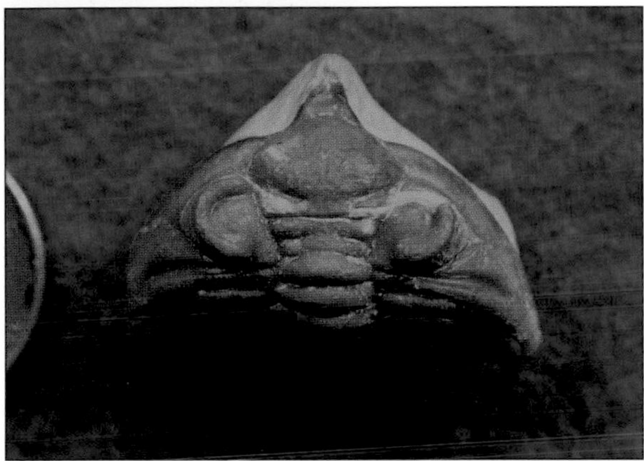

Huntonia (Neoprobolium) oklahomae. Haragan Formation, Lower Devonian, Clarita, Coal County, Oklahoma.

Dicranurus and Other Bizarre Trilobites

Dicranurus is characterized by the presence of large paired occipital spines recurved over the thorax. It is a strange and "spiny" trilobite—difficult to work out of the rock.

Coronocephalus rex. A trilobite related to *Encrinurus*—a spiny, Silurian trilobite. Lower Silurian, Xiushang Formation, south part of Sichuan Province, China. (Value range E)

Dicranurus hamatus Hall. *Dicranurus,* with its pronounced paired occipital spine, is an example of a tendency for arthropods to become complexly ornamented and then go extinct. Many modern insects, like the rhinoceros beetle, are doing the same thing. Haragan Formation, Lower Devonian, Clarita, Coal County, Oklahoma. (Value range F)

Sphaerexochus romingeri. The Donald Duck trilobite. Joliet Dolomite, Grafton, Illinois.

Dicranurus hamatus. The cephalon of this bizarre Devonian trilobite. Haragan Formation, Clarita, Oklahoma. (Value range G)

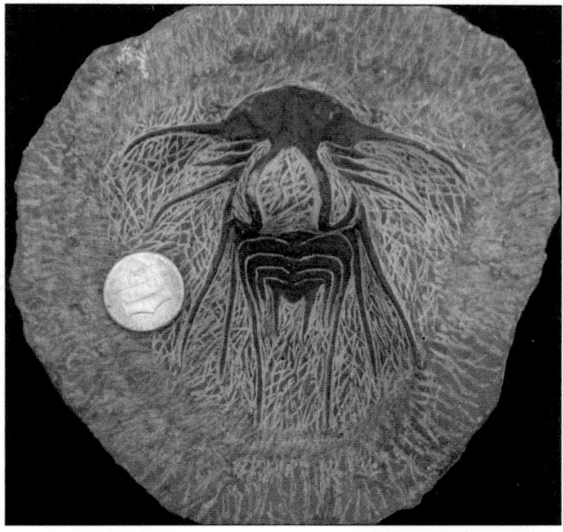

Dicranurus monstrosus Barrande. Lower Devonian, Morocco. Many of these *Dicranurus* specimens from Morocco are either reconstructions or polyester casts (**fakes**). The polyester resin cast is often cleverly placed into a depression carved in the limestone in which *Dicranurus* occurs. They are, however, excellent reproductions of this interesting trilobite and are sold at a low price by Moroccan fossil dealers. Caveat emptor! (Value range F, as cast)

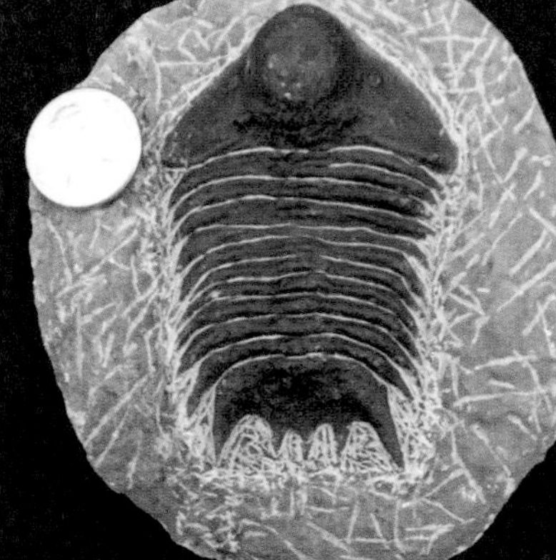

Undetermined, Hamar Lagndad Formation, Lower Devonian, Morocco.

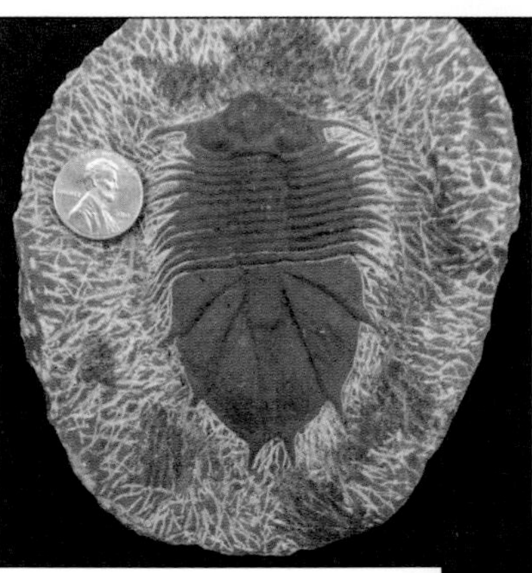

Undetermined, Hamar Lagndad Formation, Lower Devonian, Morocco.

Psychopyge elegans. Lower Devonian, southern Morocco. Another example of a highly ornamented trilobite. The Early Devonian appears to be a time of maximum diversity in highly ornamented trilobites like this. Some of these offered from Morocco are resin casts. (Value range E)

Proetid Trilobites

Protetid trilobites are especially characteristic of the Devonian and the Lower Carboniferous (Mississippian) Periods.

Crassiproetus (Proetus) crassimarginatus. Cedar Valley Limestone, Middle Devonian, Fairfax, Iowa. (Value range F)

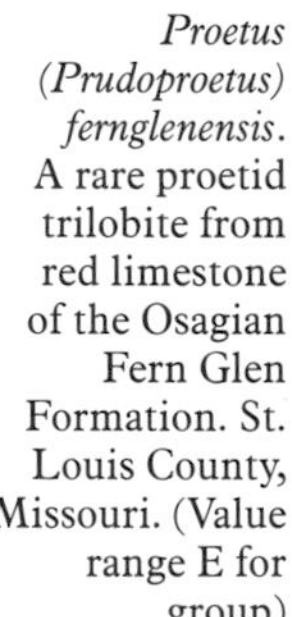

Proetus (Prudoproetus) fernglenensis. A rare proetid trilobite from red limestone of the Osagian Fern Glen Formation. St. Louis County, Missouri. (Value range E for group)

Late Paleozoic Trilobites

Trilobites become rare after the Devonian. Not only were they less common, but their diversity was also much reduced after the Devonian until they disappear in the Permian.

Outcrop of Lower Mississippian Chouteau Limestone, Salt River, Missouri. The Chouteau Limestone (or Formation) is the source of the following small Mississippian trilobites. Most of these have come from quarries near Glasgow, Missouri.

Breviphillipsia sampsoni. Chouteau Formation, Lower Mississippian. Left, unprepared, right prepared specimen. *Phillipsia* and related genera are especially characteristic of the Mississippian Period.

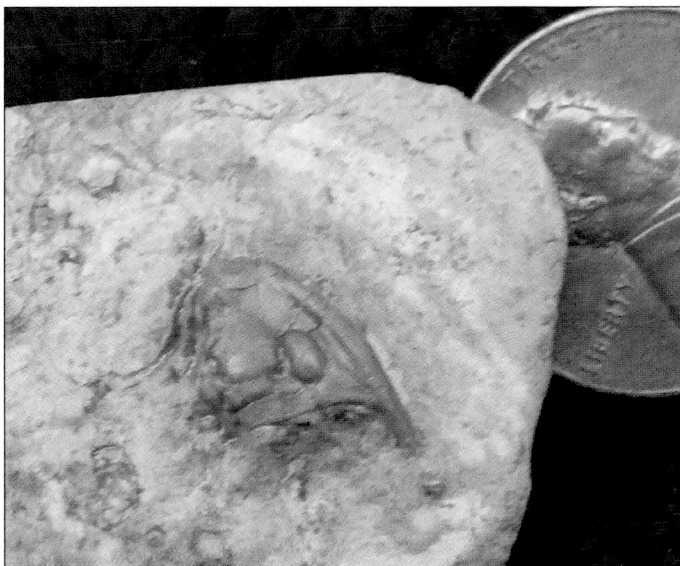

Paladin sp. A partial cephalon of a Pennsylvanian trilobite. This is the norm for late Paleozoic trilobites. They are usually incomplete. Middle Pennsylvanian, Grand River, northeast Missouri. (Value range H)

Group of *Breviphillipsia sampsoni* Chouteau Formation, Lower Mississippian, Glasgow, Missouri. (Value range D)

Eurypterids

Eurypterids are non-trilobite arthropods which can locally be relatively abundant. Those from New York and eastern Ontario from the Bertie Formation are the ones most widely known among collectors. Eurypterids are relatives to scorpions. They went extinct at the end of the Permian Period along with many other life forms.

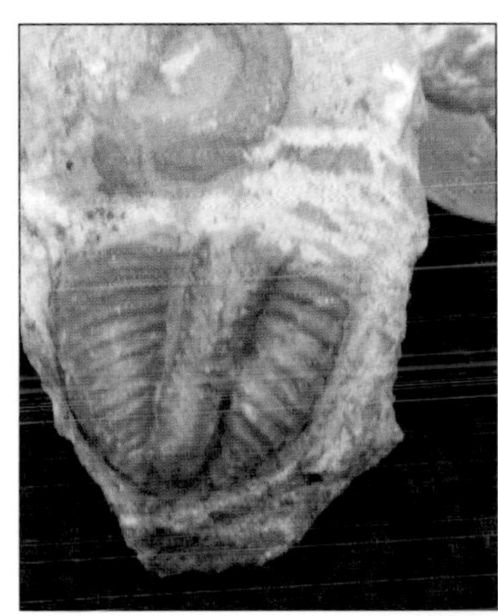

Phillipsia sp. One of the most common trilobites of the Mississippian Period. The pygidium (like this) is what is usually found. Complete specimens are quite rare. (Value range G)

Eurypteris remipes. A group of Silurian eurypterids. Silurian strata in upstate New York and eastern Ontario yield some exquisite specimens of these "sea scorpions." To find these animals clustered together like this is uncommon. (Value range D)

Ditomophyge sp. A complete specimen of a rare late Paleozoic (Pennsylvanian) trilobite. Limestone of the Marmaton Group, St. Louis County, Missouri. (Value range E)

Diorama of Silurian sea-scape. A eurypterid is lurking at the left. The colonial organisms to the right are corals.

Life-sized casts of Devonian eurypterid (left) and *Terataspis* sp. (Silurian trilobite) at MAPS EXPO, 2011.

Eurypteris remipes. Bertie Formation, Upper Silurian. (Value range E)

Eurypteris remipes. Bertie Formation (waterlime), Herkimer County, New York. A large, dark, and well preserved Silurian eurypterid. (Value range D)

Non-trilobite Arthropod Trackways

Non-trilobite trackways are relatively uncommon in Paleozoic strata. Among the most interesting are large trackways made by animals which had a distinct telson. These are given the trace-fossil name of *Protichnites*. *Protichnites* is believed to have been made by some type of air breathing arthropod.

Blanket sandstone. Blanket sandstones are relatively thin sequences of sandstone inter-bedded with dolomite and limestone, deposited in shallow water on the craton. They often exhibit desiccation cracks as the sand flats where they formed were commonly exposed to drying, especially during low tide. Unlike sandstone deposited in deeper marine waters, blanket sandstones contain few fossils—especially if they are of early Paleozoic age. This is because few organisms at this time existed that could tolerate low-tide exposure and its desiccation, could utilize available atmospheric oxygen, and tolerate exposure to the sun. In later geologic time, insects, crabs, and vertebrates frequently left trackways (if not body fossils) on these surfaces, but in the early Paleozoic these animals had not yet appeared.

Bedding surfaces of blanket sandstone (Roubidoux Formation) exposed in a creek bed near Rolla, Missouri.

Fossil desiccation cracks on sandstone slabs set into a masonry wall. These make interesting rock surfaces, prized and extensively used (or used to be) in Ozark masonry. Such desiccation tracks indicate that the bedding surface at times was exposed to the sun. What are believed to be layers of algae present on this surface shrunk upon desiccation, developing cracks that then were filled (by sand) when this cracked surface was covered by sand. Because such desiccation tracks are sometimes associated with trackways like *Protichnites*, the animals responsible for them are suspected to have been early air breathers (air breathing animals are considered to have first appeared in the Devonian in the form of insects and amphibians).

Modern desiccation (mud) cracks. What has cracked here is actually mud—desiccation cracks are proof that this sediment was exposed to the sun and its drying effects.

"Fossil" ripple marks. Ripple marks indicate that the sediment carrying the ripples was submerged periodically (and deposited) in shallow water. Sequences bearing ripple marks like this sometimes alternate with layers having desiccation cracks.

Fossil desiccation tracks, but what has cracked here? These are the fillings of desiccation cracks; however, no mud was present in the underlying layer. What is believed to have cracked was a layer (or mat) of algae. This mat of cyanobacteria, on desiccation, shrunk and thus developed cracks. The cracked mat was then covered by sand, forming these "mud" cracks composed of sand while the algal mat and other organic material was destroyed under oxidizing conditions.

Protichnites sp. This is a trackway associated with Cambrian blanket sandstones. Two *Protichnites* trackways are converging at the right. The track made by the animal's **telson** (tail) is distinct. Because of this tail, these trackways were not made by trilobites or related trilobitomorphs (soft bodied trilobites) but rather were made by some other type of arthropod—one more like a horseshoe crab. Upper Cambrian (or lowermost Ordovician) Gunter Sandstone near Williamsville, Missouri.

Protichnites sp. Gunter Sandstone, Williamsville, Wayne County, Missouri.

Protichnites sp. Trackway from a small *Protichnites* animal. Potsdam Sandstone, Keysville, New York. (Value range E)

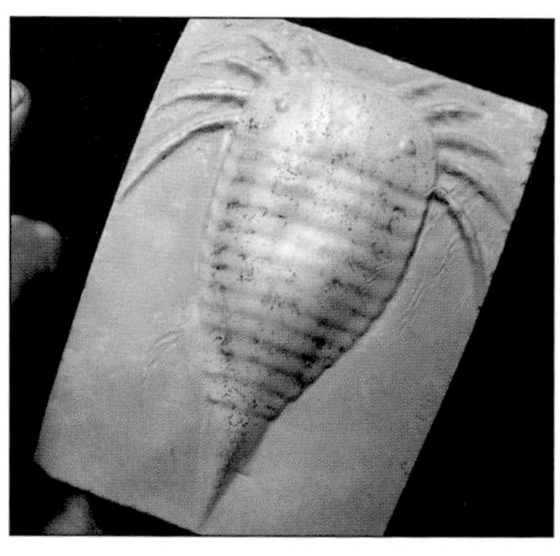

"The *Protichnites* animal?" Aglaspids, extinct relatives to horseshoe crabs, are rare Paleozoic arthropods with a non-calcareous, delicate exoskeleton. They are especially characteristic of the Cambrian, where they still are rare. This is a cast of an aglaspid reconstruction.

Strabops sp. Small, enrolled specimens of an aglaspid. Davis Formation, Elvins (Park Hills), Missouri. (Value range F, single specimen)

Trilobitomorph? trackway in blanket sandstone. Unlike the following trackways, this (presumed) trilobitomorph trackway occurs in a blanket sandstone. It's like the previous trackways of *Protichnites* but lacks evidence of a telson. This trackway may not have been produced by a trilobitomorph, but rather by some other type of arthropod. This is because the very shallow water environment of blanket sandstones frequently were exposed to desiccation, conditions requiring an arthropod whose gills could utilize atmospheric oxygen—gills efficient enough to enable them to walk on exposed sand surfaces during low tide. Everton Formation, Ste. Genevieve County, Missouri.

Trilobitomorph Trackways

Most (or at least many) of the Paleozoic trackways found in marine strata are believed to have been made by soft bodied, trilobite-like arthropods. Soft bodied trilobite-like arthropods appear to have been common along with trilobites themselves and such forms are known as trilobitomorphs. Tracks and trails of trilobitomorphs appear in shale and sandstone beds often deposited under relatively deep sea conditions, sediments deposited on what was at the time the edge of the continent.

Trilobitomorph trackways in red sandstone (Swan Creek Sandstone). Notice the large ripple marks, they indicate that the sand was deposited under shallow water. This is from a blanket sandstone of the type which might have trackways like *Protichnites*. As this sandstone is mid-Lower Ordovician in age, *Protichnites* may have been extinct by this time as *Protichnites* is characteristically a Cambrian trace fossil.

Crossopodia sp. A frequently found trace fossil attributed to trilobitomorphs. Mississippian, Gilmore City Limestone, Gilmore City, Iowa. (Value range F)

Arthropod (trilobitomorph) trackway, Chester Group sandstone, southern Indiana. No trilobites have been found with these trackways which cover bedding planes of fine grained sandstone. They may have been made by soft bodied trilobite-like arthropods known as trilobitomorphs.

Palmichnium sp. Trilobitomorph trackways. A presumed arthropod trace fossil from Lower Devonian strata of Morocco, which yields a variety of fine and complete trilobites. Trackways like this probably were made by soft-bodied arthropods, possibly soft-bodied trilobite-like arthropods. (Value range G)

Arthropod (trilobitomorph) trackway, Chester Group sandstone of the Upper Mississipian, southern Indiana. (Value range F)

Rusophycus sp. (Trilobite resting pits). These tracks were thought by quarrymen to be a fossil calf track. They represent depressions dug in sand by some sort of trilobite-like animal (trilobitomorph). They occur in blanket sandstone, the Gunter of latest Cambrian (or early-most Ordovician).

Arthropod (trilobitomorph) trackway, Davis Formation, Upper Cambrian, southern Missouri. (Value range F)

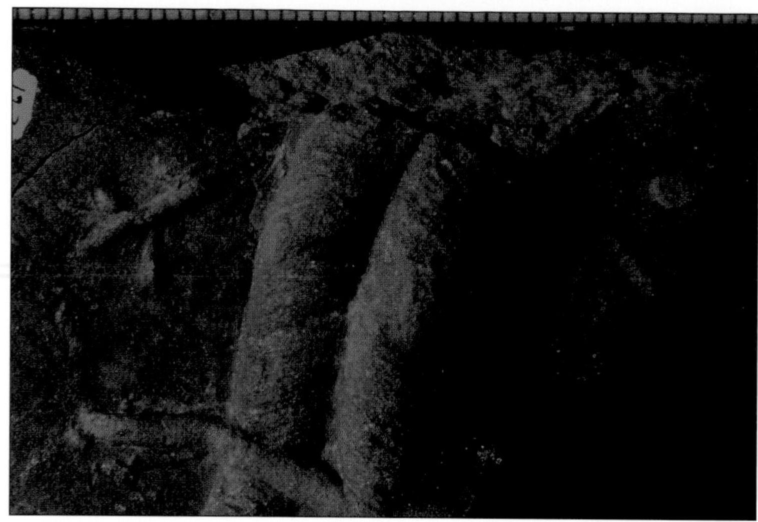

Cruziana sp. This cast of a track is believed to have been made by trilobites. It's a natural sandstone cast of the track made in mud over which sand was deposited to form what is known as a sole cast. *Cruziana* casts like this can be locally common trace fossils. Some confusion exists as to what is *Cruziana* and what is *Rusophycus*, the later being a shorter form of the same type of trace-fossil. Gros Ventre Formation, Middle Cambrian, Big Horn Mountains, northern Wyoming. (Value range F)

Cruziana sp. Gros Ventre Formation, Middle Cambrian, Wyoming.

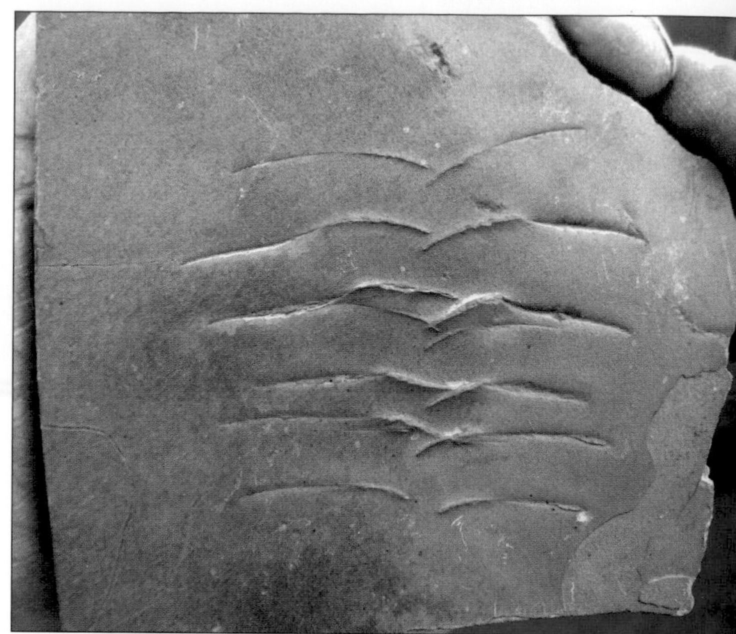

Arthropod (trilobitomorph) trackway. Sole impressions of what was a fairly large, soft-bodied, trilobite-like arthropod (trilobitomorph). Lower Pennsylvanian, Atoka Formation, foreland facies, Ben Hur, Arkansas. (Value range G)

Arthropod (trilobitomorph) trackway. Middle Pennsylvanian, Labette Shale, northern St. Louis County, Missouri. (Value range G)

Rusophycus sp. This trace fossil is similar to *Cruziana* shown above, but **shorter**. Some trace fossil workers consider these to be "resting pits" dug by trilobites or trilobitomorphs. Gros Ventre Formation, Middle Cambrian, Big Horn Mountains, northern Wyoming.

Trilobitomorph trackway, Middle Pennsylvanian, Labette Shale, northern St. Louis County, Missouri.

Ostracodes

Ostracodes (or clam-shrimp as they are also called) are arthropods resembling clams. Ostracodes are still living—most are very small with fossil forms usually considered to be microfossils. In the Ordovician ostracodes of the genus *Leperditia* and *Isochilina* are megafossils, some being giants compared to most other ostracode genera.

Marine Arthropods (Crustaceans)

Fossil crustaceans (shrimp, lobsters, etc.) are usually uncommon fossils in Paleozoic rocks. This is probably because, at this time, they had unmineralized exoskeletons that normally were not preserved. Under ideal conditions, as with the "Mazon Creek" ironstone nodules, they locally can occur in abundance.

Leperditia fabulites. Numerous specimens of these jelly-bean-like arthropods occur in a black, petroliferous limestone. Dutchtown Formation, Lower Middle Ordovician, Dutchtown, Missouri. (Value range G)

Spoil piles of the "Mazon Creek" fossil beds.

Leperditia cf. *L. scalaris*. Ostracodes en mass. Everton Formation, Lower Middle Ordovician, Calico Rock, Arkansas.

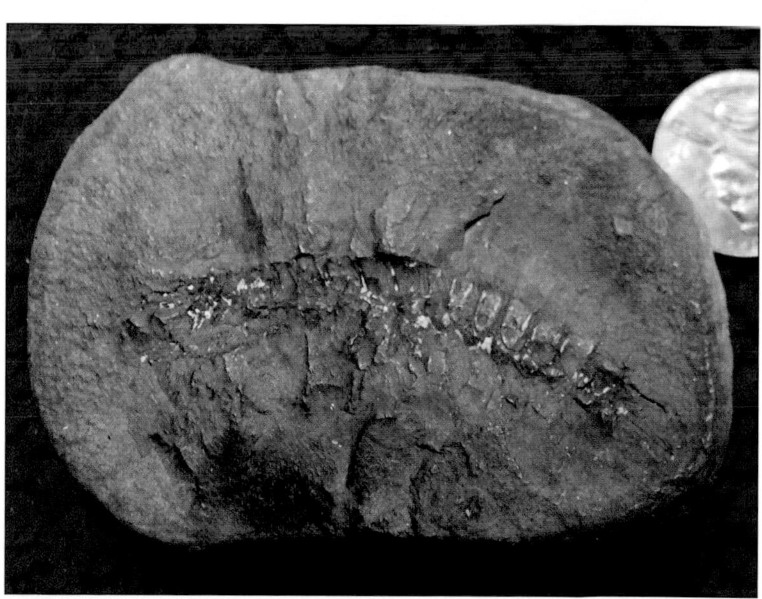

Acanthotelson stimpsoni. A land living crustacean found in ironstone concretions associated with Pennsylvanian coal swamps.

Cyclas americanus. These are small, round arthropods found in small, round, ironstone concretions.

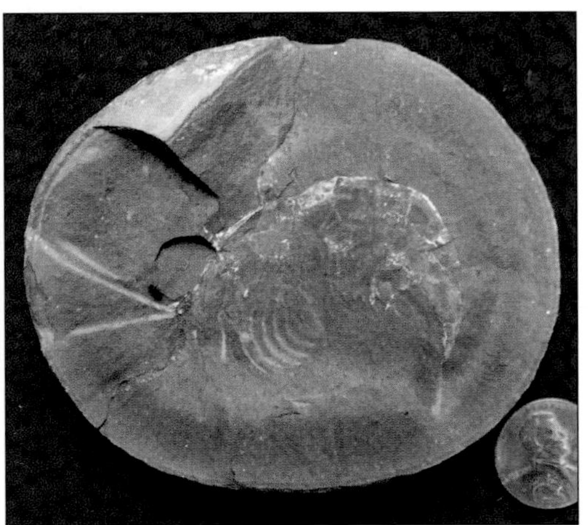

Belotelson magister. A shrimp. One of the more frequently found crustaceans in Pennsylvanian ironstone concretions. Shrimp occur in the Paleozoic, however, because of their non-mineralized exoskeleton, they usually are rare fossils. The marine Essex Fauna ("Mazon Creek" ironstone nodules) of northern Illinois has yielded numerous specimens. This is an especially nice example. (Value range E)

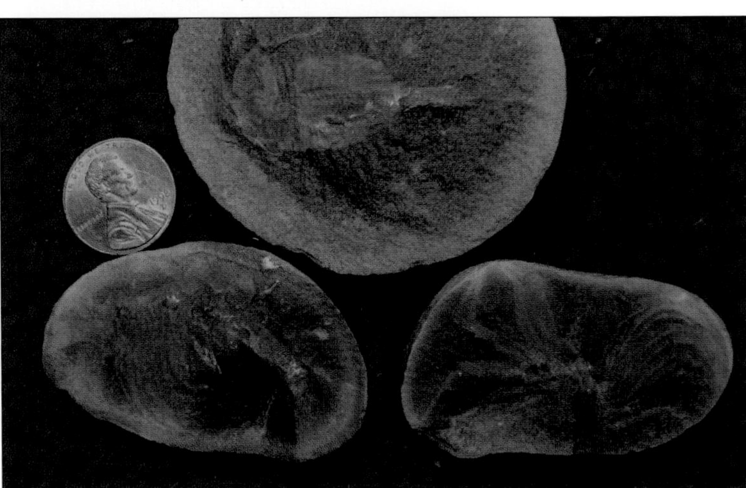

Shrimp. (Top) *Palarocaris typus*, (bottom) *Kallidecthes richardsoni*. This is the usual occurrence of fossil shrimp in nodules of the Essex locality (Value range G, single specimen)

Land Arthropods

Land living arthropods like insects, millipedes, and spiders usually are rare fossils in Paleozoic rocks. One of the most extensive faunas of Paleozoic land arthropods occur in the ironstone concretions (or nodules) of the Braidwood and Essex regions of northern Illinois ("Mazon Creek" fossils). Here occur centipedes and millipedes, primitive worm-like arthropods including the huge *Arthropleura*, a five foot long giant millipede. Arachnids are known from primitive spiders and land meristromes (relatives to horseshoe crabs) of the genus *Euproops*. Insects are also present in considerable diversity, including large cockroaches.

Euproops danae Meek. An arthropod related to the horseshoe crab and associated with the well known plant fossils of Pennsylvanian coal swamps. It is hypothesized that *Euproops* may have lived near the top of tree ferns and other vegetation of the coal swamps.

Modern Millipede embedded in leucite. The many legs on this primitive arthropod would make trilobitomorph-like trackways however, millipedes lived (even in the Paleozoic), in non-marine environments.

Eupohoberia sp. Millipede in ironstone concretion. Millipedes are **primitive arthropods**. Their obvious segmentation and worm-like body links them with segmented worms, the annelids.

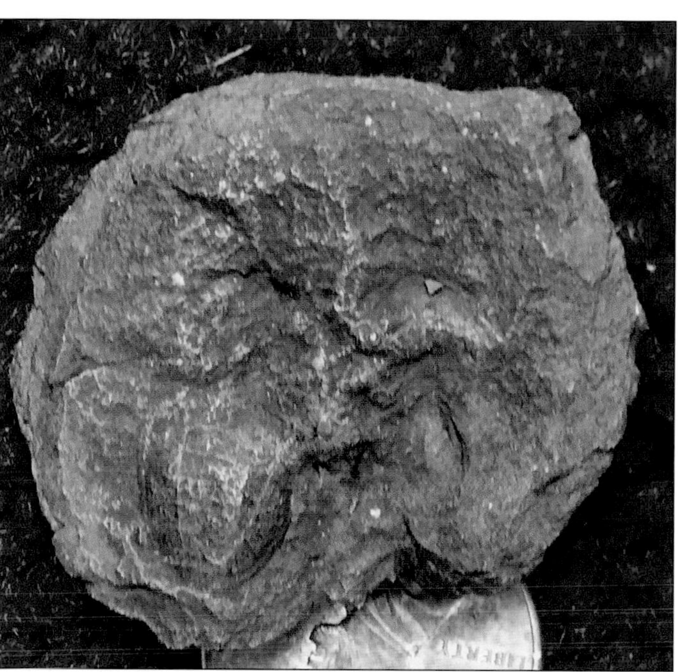

Spider. *Architarbus rotundatus*. Spiders appeared concurrently with insects. They are rare fossils in Paleozoic strata. This is one in a Pennsylvanian ironstone concretion. (Value range F)

Eupohoberia sp. Small millipede in ironstone concretion.

Acanthepestes sp. A millipede preserved in freshwater limestone (Topeka Limestone), Upper Pennsylvanian, Hamilton, Greenwood County, Kansas.

Architarbus sp. (Spider). Latex cast of nice specimen.

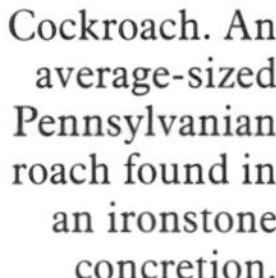

Cockroach. An average-sized Pennsylvanian roach found in an ironstone concretion.

Hermit arthropods. This snail-like fossil (*Scaevogyra swezeyi*) was found associated with strata deposited under what are believed to have been hypersaline conditions (exceptionally salty seawater). Such conditions generally exclude most animals. When fossils are found associated with such environments, they possibly were introduced into this environment in some unusual manner. These mollusks are suggested to have been introduced into it by arthropods, which used the large shells for protection in the same manner as do living hermit crabs. Such "hermit arthropods" thus may have introduced the shells artificially into an environment in which they otherwise would not be found. Upper Cambrian, Potosi Formation near Palmer, Missouri.

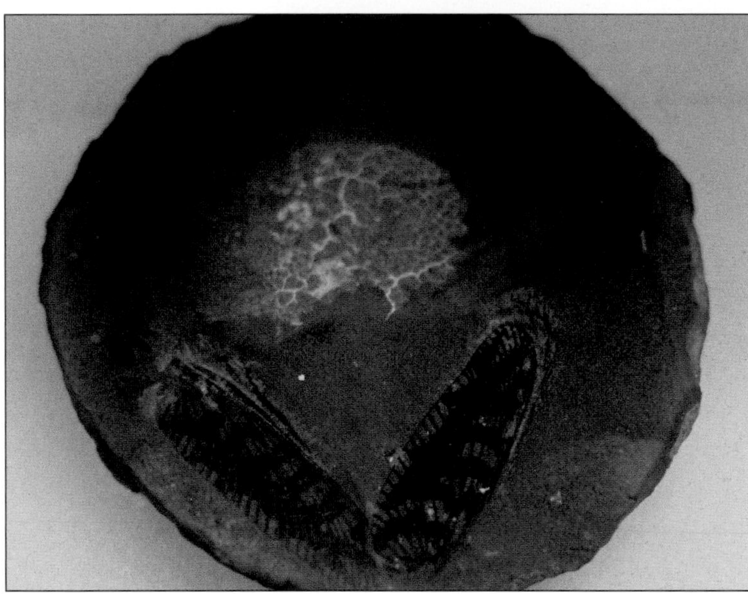

Homaloneura dabasinskasi. Superbly preserved wings of a Pennsylvanian insect preserved in an ironstone concretion or nodule. Photo taken from specimen on display at 1st North American Paleontological Convention 1969, Field Museum, Chicago.

Another relatively large fossil mollusk found associated with hypersaline-deposited strata and believed to have been carried into this environment by a hermit arthropod. Upper Cambrian, Potosi Formation, Piedmont, Missouri.

Hermit Arthropods

Hermit crabs are arthropods which utilize abandoned shells of mollusks for protection. In doing so they may carry these shells into areas where otherwise they would not occur. Relatively large shells of the Cambrian gastropod-like mollusk *Scaevogyra* are sometimes found in strata where they normally would not be found. These large and rarely occurring fossils are hypothesized to have been transported hermit-crab-style by some type of arthropod, possibly a type of soft bodied form which otherwise could not have lived in what was a hostile environment without the protective shell.

Glossary

Atlantic faunal province. Fossils (especially trilobites) found in sediments of the former Iapetus Ocean. Different trilobites lived in the waters separated by land masses existing during the early Paleozoic. These land masses were quite different in shape from those of today as this was prior to the existence of Pangea.

North American Faunal Province. A fauna of marine organisms unique to the Cambrian seaways covering that portion of North America which existed in the Cambrian and known as Laurentia.

Bibliography

Briggs, Derek E. G., Douglas H. Erwin and Frederick J. Collier, 1994 *The Fossils of the Burgess Shale*. Smithsonian Institution Press. Washington and London. ISBN 1-56098-364-7.

Burns, Jasper, 1999. *Trilobites-Common Trilobites of North America*. Nature Guide Books. ISBN-9669157-0-4.

Snajdr, Milan, 1990. *Bohemian Trilobites*. Czech Geological Survey, Prague. (Ustredni Ustav Geologicky) ISBN 80-7075-001-4.

Whiteley, Thomas E., Gerald J. Kloc and Carlton E. Brett, 2002. *Trilobites of New York, an Illustrated Guide*. Comstock Publishing Associates, a division of Cornell University Press. Ithaca and London.

Echinoderms

Echinoderms, which live exclusively in modern oceans, represent a phylum of interesting and well known animals. They include the living starfish (asteroids), brittle stars (ophiuroids), sea cucumbers (holothurians), as well as the crinoids, an echinoderm class that, while still living, were much better represented in the Paleozoic and Mesozoic Eras than they are today. In the Paleozoic, a large number of now extinct echinoderm classes existed, most of these living during the early Paleozoic (Cambrian and Ordovician periods). Early Paleozoic echinoderm body-plan-diversity (classes) were at their maximum during this time. Whatever happened in the way of species diversity near the end of the Precambrian, resulted in numerous echinoderm body plans spewing off (to quote Ellis Yochelson) like "sparks from a St. Catherine's Wheel." **Extinct echinoderm classes** in the Cambrian includes the **eocrinoids** and **edrioasteroids,** and in the Ordovician, the **cystoids, carpoids, paracrinoids, edrioblastoids, stylophorans,** and other forms. **Of extant forms** it consists of the **asteroids, opihuroids, holothurians, echinoids,** and **crinoids**. These classes obviously avoided extinction while the eocrinoids, paracrinoids, cystoids, edrioasteroids, and blastoids (to name a few extinct body plans covered in this chapter) went extinct sometime either during or at the end of the Paleozoic Era.

The underside (ventral) portion of an ophiuroid (serpent star). Modern echinoderms are characterized by five fold symmetry, as illustrated by this modern serpent star. The body of most echinoderms is composed of small plates or granules composed of calcium carbonate embedded in living tissue. Because of this mineralization, much of an echinoderms body is preserved completely as a fossil. Echinoderms have thus left an excellent fossil record, which, like many other marine phyla, has its earliest members appearing during the Cambrian Period of the Paleozoic Era.

Eocrinoids and Puzzling Cambrian Pelmatozoan Echinoderms

Like many forms of life of the Cambrian, echinoderms during this period were odd. Most abundant were the eocrinoids, relatives of, but apparently not direct ancestors to crinoids. Eocrinoids, like all of the following categories, belong to what are considered by most paleontologists to be specific echinoderm classes.

Cambrian Echinoderms. Cambrian echinoderm fragments are made up of single crystals of calcite, a characteristic of all echinoderms. Echinoderms, as a phylum, go back to the Early Cambrian. These fossils are probably fragments of eocrinoids, one of the first classes of echinoderms to leave a good fossil record. Pelmatozoan echinoderms (stalked forms), usually leave fragments resembling Cheerios. Note the five-sided (star-shaped) fragments, pentagonal symmetry (five-sided symmetry), a characteristic of the phylum.

Cambrian pelmatozoan fragments, southern Missouri. Zones of these pelmatozoan fragments were uncovered when a dam broke on Missouri's Profit Mountain pump-back electrical storage facility, scouring the hillside. When this rush of water was released, it exposed some interesting geology, including zones of fossil bearing shale. (*Courtesy of Tim Vogt, Missouri State Parks*)

Attachment bases of Cambrian pelmatozoans. Davis Formation, Ste. Francois County, Missouri. Pelmatozoans are held to the sea floor by a holdfast, which may look like a root system or (as seen here) like a button attached to hard-ground (lime muds that had become packed and somewhat indurated). (Value range G)

These small calcareous buttons occur in large numbers in a layer of Cambrian limestone near Bonneterre, Missouri. They are from some unknown type of Cambrian echinoderm. They appear to be pelmatozoan stem fragments as each button is made up of a single crystal of calcite, a characteristic of all echinoderms.

Cambrian stalked echinoderm. A peculiar stalked echinoderm (pelmatozoan) associated with the button-like holdfasts of the previous photo and also associated with "hard ground" stromatolites.

Eocrinoid impression. Spence Shale, Antimony Canyon, Idaho. Eocrinoids are early and primitive pelmatozoan echinoderms where the stem is an extension of the plated body.

Hard ground produced by blob-like stromatolites to which the numerous button-like holdfasts of Cambrian pelmatozoan echinoderms were attached.

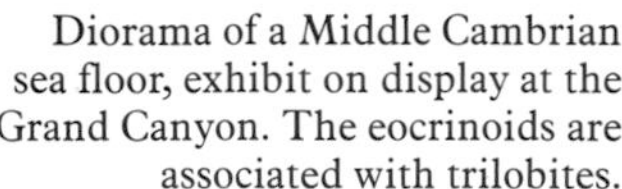

Diorama of a Middle Cambrian sea floor, exhibit on display at the Grand Canyon. The eocrinoids are associated with trilobites.

Crinoids

Crinoid fragments represent some of the most common and widespread fossils found in Paleozoic marine strata. Crinoids are often confused with plants—**which they are not!** They resemble plants only in that they were filter feeders, feeding upon micro-plankton which thrived in the clear shallow seas so favorable for them. The Paleozoic fossil record of crinoids is a large one. Only a small sample can be shown here.

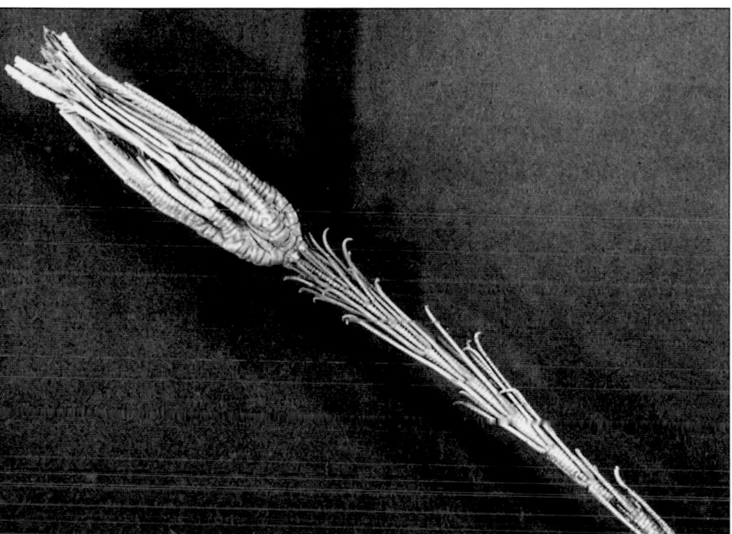

Modern Crinoid (or sea lily). Crinoids are stalked animals (pelmatozoans) still living in modern oceans. They are much less common today then they were during the geologic past, partially for the reason that there are fewer shallow water regions in today's oceans than existed during the past, especially during the Paleozoic era. Epicontinental seaways were much more common during the Paleozoic than today as there was more shallow water habitat available for them. Note the cirri on the crinoids stem. The crinoid's "head" or calyx is to the left, this filters plankton upon which the animal feeds. Crinoids are (and were) filter feeders.

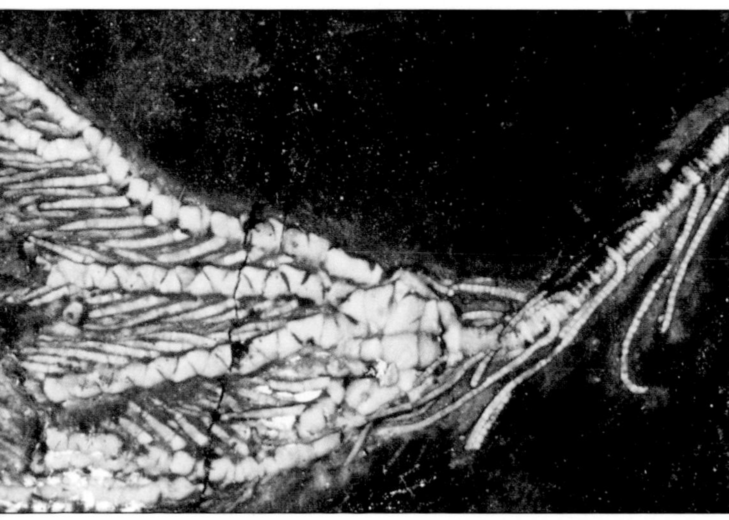

Fossil crinoid. In this crinoid the calyx is splayed out to the left. Note the cirri on the animal's stem. This crinoid is from the Mississippian Period; it's not too different from the modern crinoid shown in the previous photo.

Cupulocrinus polydactylas. Crinoid "heads" or calyxes are embedded in fossiliferous limestone from Richmond Indiana. Richmond Group, Upper Ordovician.

Crinoid bearing limestone of Mississippian age near Bozeman, Montana. The Lower Carboniferous of Europe (that is the Mississippian Period) was probably the height of Paleozoic crinoid diversity. Here crinoidal limestone of the Lower Carboniferous (Mississippian Period) crop out on a mountainside. *Photo by Warren Wagner*

Crinoid stems. These uncleaned (just as they were found) crinoid stem fragments came from an Upper Carboniferous (Pennsylvanian) outcrop. Crinoid stem fragments can be some of the most abundant Paleozoic fossils. They sometimes are known as **"Indian Beads,"** as multiple specimens with a center hole (like that at the bottom-left) were strung by Native Americans to produce a crinoid-stem-necklace. (Value range G for all)

Glyptocrinus sp.
An early Paleozoic crinoid from Middle Ordovician strata. The splayed arms have the pinnules, used to filter micro-organisms, attached to the arms. Crinoids older than the Middle Ordovician are rare. Crinoids form part of GODE (the **G**reat **O**rdovician **D**iversification **E**vent).

Ptychocrinus splendens. Another group of crinoids from the same locality as above. (Value range D).

Glyptocrinus sp. Slab of Middle Ordovician limestone from northeastern Missouri with part of a small colony of this Ordovician crinoid. (Value range E)

Close-up of one of the crinoids on the above slab.

Ptychocrinus splendens.
A group of complete, delicate crinoids—arms with pinnules can be seen. Crinoids were gregarious animals. Complete crinoid specimens are relatively uncommon fossils, as when the animal died plates which composed it disarticulated (scattered) unless the organism was quickly buried by sediment. Crinoids therefore usually are found either as stem fragments or as a scattering of stem and calyx plates known as crinoidal limestone if the fragments compose most of the rock. Girardeau Formation, Lower Silurian, Cape Girardeau, Missouri.

Scyphocrinus elegans. A fine specimen from Morocco of a crinoid genus, which had worldwide occurrence at the end of the Silurian Period and at the beginning of the Devonian. *Scyphocrinus,* like other crinoids, is found in colonies or groups. *Scyphocrinus,* however, was a floating crinoid whose stem was attached to a hollow float (lobolith), which enabled a group of these echinoderms to float at the surface of the sea and thus be carried over long distances by drifting. It is for this reason that the genus (and species) is so widespread.

Scyphocrinus elegans. A slab with multiple specimens from Morocco. (Value range D)

Scyphocrinus elegans. A group of crinoids from Morocco that has, in the author's opinion, been somewhat "doctored" up. The slab is attractive, but appears to be a clever composite. This is understandable as complete crinoids are rare. Moroccan collectors have to maximize available material to be competitive. Only partial destruction of the slab would prove this. As with many of the Moroccan fossils, it's "Caveat Emptor." Silurian-Devonian boundary, Morocco. (Value range D if authentic slab, E if it is a composite)

Scyphocrinus elegans. A slab with multiple specimens. The red matrix in which the crinoids are embedded is characteristic of Middle and Late Silurian strata over a large portion of the northern hemisphere. Silurian seaways were apparently supplied with large quantities of iron oxide, which may have originated from large exposures of Precambrian iron formation exposed at that time and undergoing weathering; this scenario thus contributing a lot of dissolved iron to the Late Silurian seas. The iron deposits around Birmingham, Alabama, are of this age and probably are of similar origin. These large crinoids do not occur there (so far as is known), but similar ones occur in iron-rich strata of southeastern Missouri. (Value range D)

Camerocrinus. Also known also as loboliths, *Camerocrinus* is believed to be the float of *Scyphocrinus*. A single crinoid or a group of them was attached to one of the floats where the group could then drift over the sea and become dispersed over a large area. Earlymost Devonian, Harrigan Formation, Arbuckle Mountains, Oklahoma. (Value range F, single specimen)

Group of large silicified crinoid stems. Most likely large stems like this were a part of the crinoid's holdfast. Probably a number of individual crinoids grew from such a holdfast. Osagian Group, Middle Mississippian, central Kentucky. (Value range G)

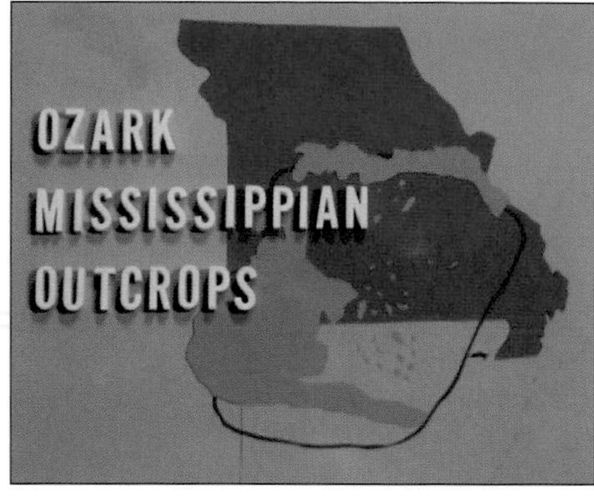

Mississippian limestone, which may be nearly composed of crinoid fragments, surrounds the Ozark Uplift. Most of this limestone (as is the case with the Burlington, Keokuk, and Boone formations) is chert-bearing and well preserved crinoids can sometimes be found in these cherts. These cherty limestones also extend in the subsurface over a large portion of the US Midwest and represent one of the world's largest (if not the largest) concentrations of echinoderm generated rock.

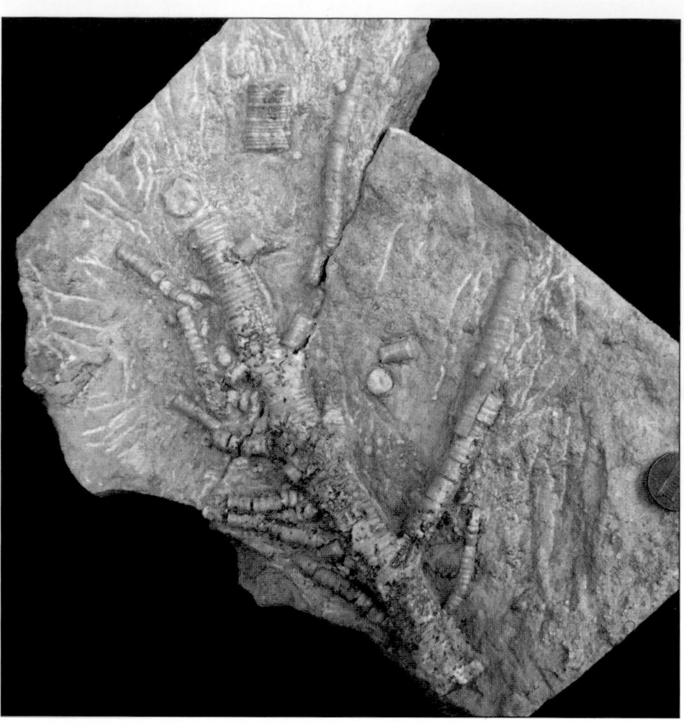

Crinoid holdfast section. Keokuk Limestone, Middle Mississippian. The Mississippian Period of the Paleozoic Era saw some of the largest concentrations of crinoids ever to exist. A holdfast like this probably hosted multiple crinoids.

Cherty limestone of the Burlington-Keokuk Formations. Crinoids are found both in the limestone and in cherts, which weather out from this thick limestone sequence of the US Midwest.

Crinoid calyx exposed during highway construction being cut out of a large boulder by use of a masonry saw. Construction projects in the US (and elsewhere) sometimes encounter whole colonies of crinoids. Often, however, they are very difficult to see in the fresh rock as the rock usually has to weather somewhat before the crinoids or other fossils become visible. Burlington Limestone, Middle Mississippian Highway 65 cuttings, 1975, Springfield, Missouri.

Crinoid stem impression (with cirri) in chert. The small "stems," branching off of the main stem, are known as cirri. This chert slab from the Mississippian Period is unusual. Crinoid stem impressions, although being common in such chert, usually don't show cirri, especially with those of Mississippian age. (Value range F)

The specimen in previous photo (prepared) and cut. (Value range E)

A group of crinoids from the same bedding surface that produced the previous specimen. Burlington Limestone, Middle Mississippian, Springfield, Missouri.

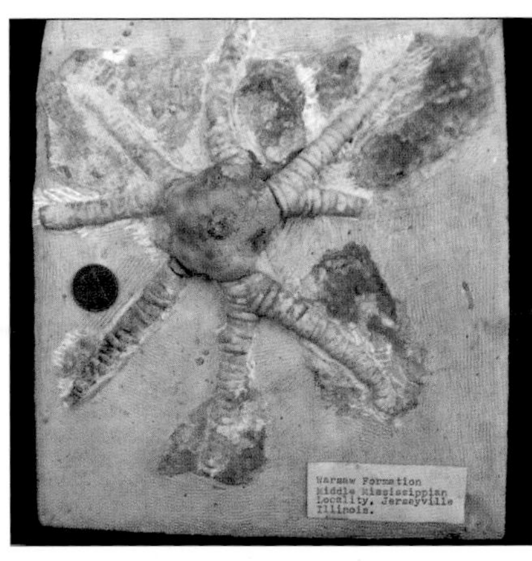

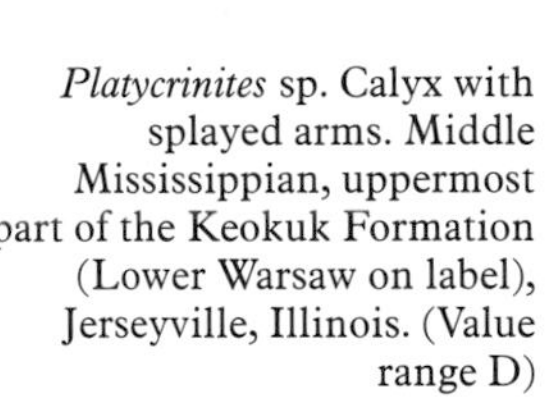

Platycrinites sp. Calyx with splayed arms. Middle Mississippian, uppermost part of the Keokuk Formation (Lower Warsaw on label), Jerseyville, Illinois. (Value range D)

Physetocrinus sp. The calyx of a crinoid (the stem was attached to the circular area in the center). Burlington Limestone, Springfield, Missouri.

Eutrochocrinus sp. Internal and external molds of a crinoid calyx "popped" out of Osagian (Burlington) chert. Mississippian rocks of the US Midwest can include a lot of chert and flint concentrated by weathering from the Burlington and Keokuk Formations. Often these internal molds show crinoid features in a manner quite different from specimens preserved in limestone. Burlington Limestone, Callaway County, Missouri. *Courtesy of Patricia Eicks*

Platycrinites sp. A small, complete crinoid of Middle Mississippian age. Burlington Limestone, Hannibal, Missouri.

Mississippian crinoid "garden." The Burlington-Keokuk formations of the US Midwest have produced one of the largest faunas of fossil crinoids known. Large quantities of crinoid biomass produced crinoid hard parts, which contributed to forming the extensive limestone beds of the Burlington and Keokuk formations. The shallow seaways in which the crinoids lived were very clear. Two lone trilobites are shown which, compared to crinoids, were a relatively uncommon animal by this time in the Paleozoic. *Artwork by Virginia M. Stinchcomb, 1962*

Steganocrinus sp. Internal molds in chert of a large crinoid calyx from the Burlington Limestone. This is an excellent example of a spectacular interior and exterior mold of a crinoid calyx in chert. The specimen was found while breaking chert to prepare "cores or blanks" used in flint knapping. (Value range E)

Steganocrinus sp. Close-up of specimen in previous photo. Note the quartz crystals formed in the crinoid's interior where it has produced a small geode.

Dorycrinus sp. Interior chert mold of a Burlington crinoid. As the plates of Mississippian crinoids often are thick, an interior mold of a crinoid calyx is totally different from the calyx's external appearance. Burlington Limestone, Callaway County, Missouri. (Value range E)

Actinocrinites sp. A large calyx of this Mississippian crinoid genus. The crinoid head (calyx) has been silicified (replaced with silica) and the plates are rounded as it has begun to form a geode. Some geodes found in Mississippian limestones of the US Midwest are attributed to originally being crinoid "heads" (or calyxs). Fort Payne Formation, Laurence County, Tennessee. (Value range E)

Steganocrinus sp. Internal molds of smaller specimens of this crinoid preserved in Osagian chert. Jefferson County, Missouri. (Value range F for single)

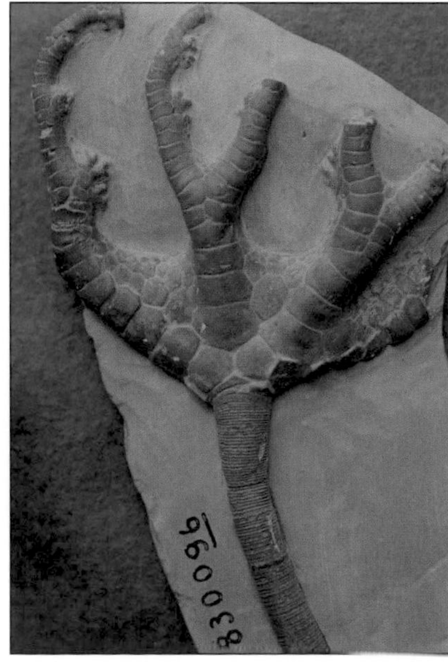

Onychocrinus exsculptus. Bordon Formation, Crawfordsville, Indiana. This specimen, from the Cory's Bluff locality on Sugar Creek near Crawfordsville, Indiana, has yielded a large number and variety of fine crinoids. This specimen was collected early in the twentieth century. *Courtesy Dept. of Earth and Planetary Sciences, Washington University, St. Louis, Mo.*

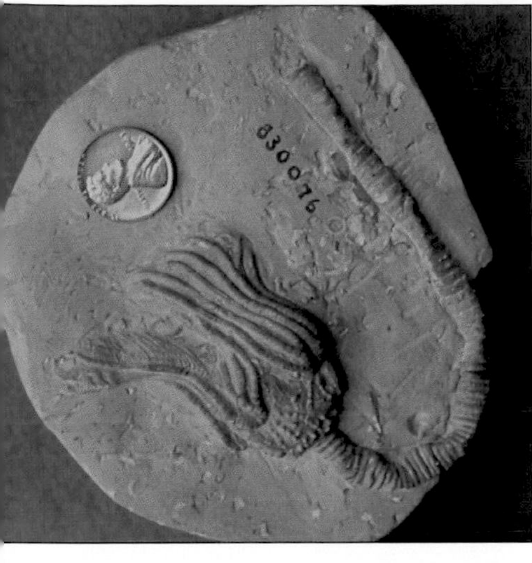

Taxocrinus multibrachiutus. Cory's Bluff, Crawfordsville, Indiana. A hand-cleaned specimen collected from this classic locality about a century ago.

Actinocrinus shellaris. Lower Carboniferous, Belfast, Ireland. A large part of the country of Ireland is underlain by Carboniferous (both Lower and Upper) rocks. Occurrence of these rocks is very similar to the same aged rocks in eastern North America. This crinoid is also very similar to Mississippian crinoids in the eastern US for during the Lower Carboniferous. A continuous shallow sea covered both Europe and North America, the deep Atlantic Ocean still being in the geologic future.

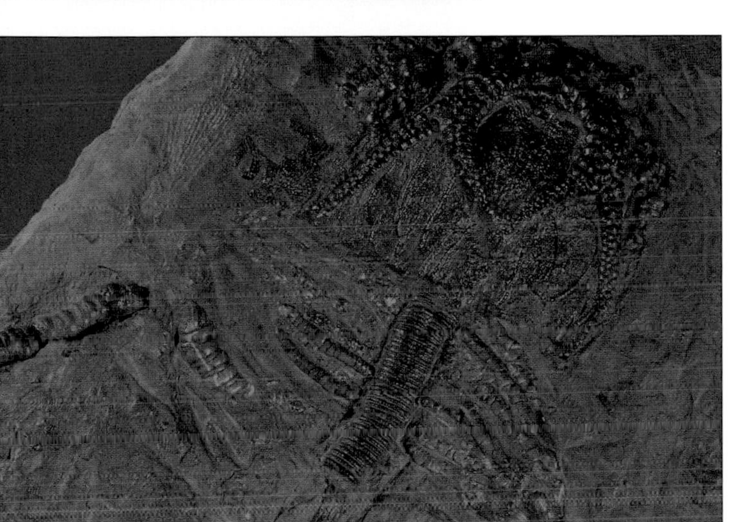

Taxocrinus multibrachiutus. Cory's Bluff, Crawfordsville, Indiana. A specimen collected about a century ago (c. 1910). Today modern air abrasive machines enable these crinoids to be cleaned more thoroughly than is the case with this specimen. *Courtesy Dept. of Earth and Planetary Sciences, Washington University, St. Louis Mo.*

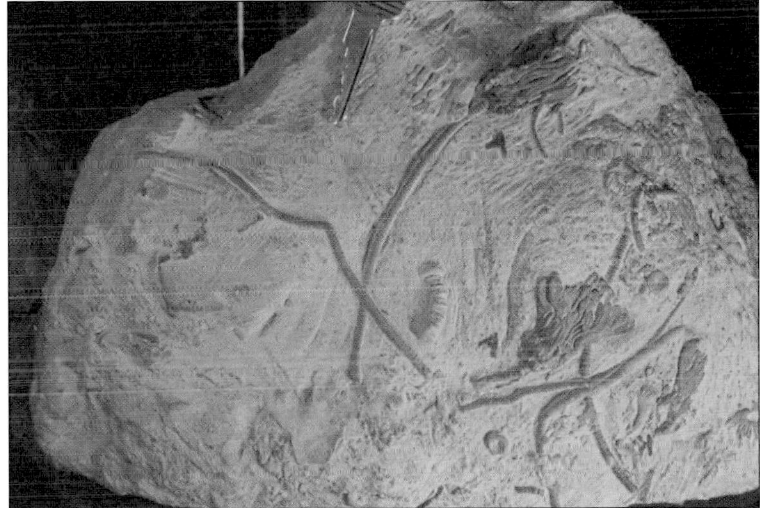

Platycrinites sp. From a classic crinoid locality. A large number of crinoids came from quarries near LeGrand, Iowa, from the 1910s to the 1940s. Lower Mississippian, Kinderhookian Series.

Cyathocrinites sp. Specimen cleaned with an air abrasive machine. Ramp Creek Formation, Crawfordsville, Indiana. (Value range E)

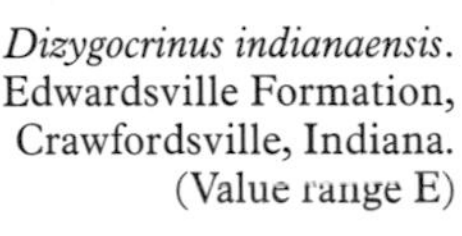

Dizygocrinus indianaensis. Edwardsville Formation, Crawfordsville, Indiana. (Value range E)

Caraifornia sp. A peculiar Devonian crinoid calyx resembling a "fossil" green pepper. Bahaban, Germany.

A specimen similar to the previous example from the Lower Devonian of Morocco. (Value range F)

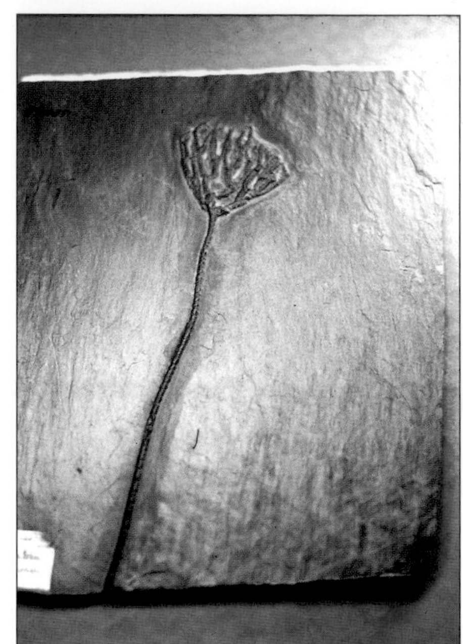

A Lower Devonian crinoid in slate from the classic Konserva-Lageratatten of the Hunsruckschiefer, Bundenbach, Germany.

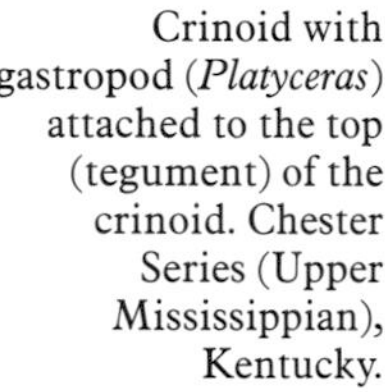

Crinoid with gastropod (*Platyceras*) attached to the top (tegument) of the crinoid. Chester Series (Upper Mississippian), Kentucky.

Unbekamite tri. Hunsruckschiefer (Bundenbach Slates), Lower Devonian, Bundenbach, Germany.

An Ophiuroid (brittle star) wrapped around a crinoid tegumen. Warsaw Formation, Kirkwood, Missouri. From a locality which produced numerous specimens with ophiuroids and starfish attached to the tegumen of the crinoid. (Value range F)

Zeacrinites wortheni. Paint Creek Formation, Floraville, Illinois. An attractive and somewhat common Upper Mississippian crinoid from the US Midwest. (Value range E)

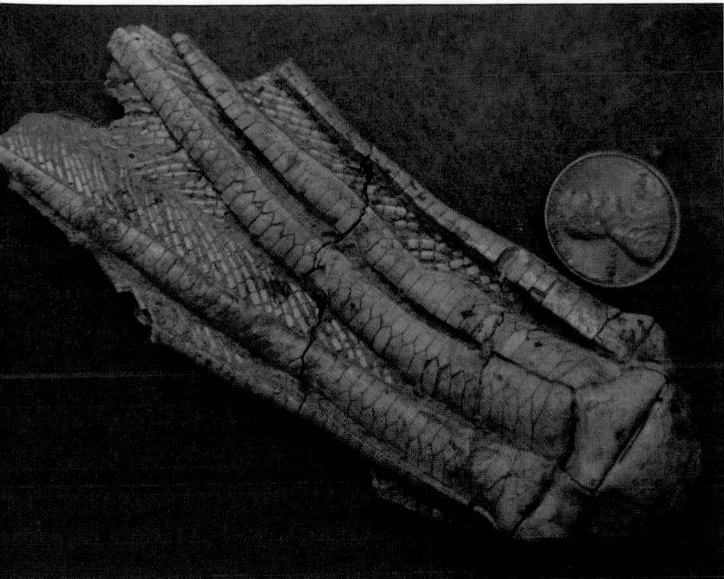

Erisocrinus typus. From a locality which produced a large number of excellent Pennsylvanian crinoids. LaSalle Formation, Pontiac, Illinois. (Value range F)

Orophocrinus stelliformis. Burlington Formation, Springfield, Missouri. This is one of the more bizarre blastoids, with its distinct star-like shape. (Value range F)

Metablastus bipyramidalis (Shumard). Burlington Limestone, Fenton, Missouri. (Value range F)

Blastoids

Blastoids represent an echinoderm class which went extinct at the end of the Paleozoic. The first blastoids appeared in the Silurian; edrioblastoids (considered as a related class) appear during the Middle Ordovician. Blastoids locally can be common fossils, especially in marine strata of Late Mississippian (Chesterian) age.

Pentremites sulcatus. The large hole at the bottom is the blastoid's anus. Golconda Formation, Chester Series, Star Landing, Perry County, Missouri. (Value range F)

Pentremites sp. This is the most commonly found blastoid. The blastoid genus *Pentremites* is especially common in Late Mississippian age (Chesterian) strata. The two blastoids illustrated below are much rarer and therefore less widely distributed in collections. Middle Mississippian, Keokuk Formation, Springfield, Missouri. (Value range F)

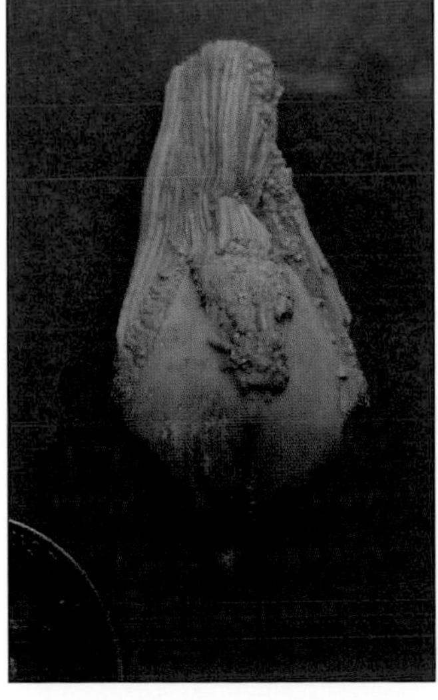

Pentremites sp. Specimen showing pinnules. Paint Creek Formation, Prairie du Long Creek, St. Clair County, Illinois. Blastoids showing pinnules are relatively rare. (Value range F)

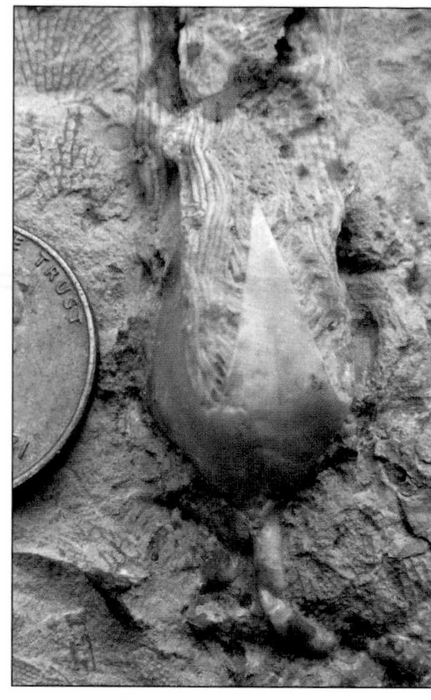

Pentremites with pinnules. Prairie du Long Creek, St. Clair County, Illinois. (Value range F)

Pentremites godoni. Specimens replaced with red chert. Chester Series, Waterloo, Illinois.

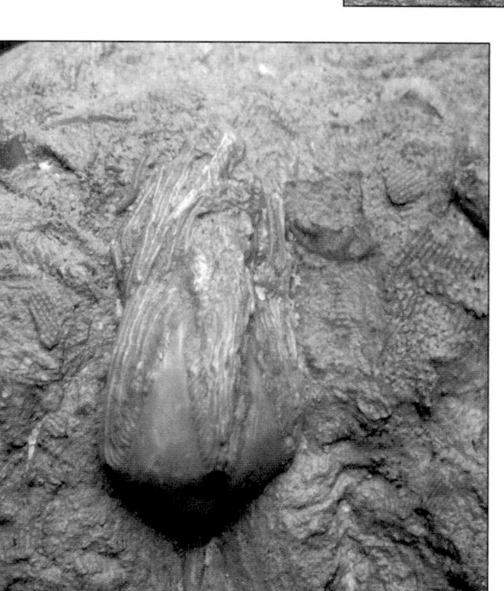

Pentremites godoni with pinnules from the Paint Creek, Illinois locality. (Value range E)

Pentremites brentwoodensis. Brentwood Limestone, earliest Pennsylvanian, Fayetteville, Arkansas. Pennsylvanian blastoids are almost non-existent, these come from the lowermost Pennsylvanian, which lies just above Upper Mississippian strata also containing *Pentremites*. (Value range F)

Pentremites godoni. Paint Creek Formation, Waterloo, Illinois. A typical specimen from this extensively collected locality.

Deltoblastus batheri. These peculiar blastoids come from the island of Timor in the southern hemisphere. They are the only known Permian blastoids. Blastoids, along with most other life forms of the Paleozoic, go extinct at the end of the Permian (the terminal Paleozoic Extinction Event). *Specimens courtesy of Larry Osterberger*.

Echinoids

Echinoidea, an echinoderm class thriving today, first appears in the Middle Ordovician as part of GODE (The Great Ordovician Diversification Event). Echinoids are probably the most abundant echinoderms in today's oceans.

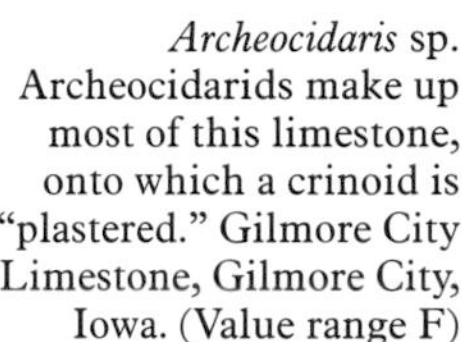

Archeocidaris sp. Archeocidarids make up most of this limestone, onto which a crinoid is "plastered." Gilmore City Limestone, Gilmore City, Iowa. (Value range F)

Living echinoids photographed in a marine aquarium. The sunflower-like object at the bottom is a sea anemone, a cnidarian, **not** an echinoderm. Echinoids thrive in the oceans of today. They represent one of the most successful echinoderm classes.

Archeocidaris wortheni Hall. Two archeocidarids reconstructed from concentrated, disarticulated specimens from a (now removed) limestone ledge and bedding surface covered by them on I-55, Arnold, Missouri.

Archeocidaris (*Echinocrinus*) sp. Upper Pennsylvanian, east Texas. (Value range D)

Melonechinus multiporus. A bedding surface of the St. Louis Limestone covered with plates and partial specimens of this strictly Paleozoic echinoid. Certain layers of the St. Louis Limestone in the St. Louis, Missouri, region can be covered with plates of this echinoid; however, complete specimens are rare and quite desirable. (Value range E)

Archeocidaris (*Echinocarinus*) sp. Small specimens of this urchin are surrounded by numerous spines. Gilmore City Limestone, Mississippian, Gilmore City, Iowa. (Value range F)

Oligoporous sp. This is the large echinoid found in Osagian Mississippian age limestone. Keokuk Formation, Springfield, Missouri. (Value range E)

Starfish and Serpent (or Brittle) Stars

These two classes are some of the most common and successful echinoderms in modern oceans. Both have a long geologic history, dating back to the Ordovician Period. Most Paleozoic starfish and brittle stars are smaller in size than those living today—both are also desirable fossils.

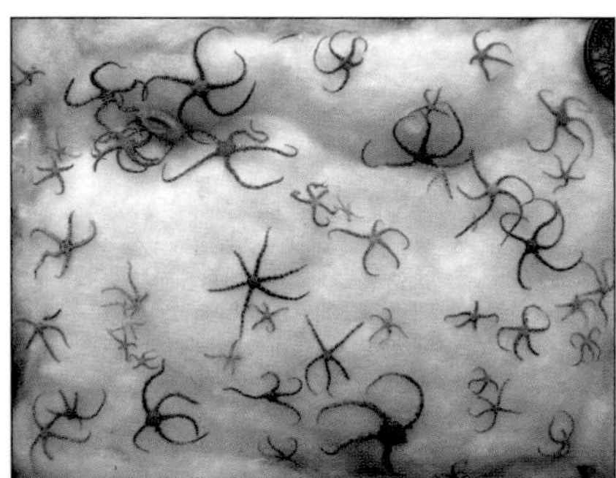

Modern juvenile ophiuroids (serpent stars) and asteroids (starfish). These and echinoids are probably the most abundant and widespread echinoderms in modern seas.

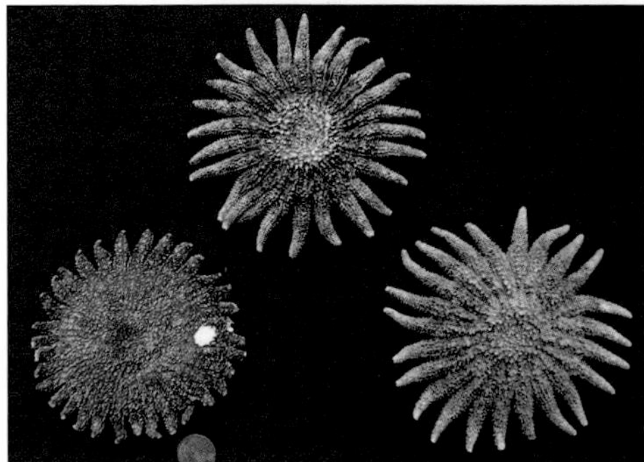

Modern sun-stars. Multi-armed asteroids with twenty-five arms (top and lower right). The sun star to the left has thirty three arms—two apparently have been lost as all living echinoderms have multiples of their five-fold symmetry.

Asteroids (Starfish)

Starfish first appear during the Middle Ordovician as part of the great Ordovician diversification event (GODE). In the Paleozoic, they rarely were abundant, being greatly overshadowed in number by crinoids and blastoids.

Starfish (*Onychaster*). Looking much like a modern starfish, this specimen comes from Upper Ordovician sandstone of the Bani Formation of the Anti-Atlas Mountains of Morocco. Fossils in this reddish Ordovician sandstone have been recognized as representing elements of an Ordovician Konservat-Lagerstatt. (Value range D)

Side view of the previous specimen.

Encrinaster roemeri. A superb specimen of this Lower Devonian asteroid in slate from the Hunsruchschiffer, Bundenbach, Germany. *Courtesy Dept. of Earth and Planetary Sciences, Washington University.*

Hallaster sp. A widespread asteroid from the Late Ordovician and early Silurian. Girardeau Formation, Cape Girardeau, Missouri. Paleozoic starfish are generally small like this. Large examples like those shown in the previous photos are the exception. (Value range F)

Ursoma sp. Impressions of numerous starfish in yellow sandstone have come from the Lower Silurian of eastern Australia. (Value range F)

Stenaster obtusus + trilobite pygidium. Galena Formation, Middle Ordovician. Cannon Falls, Minnesota. Identified by F. Hotchkiss. Paleozoic starfish can be tricky to identify.

Hudsonaster sp. Galena Formation, Middle Ordovician, Cannon Falls, Minnesota. Identified by F. Hotchkiss.

Hudsonaster cylindricus. Trenton Formation, Kirkfield, Ontario, Middle Ordovician. Identified by F. Hotchkiss. (Value range F)

Hudsonaster sp. Decorah Formation, Middle Ordovician, Salt River, Ralls, County, Missouri. (Value range F)

Asterophyllites sp. Presumed asteroid trace fossil impressions. A large number of these have entered the collector community from outcrops in eastern Kansas. Tongonoxie Sandstone, Upper Pennsylvanian, eastern Kansas. (Value range F)

Asterophyllites sp. Presumed asteroid trace fossil impressions. Upper Pennsylvanian, Tongonoxie Sandstone, eastern Kansas. (Value range F)

Asteroid impression. Golconda Formation, Chester Series, Waterloo, Illinois. (Value range G)

Ophiuroids (Brittle Stars)

Brittle stars, like starfish, first appear in the Middle Ordovician as part of GODE (Great Ordovician Diversification Event). Good specimens of these echinoderms are also desirable fossils. Brittle-star fossils become more common in the Mesozoic and Cenozoic Eras, however some large, excellent specimens have recently (2011) come from the Ordovician of Morocco.

Ophiuroid—family Protasteridae. Small Mississippian brittle stars. Glen Dean Formation, Chester Series, Ste. Genevieve County, Missouri. (Value range F)

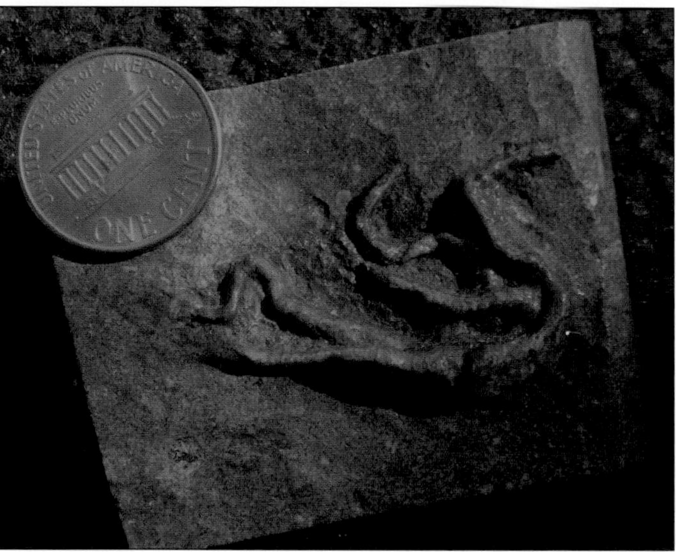

Long-armed ophiuroid. Suborder Zengophlurina. This and the specimen of the previous photo were found on the same bedding plane of a large slab exposed along the Mississippi River. Ste. Genevieve County, Missouri. (Value range F)

Echinoderm group. Two crinoids and an ophiuroid (top right). Girardeau Formation, Cape Girardeau, Missouri. (Value range E)

Close-up of ophiuroid shown in the previous photo.

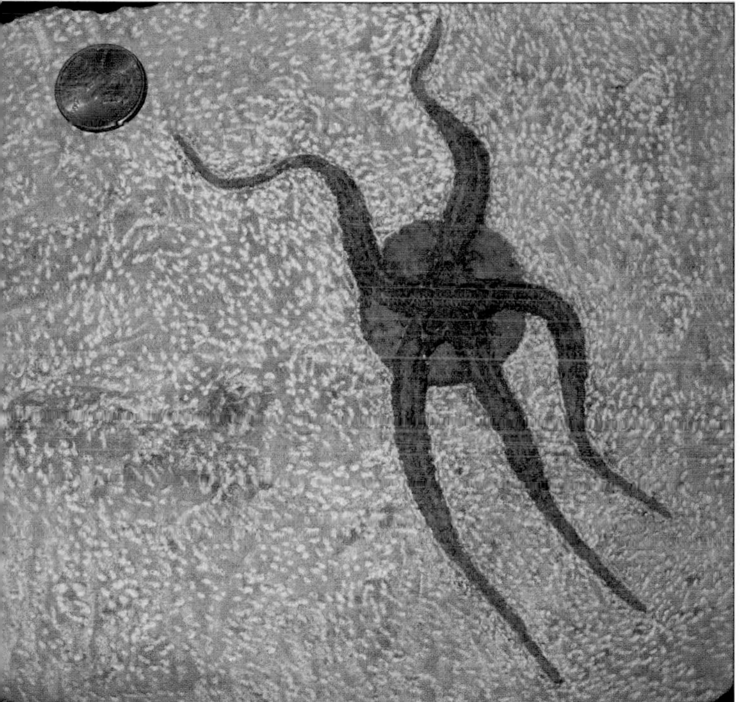

Ophiuroid from Upper Ordovician, Bani Formation, Konservat-Lagerstatt of Morocco. (Value range E)

Edrioasteroids

Edrioasteroids are some of the earliest appearing echinoderms. Representatives of the class first appear in the Lower Cambrian along with eocrinoids. Edrioasteroids, especially well preserved ones, are rare and desirable fossils.

Stromatocystites walcotti. A Lower Cambrian edrioasteroid in slate. Edrioasteroids are one of the first echinoderms to appear in the rock record. Norris Point, western Newfoundland. (Value range E)

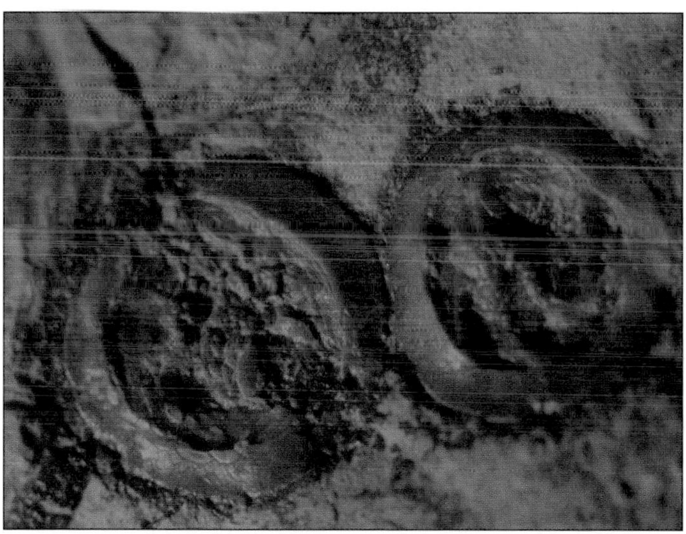

Agetacrinites hanoveri. Edrioasteroids which grew on a late Devonian hard ground. A large number of these entered collections from a quarry near Nora Springs, Iowa, in the mid-1960s. (Value range F)

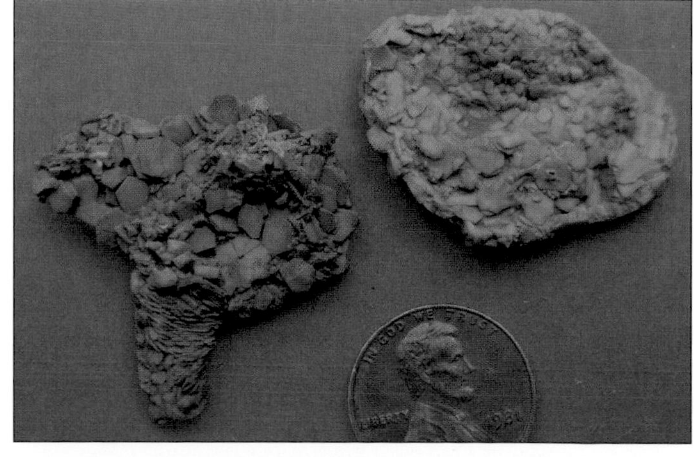

Discocystis sp. Partially articulated edrioasteroid. This type of preservation is the norm for edrioasteroids. Complete specimens are rare and very desirable. Upper Mississippian, Prairie du Long Creek, St. Clair County, Illinois.

Discocystis kaskaskiensis. Two specimens of a Mississippian edrioasteroid, which is rare and desirable from Chesterian age strata. Millstadt, Illinois. (Value range D for both)

Comarocystites missourensis. A group of these unique echinoderms resembling morel mushrooms. The concave plates and their irregular configuration is typical of the class. (Value range D for group)

Paracrinoids

Paracrinoids are an extinct stemmed echinoderm class known only from the Middle Ordovician. They had a very short range of existence compared to most other echinoderm classes. Paracrinoids are rare and desirable fossils, especially complete specimens.

Omarocystites missourensis. Specimen removed totally from matrix. (Value range E)

Comarocystites missourensis. An Ordovician stalked echinoderm (pelmatozoan) which lived only during the Middle Ordovician. Paracrinoids are examples of organisms appearing in the GODE "Great Ordovician Diversification Event," but unlike crinoids and asteroids existed for only a short span of geologic time before going extinct. Kimmswick Limestone, Middle Ordovician, Jefferson County, Missouri. (Value range F)

Canadocystites sp. Kimmswick Limestone, Fruitland, Missouri. I-55 cuttings. (Value range F)

Paracrinoid. Probably an undescribed genus of paracrinoid which came from I-55 excavations near Fruitland, Missouri, 1975. (An undescribed specimen should not be pegged with monetary value, **science comes first.**)

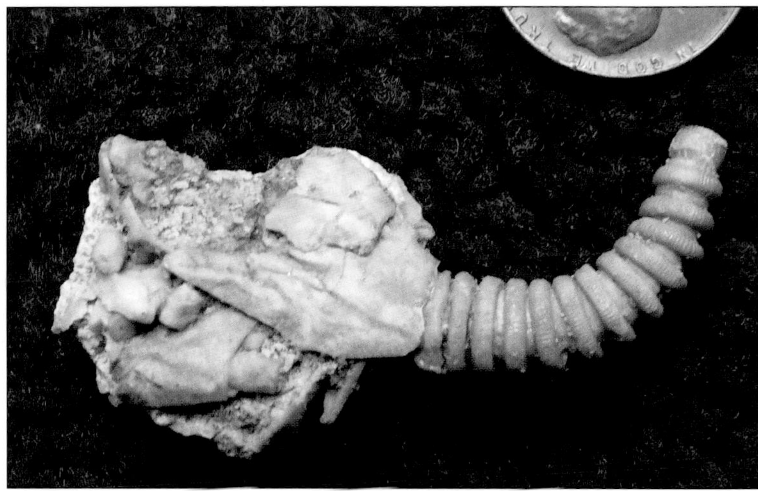

Homocystites sp. Middle Ordovician, Kimmswick Limestone, Jefferson County, Missouri. (Value range F)

Pleurocystites sp. Trenton Group, Middle Ordovician, Kirkland, Ontario. (Value range E)

Cystoids

Cystoids are representatives of an exclusively Paleozoic echinoderm class. They are a complex group which consists of a large variety of forms. Cystoids are most abundant in the Ordovician, Silurian, and Devonian periods, becoming extinct at the end of the Devonian. Like the other extinct Paleozoic echinoderm classes, complete and well preserved cystoids are quite desirable fossils.

Castericystis (*Pleurocystites*) sp. A group of these distinctive Ordovician cystoids from Middle Ordovician limestone of eastern Ontario. *Pleurocystites* is one of the most abundant and widespread of Ordovician cystoids. They are desirable! (Value range C for slab)

Glyptocystites sp. (bottom) and *Hybocrinus nitidus* (top). Bromide Formation, Middle Ordovician, Johnston County, Oklahoma. (Value range F)

Regulacystis pleurocystites. A Devonian cystoid in slate. These come from the famous Lower Devonian Hunsruckschiffer (Bundenbach Slates) of southern Germany. They are some of the last of the cystoids as well as one of the most widely occurring cystoids, hundreds having come from the roofing slate quarries of Bundenbach. (Value range F)

Echinosphaerites aurantium. These nearly spherical cystoids are restricted to the Ordovician Period. They are one of the more commonly seen cystoids. Benbolt Limestone, Middle Ordovician, Scott County, Virginia. (Value range F, single specimen)

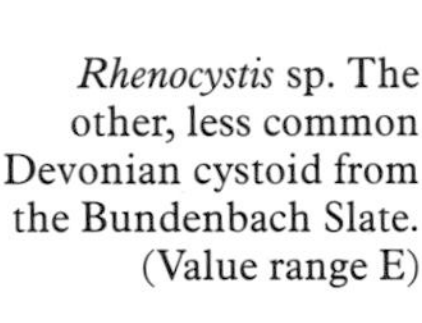

Rhenocystis sp. The other, less common Devonian cystoid from the Bundenbach Slate. (Value range E)

Sinocystis sp. An egg-shaped, internal mold of a Silurian cystoid. Yunnan Province, China.

Stylophorans

Stylophorans previously were placed in the cystoids. They have a number of anatomical features making them distinct from other echinoderms, some of which appear to link them to the Phylum Chordata.

Caryocrinites pleurocystites. Beech River Formation, Brownsport Group, Middle Silurian, Decatur County, Tennessee.

Sclenocystites strimplei. An extinct class of free swimming echinoderms which some paleontologists consider to be related to some of the earliest vertebrates. These fossils have been placed into their own phylum by some paleontologists, who consider them representative of a phylum intermediate between chordates and echinoderms known as the calcichordata. Galena Formation, Middle Ordovician, Cannon Falls, Minnesota. (Value range E)

Sclenocystites strimplei. Two specimens below a crinoid stem. Galena Formation, Cannon Falls, Minnesota. The species is named after echinoderm collector and worker Harold Strimple.

Sclenocystites strimplei. Galena Formation, Cannon Falls, Minnesota.

Holothurians (Sea Cucumbers)

Holothurians rarely leave good fossils as they are soft-bodied. As such they are rare fossils.

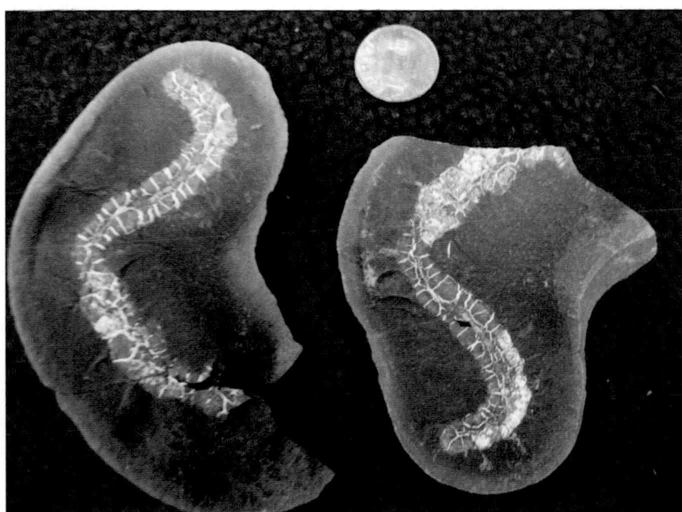

Sea cucumber with ring of calcareous plates (marked "mouth") is a support for the esophagus and body muscles. The animal's body is not well preserved—better on previous specimen, pit 11, Essex fauna. (Value range G)

Eldonia berbera. A large number of fossils of this soft-bodied animal have come from the Anti-Atlas Mountains of Morocco. *Eldonia* originally was described from the Middle Cambrian Burgess Shale of British Columbia. A number of websites state that these fossils are Devonian in age. They are **not**. They are late Ordovician in age and come from an Ordovician Conservtat-Lagerstat in the Anti-Atlas Mountains. (Value range E)

Holothurian (sea cucumber). Unlike the other echinoderm classes, the body of holothurians (sea cucumbers) is not composed or covered with calcareous plates but rather is fleshy. As a consequence of this, the fossil record of sea cucumbers is poor. They do possess small, calcareous barbs (known as sclerites) embedded in the fleshy body and these can be preserved as microfossils (holothurian sclerites). The best known fossil holothurians are those found preserved in ironstone concretions of the "Mazon Creek" + Konservat-Lagerstat (Essex fauna). (Value range G)

Eldonia berbera. Eldonia has been considered possibly as being a cnidarian, a mollusk ora holuthurian. (Value range E)

Eldonia berbera. Part and counterpart. Anti-Atlas Mountains, Morocco. (Value range E)

Rare Echinoderm Chert Fossils

Chert (or flint), weathering from marine carbonate rocks (like limestone and dolomite), sometimes can preserve and yield excellent fossils of marine life, generally marine invertebrates. Sometimes rather than being small and broken, these fossils can be relatively large and complete. Once in a blue moon, a specimen is found which for various reasons can be of significance to science. Such fossils are occasionally found by persons searching creek beds or rocky, chert covered hillsides because of the person's curiosity about rocks.

The author is familiar with this scenario since, as a boy he searched rocky stream beds in Missouri for just such chert or flint fossils. Some of the fossils found in this manner can be odd, unique, and scientifically valuable, such as a Mississippian starfish found in this manner in the Springfield, Missouri, area in 2003 being an example. This is especially true if the finder makes contact with someone knowledgeable with local fossil faunas and realizes the validity of the situation.

Among the most prolific sources of these chert fossils are the cherts and flints of the Mississippian Burlington and Keokuk limestones in the US Midwest, especially in the states of Iowa, Missouri, Illinois, and northwest Arkansas. Scientifically significant examples of such chert fossils included both the interior and exterior molds of various echinoderms. These may be crinoid calyxes and other parts of crinoids like holdfasts, stems, and cirra, blastoids, echinoids, and even starfish. Non-echinoderm fossils of note collected or seen by the author includes sponges, puzzling corals, brachiopods with internal structures, and puzzling bryozoans. Arthropods are represented by trilobites and vertebrates by impressions of both teeth and dorsal spines of shark-like fishes. Overall, the diversity of fossils found in these Mississippian cherts appear to be greater than those found in the limestones, which themselves are noted for their faunal diversity and richness, especially the crinoids and blastoids. Cherts of other periods of the Paleozoic also can produce both attractive and scientifically valuable fossils. The author has in mind abundant chert concentrated upon weathering of thick sequences of dolomite of both Late Cambrian and Early Ordovician age in the Ozark Uplift of southern Missouri and northern Arkansas. It is also noteworthy that chert fossils in these areas (as well as elsewhere) occur over large areas and often are found associated with the stones of rocky creek beds, an association making them especially attractive to many persons, including children who can wade in the water while looking for fossils.

It's unfortunate that in some regions this educational resource has been placed off limits. Such creek searching for rocks in many areas of public lands in the US today is often discouraged and in some cases is illegal. Prohibitions to such collecting, often stemming from the association by both land managers and land managing agencies of fossils with archeology—a mindset which is erroneous for reasons discussed elsewhere. Ironically, persons who find such sometimes rare and scientifically valuable fossils are usually salvaging the fossils as high water (especially in streams) not only rearranges, buries, and covers previously exposed rock, but also results in exposing new ones. In this sense, fossils are a renewable educational resource.

On the matter of creek fossil collecting, the author recently was relayed an incident where a ranger, representing a land managing authority in Missouri, told a family creek collecting that such activity was not only prohibited but was theft of public property as the rocks and fossils in the creek belonged to the state and no provisions were enacted by the legislature to convey these (as is the case with fish and game) to any individual. This concept and mindset becomes even more "sticky" when the fossils found have some monetary value. (It is for this reason that many paleontologists downplay and discourage monetary association with fossils.) On this mindset however, other occurrences of natural items of value in the past have had a precedent as to the "finders-keepers" model. Gold nuggets and dust come to mind; when found on public land these usually were the property of the person who found them. The 1877 mining law in the US also encodes this finders-keepers model with its provisions for a citizen's right to establish a mineral claim on public land. We need to rethink some of these issues. Excessive legalism can (and does) choke a lot of positive and beautiful things, especially if accompanied by a lack of common sense.

Cherty limestone of the Burlington-Keokuk Formations. Middle Mississippian, northeastern Missouri.

Collecting Mississippian chert fossils from an Ozark Mississippian outlier, 1985.

On the subject of chert (and flint, a vitreous or glassy form of chert), its origin in geology is very much debated. Chert and flint are ubiquitous rocks in the author's native Missouri, especially in the Ozarks, where vast amounts of it occur. This is a reason why streams of the Ozarks are so clear and attractive. It might not be an exaggeration to call the Ozarks the "chert and flint capital of the world." **Many explanations exist in the geologic literature trying to explain chert's origin.** The author, for sake of brevity, presents below what he considers to be the best explanation (from one of his field trip guide books).

Chert (and flint) are amorphous, microcrystalline forms of silica. The origin of such large amounts of silica came from felsic volcanoes at what at the time was the margin of the North American Continent (Laurentia). These volcanos spewed out very fine ash which fell and accumulated in shallow seas either as fine silica disseminated in carbonate rocks like limestone and dolomite or clumped together to form gelatinous masses of gel-like silica (silica gel). The later, when formed, often incorporating the hard parts of marine life, the calcareous portion of the fossil and associated limestone later being dissolved but the much less soluble silica not doing so and thus accumulating to form what is commonly known as residual chert. This is what produced the rounded chert masses and nodules commonly associated with Mississippian age cherts. This is also what can be called, primary chert. The other type of chert (secondary chert) forms upon the weathering of dolomite or limestone containing disseminated silica. In this case silica incorporated in the carbonate rock undergoes solution (which takes place upon weathering) and replaces the carbonate rock, sometimes on an almost molecular basis—this also replaces fossils with silica which might have been present in the original carbonate rock. In this manner some of the more "punky" and porous chert so often associated with Cambrian and Lower Ordovician rocks, not only in the Ozarks, but also in the southern Appalachians as well as elsewhere, were formed. Fossils associated with these cherts can also be silica replacements (casts) of the originally calcareous fossils.

Crinoid stem impressions in Mississippian chert from the previously shown locality. These are common fossils in Mississippian chert.

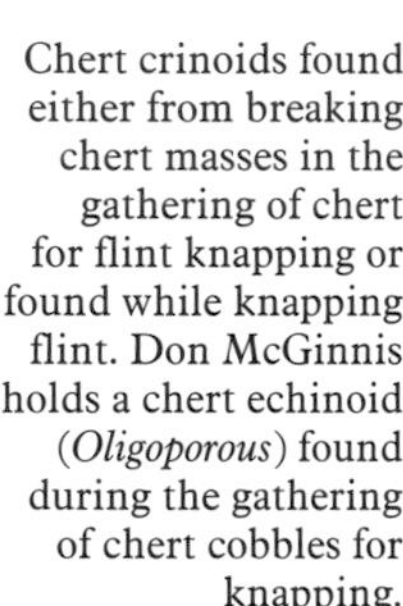

Chert crinoids found either from breaking chert masses in the gathering of chert for flint knapping or found while knapping flint. Don McGinnis holds a chert echinoid (*Oligoporous*) found during the gathering of chert cobbles for knapping.

Oligoporous sp. Close-up of this specimen of an unusual, early echinoid preserved in chert. (Value range D)

Flint is a material prized and widely used by early humans, as well as more recently by technologically challenged cultures. The author first became aware of this as a child finding chert or flint arrowheads in the St. Louis region. Pre-Columbian Native Americans, some 1,000-800 years ago, lived in what would become the St. Louis region and left numerous chert and flint artifacts which can still abound. Knapping ability necessary to produce these stone tools represents both a high degree of skill as well as an intimate knowledge of the inherent properties of the various types of flint necessary to produce the desired object. It's interesting that a number of modern persons have taken up this knapping process and also produce intricate stone objects and tools as a hobby.

Knapped flint containing a blastoid (right). The cobble has been fashioned to display the fossil in an interesting and novel manner along with an emerging flint arrowhead or projectile point. (Value range E)

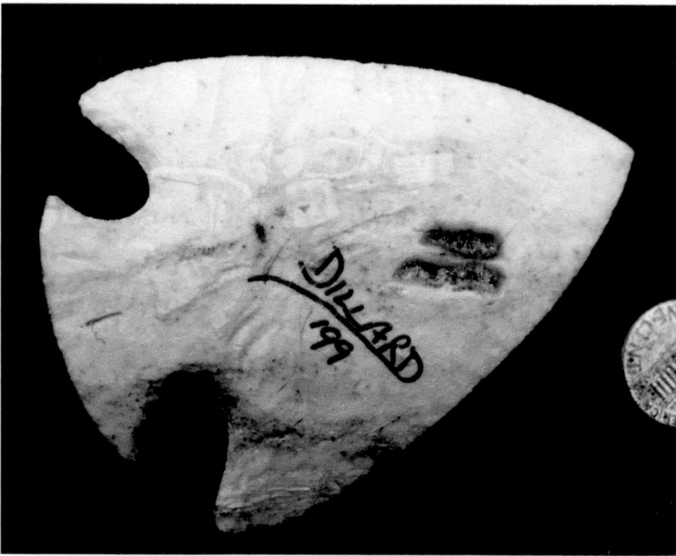

Recently knapped flint arrowhead with silica replaced crinoid stems (above the D in Dillard to the right). This is considered as primary chert, although the crinoid stem fragments had to be replaced with silica as originally they were made up of crystalline calcite. Flint and chert of Mississippian (Osagian) age in the US Midwest often show these vague crinoid fragments. Chert and flint from other parts of the globe usually lack them.

Flint and Chert

A cryptocrystalline form of the mineral quartz, flint is a vitreous (or glassy) form of chert, while chert can occur in porous and punky varieties as well as vitreous material with the hardness of quartz. The origin of both is varied and disputed—abundant chert and flint found in Mississippian rocks may have originated from silica derived from volcanic sources.

Flint hand axes made approximately 6,000 years ago. These hand axes have come from the Sahara Desert of NWA (northwest Africa) and have been collected in large quantities, along with meteorites occurring in the same areas. Both of these geo-collectibles were (are) found by traveling locals who sell them to Moroccan fossil dealers. Similar flint hand axes are found in eastern North America but are probably not this old. Unlike flint found in the central part of North America, this flint lacks fossils.

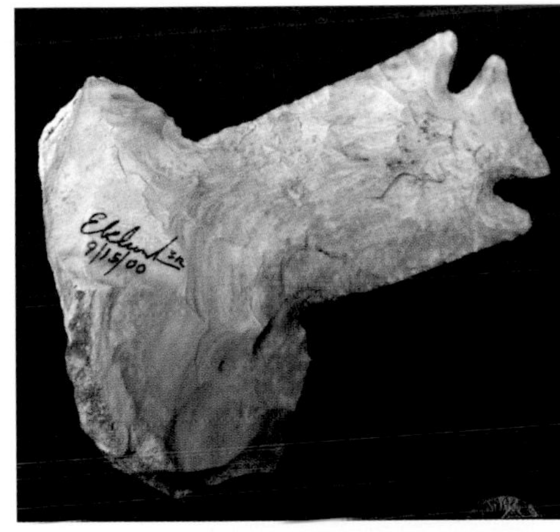

Partial arrowhead recently knapped from a chert (flint) concretion.

Native American knapped Mississippian age chert with a crinoid plate positioned in the center. This knapped piece was made by an unknown **person** some 800+ years ago and found near a spring branch in the western Ozarks. The crinoid plate impression obviously was of interest to the knapper.

Knapped Mississippian age chert containing an impression of a brachiopod. This specimen was also found near the same spring branch in Dade County, Missouri, as the previous specimen. It may have been made by the same individual who made that previous piece.

Glossary

GODE: Great Ordovician Diversification Event. This is when (some 435 million years ago) major marine invertebrate animals such as corals, bryozoans, and many echinoderms became abundant in both biomass and species diversity.

Pelmatozoan echinoderms. Those echinoderms which are attached to a pelma, a stalk or "stem," in contrast to those which are not so attached. Crinoids are the only living pelmatozoans.

Bibliography

Hess, Hans, William Ausich, Carlton E. Brett and Michael J. Simms, eds., 1999. *Fossil Crinoids*. Cambridge University Press. ISBN 0-521-52440-7.

Tarr, William Arthur, 1926. *The Origin of Chert and Flint*; University of Missouri Studies Volume 1, 54 pages.

Chordates

(Hemichordates and Vertebrates)

The phylum chordata consists of animals having a backbone (vertebrates) and those in which the notochord is primitively developed (hemichordates). In this phylum is humanity and other mammals as well as the other classes of vertebrates like amphibians, birds, and reptiles, and the various classes of gilled vertebrates collectively referred to as "fish." The phylum chordata is made up of the subphylum hemichordate and the vertebrates (some zoologists consider these to be separate phyla). Graptolites, fossils commonly found in Paleozoic rocks, are a member of the former. Graptolites were colonial organisms like corals and bryozoans. Their fossilized colonies, known as rhabdosomes, originally were composed of a protein bearing material similar to fingernails. As fossils, this material is generally preserved as a carbonaceous film.

Graptolites range in age from the Cambrian to the Mississippian and consist of two major types, the bottom dwelling dendroids and the floating graptoloids which, because they were pelagic organisms, occur widely in marine rocks and can thus serve as excellent guide fossils.

Dictyonema retiforme. Silurian denderoid graptolites, Gosport Channel in the Lockport Formation, Middle Silurian, western New York. (Value range G)

Hemichordata (Dendroid Graptolites)

These are the earliest graptolites as well as the earliest hemichordates. They were bethonic (bottom dwellers).

Collecting graptolites from (shallow-water-deposited) Cambrian siltstone, Afton, Minnesota.

Graptolites are now known to be colonial hemichordates, a subphylum of the Phylum Chordata. Denderitic graptolites represent the earliest and most primitive graptolites, first appearing in the Lower Cambrian.

Hemichordata (Graptoloid) Graptolites

Graptoloids were pelagic colonies which have a wide distribution in Ordovician and Silurian strata. Their stipes and rhabdosomes are often the only fossils found in Ordovician and Silurian strata of deep sea origin.

Thick graptolite-bearing Ordovician shale, Montmorency Falls, Quebec. These thick, carbon-rich shales were deposited in deep water. They can be rich in graptolites. Some pelagic trilobites can also be associated with these fossils.

Monograptus sp. Graptolites preserved three-dimensionally in limestone from the previously shown locality. Graptolites preserved in this manner can be etched from limestone by acid. Specimens prepared in this way show features which align them with the hemichordates. Middle Ordovician, Montmorency Falls, Quebec, Canada.

Didymograptus sp. Graptolite stipes preserved as iron oxide films in shale. These shale fossils are characterized by being associated with deep sea environments. Lower Ordovician, Mazern Shale, Crystal Springs, Arkansas.

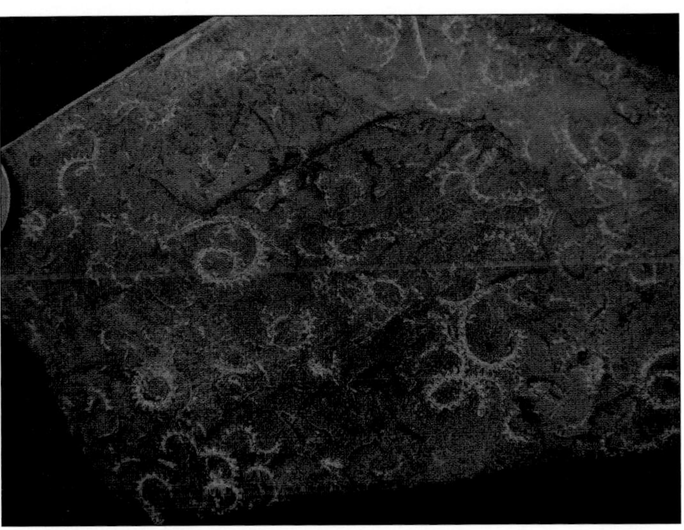

Spirograptus sp. Silurian, Guadalajara, Spain. (Value range F)

Didymograptus colony. A sketch of a floating graptolite colony is to the left, the tennis ball represents the float on this fossil graptolite colony. Mazern Formation, Lower Ordovician, Ouachita Mountains, Arkansas.

Folded and metamorphosed graptolite bearing, deep sea slatey shale. Ouachita Mountains, Arkansas. Deep sea sediments can be almost devoid of fossils. Graptolites are an exception to this as they floated on the ocean's surface, falling to the ocean's depths only when a colony died.

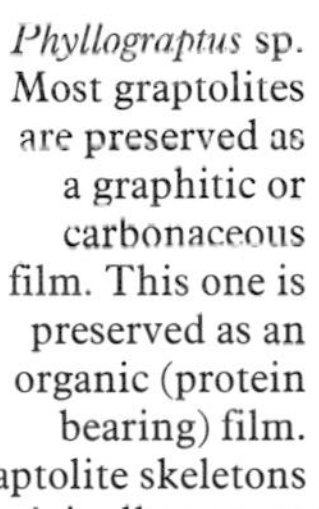

Phyllograptus sp. Most graptolites are preserved as a graphitic or carbonaceous film. This one is preserved as an organic (protein bearing) film. Graptolite skeletons originally were composed of keratin, the same material which composes finger and toenails. This graptolite material appears to have been changed little from its original composition—far from the carbon or graphite films characteristic of most other graptolites. (Value range F)

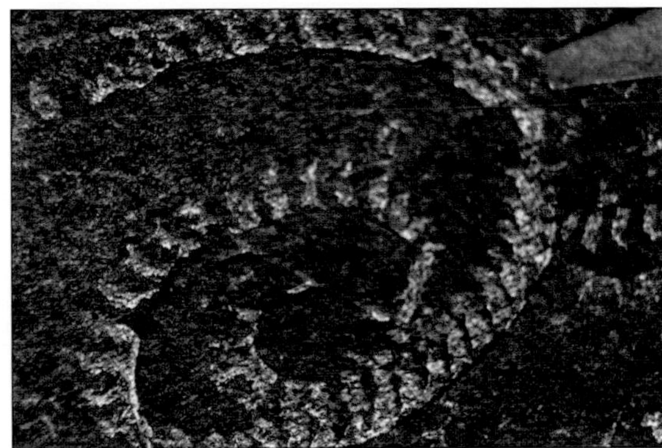

Spirograptus sp. These coiled graptolites are characteristic of the Silurian Period of the Paleozoic Era.

Agnathids (Jawless Vertebrates)

These are the most primitive vertebrates. They lack jaws and living examples, like the lamprey and hagfish, are parasites. This, however, does not appear to be the case with those of the Paleozoic Era.

Lamprey? Primitive jawless fishes with bony armor plate are the oldest undoubted fossil vertebrates (the graptolites are hemichordates, *Pikea* of the Burgess Shale being a possible exception). Vague (like this), and rare but not-so-vague jawless fish from the "Mazon Creek" ironstone nodules are the only known representatives of the agnathans (jawless fishes) which lack body armor.

Astraspis sp. Fragments of Ordovician jawless bony armor fish (agnathans). Hardin Sandstone, Cannon City, Colorado. These represent some of the earliest evidence of vertebrates in the fossil record, especially armor plated, jawless fish.

Chondricthyes (Sharks, Rays, and Shark-like Fishes)

A bewildering variety of teeth, teeth-like structures, and dorsal spines believed to be from shark-like fishes (bradyodonts) occur with some abundance (but not in the abundance of undoubted sharks of the Mesozoic and Cenozoic). These fossils are puzzling and their exact taxonomic position is still unknown.

Devonian primitive land plant and jawless-fish-bearing strata deposited in a channel fill. Beartooth Butte, northern Wyoming.

Cladotus sp. St. Louis Limestone, St. Louis, Missouri. Cladontid teeth were different from the teeth of later sharks. They have two small extensions, one at each side of the tooth. These often are broken off on fossils. (Value range F)

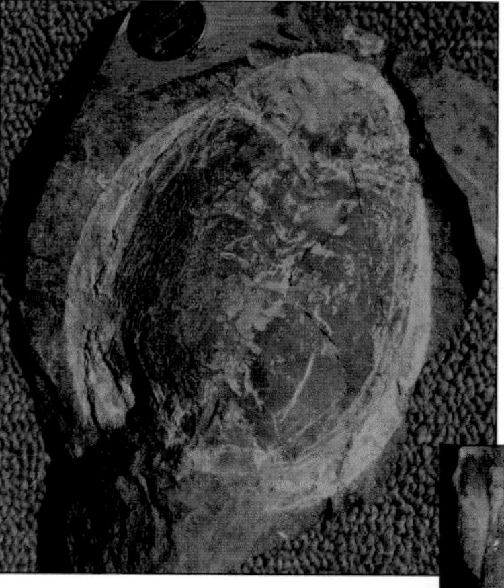

Ptychaspis bucheri. An ostracoderm, a jawless bony armor fish from the aforementioned Wyoming locality. A tail extended from the posterior (bottom of image), which as it was soft-bodied and lacked bony armor, was not preserved.

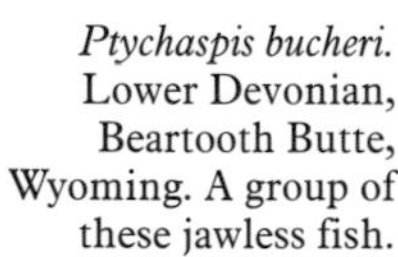

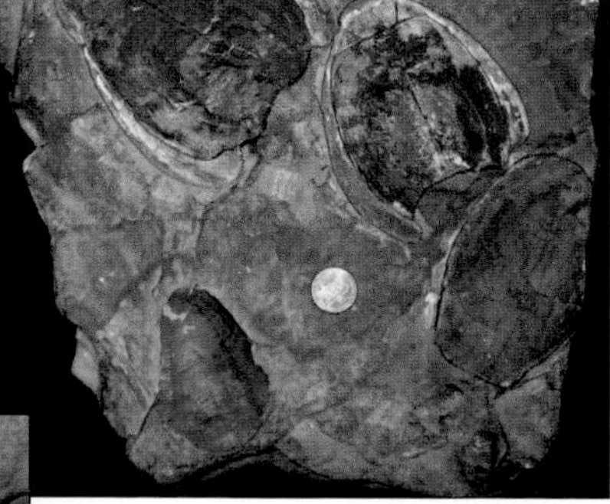

Ptychaspis bucheri. Lower Devonian, Beartooth Butte, Wyoming. A group of these jawless fish.

Chomatodus sp. St. Louis Limestone, St. Louis, Missouri. These peculiarly shaped teeth, like others from bradyodonts, were present as a "battery" of teeth, which periodically were lost in the same manner as are those of the sharks today, although sharks teeth in Paleozoic strata are much rarer than are those of the Mesozoic and Cenozoic eras.

Ptychaspis sp. A weathered specimen of this bony armor fish from Beartooth Butte. (Value range F)

Deltodus sp. St. Louis Limestone, St. Louis, Missouri. *Deltodus* is a flattened, shell crushing tooth, which often show extensive wear. It's hypothesized that the possessor may have fed of the calyxes of crinoids, which lived in vast numbers during the Mississippian Period. (Value range F)

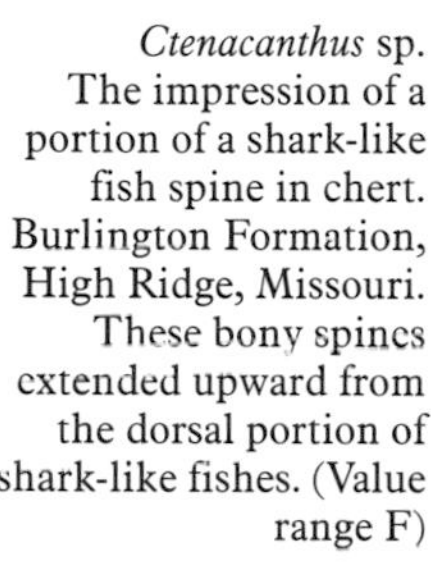

Ctenacanthus sp. The impression of a portion of a shark-like fish spine in chert. Burlington Formation, High Ridge, Missouri. These bony spines extended upward from the dorsal portion of shark-like fishes. (Value range F)

Leptacanthus sp. A small dorsal spine of a shark-like fish with spicules. Salem Formation, Waterloo, Illinois.

Group of Mississippian age shark-like fish (bradyodonts) hard-parts. St. Louis Limestone, St. Louis, Missouri. ***Upper left to right:*** *Ctenacanthus* fragment, *Dactylodus* sp., *Psammodus* sp., *Helodus* sp. ***Botton left to right:*** *Deltodus* sp. (dorsal spines) *Homacanthus* sp., *Ctenacanthus* sp. fragment. (Value range D for group {rare})

Xenacanthus sp. Freshwater shark teeth. These distinctive teeth came from Lower Permian freshwater deposits. Waurika, Oklahoma. (Value range F for group)

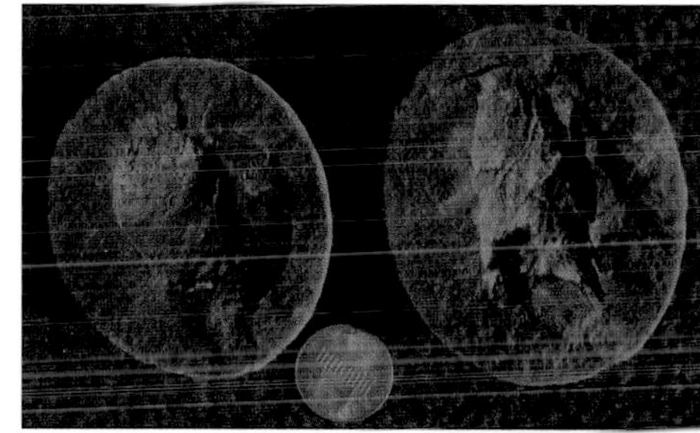

Impression of shark coprolite. Shark coprolites usually exhibit somewhat of a "twirl." This one formed the nucleus of an ironstone concretion. Essex fauna, Pit 11, Essex, Illinois. (Value range G)

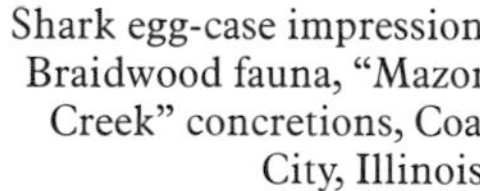

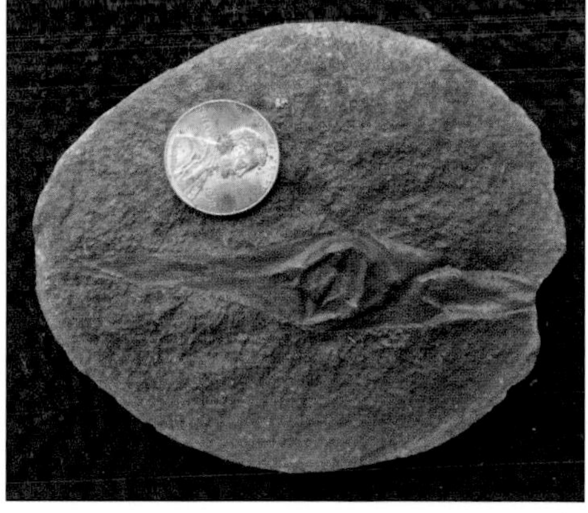

Shark egg-case impression. Braidwood fauna, "Mazon Creek" concretions, Coal City, Illinois.

Listracanthus sp. A spine-like surface "ornament" of a shark-like fish. Carbondale Group, Middle Pennsylvanian, Moberly, Missouri. (Value range E)

Plaacoderms (Bony Armor Fish with Jaws)

Placoderms are strictly Paleozoic organisms. They usually are associated with sediments believed to have been deposited in brackish water. They range from the Devonian (sometimes called the age of fishes) to the Permian when they go extinct.

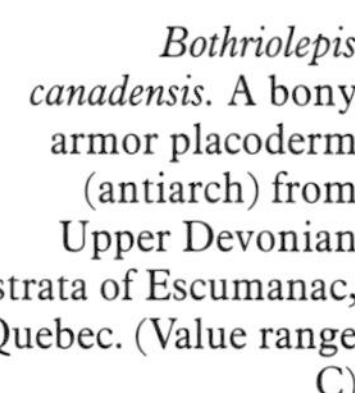

Bothriolepis canadensis. A bony armor placoderm (antiarch) from Upper Devonian strata of Escumanac, Quebec. (Value range C)

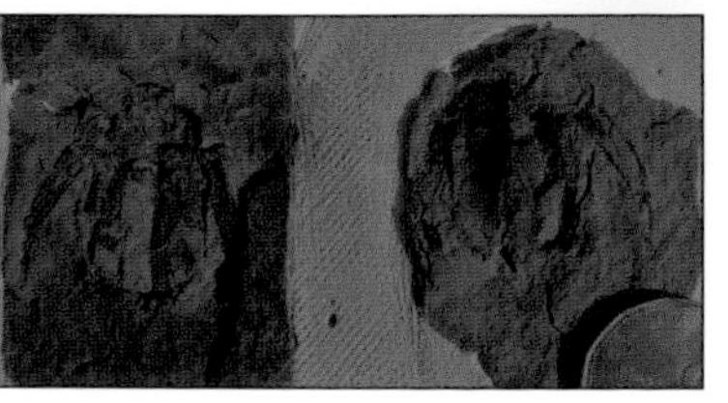

Bothriolepis canadensis. Part and counterpart of a small specimen of this jawed, bony armored fish. (Value range D)

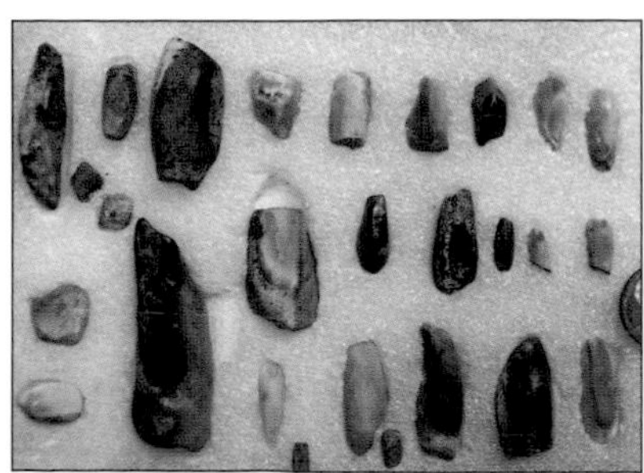

Ptychodus calceolus. Worn placoderm teeth. These teeth are found locally in abundance in Late Devonian sandstones of the US Midwest, where they often are associated with phosphate pebble zones. They have a tooth structure different from the shark-like fishes or bradyodonts, a microstructure characteristic of placoderms. Bushberg Sandstone, High Ridge, Missouri. (Value range E for group)

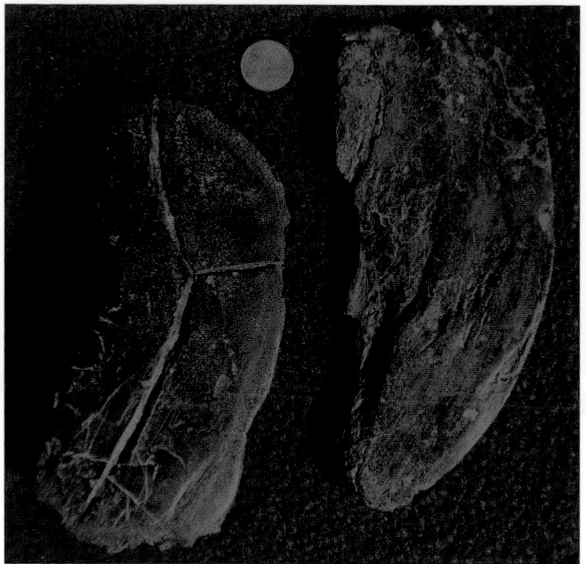

Dunkleostus. Upper Devonian, Chattanooga Shale, Central Kentucky. Parts of bony armor plate of this gigantic bony-armor fish.

Late Devonian seascape reconstruction. A large placoderm is to the left.

Dipnoans (Lungfish)

Lungfish belong to a group of fishes which flourished from the Devonian to the Permian Period and still exist today.

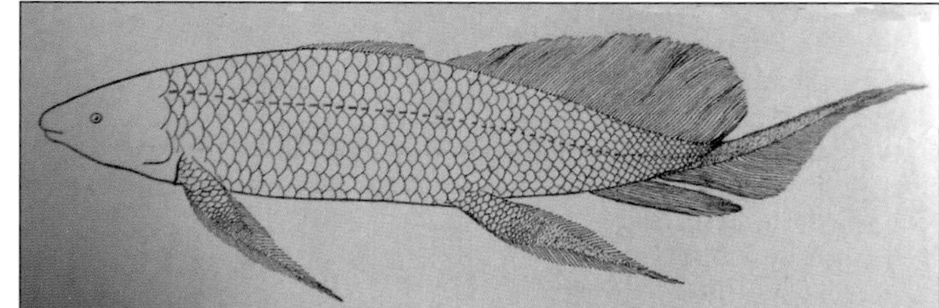

Lungfish schematic showing distinctive heterocercal tail and dorsal "fringe" characteristic of dipnoans.

Scaumenacia curta. (Whiteaves). An especially nice and complete lungfish from Upper Devonian strata of Magasha (Escumanac), Quebec. (Value range A)

Coelacanths (Lobe-finned Fish)

The lobe finned fish are believed to represent that group which gave rise to the amphibians and then ultimately to the mammals (including man). They are especially characteristic of the Paleozoic Era (Devonian through Permian). They are very desirable fossils!

Dipteris valenciennesi. A lungfish from the Devonian Old Red Sandstone, Scotland. The "Old Red" is a series of sandstone and shale beds of fresh water origin which occur extensively in Scotland. The Escumanac and other Devonian fish bearing strata of eastern North America are extensions of the Old Red Sandstone of Scotland. (Value range D)

Ctenodus sp. Lungfish scale. Large scales like this occur in concretions of the "Mazon Creek" fossil beds. Some have considered these scales to be from coelacanths. More recent evaluation considers them to be scales of large lung fish (which are closely related to coelacanths). (Value range E)

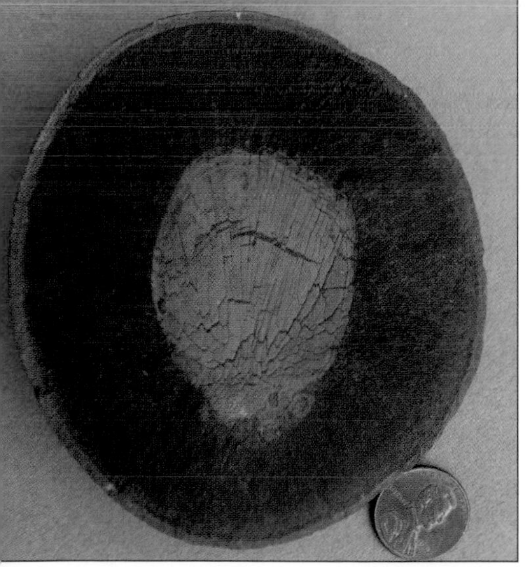

Lungfish scale, Braidwood area of the "Mazon Creek" fossil beds. (Value range E)

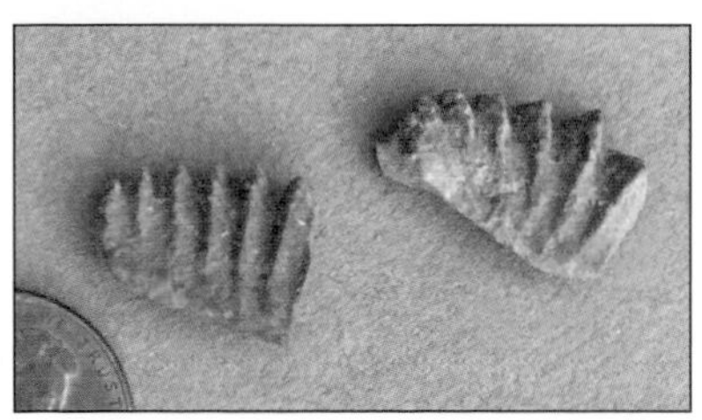

Lungfish teeth. The teeth of lungfish can be distinctive. These come from Permian fresh water deposits near Seymour Texas. (Value range F for group)

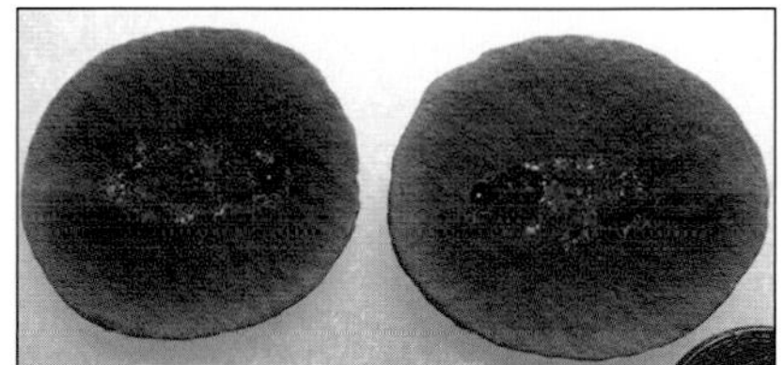

Rhabdoderma so. A coelacanth. Usually not very clear, as is the case with this specimen, small coelacanths have been found in the "Mazon Creek" concretions (Essex fauna). This example shows an attached egg sac. (Value range E)

Coelacanth? A questionable coelacanth in an ironstone nodule from the "Mazon Creek" Essex fauna. (Value range E)

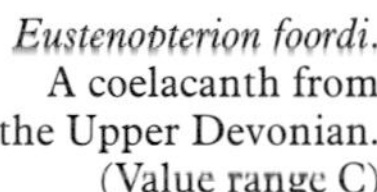

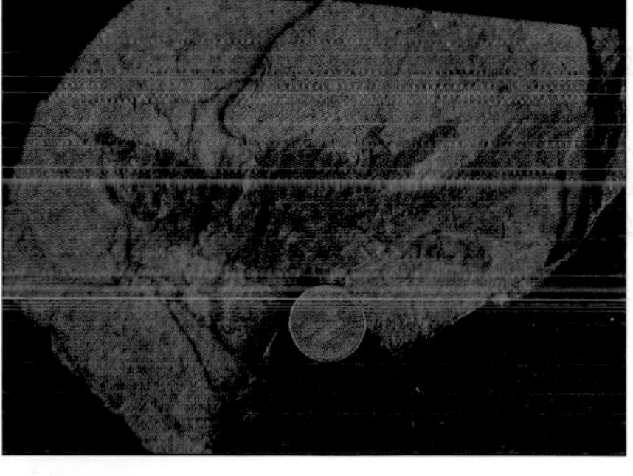

Eustenopterion foordi. A coelacanth from the Upper Devonian. (Value range C)

Eustenopterion foordi. Close-up of the distinctive homocercal tail of this and other coelacanths, including the living *Latimaria* of the Indian Ocean.

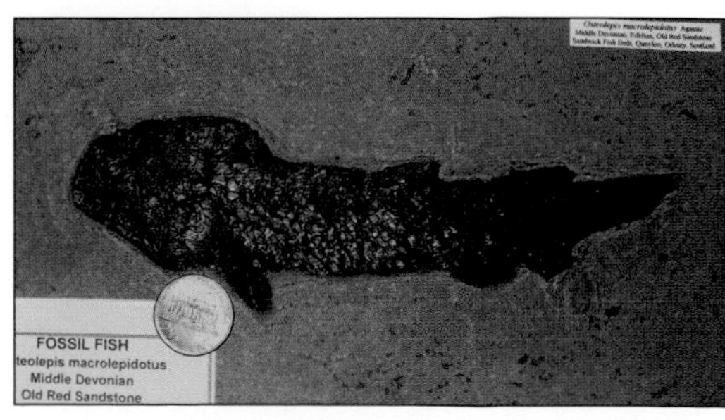

Osteolepis macrolepidotus Agassiz. Middle Devonian, Old Red Sandstone, Sandwick fish beds, Quayloo, Scotland. An "Old Red" coelacanth that has been widely distributed among collectors. (Value range E)

Osteichthyes (Ray Finned Fishes)

The ray finned fishes consist of two groups, the paleoniscids and the teleosts, the later of which didn't appear until the mid-Mesozoic and are the common fishes of today. Paleoniscids are primarily Paleozoic in age and are the most commonly seen Paleozoic fish fossils.

Elonichthys sp. A small paleoniscid in an ironstone nodule of the Essex fauna, Pit 11, northern Illinois. Most "Mazon Creek" fossil fish are small like this. (Value range D)

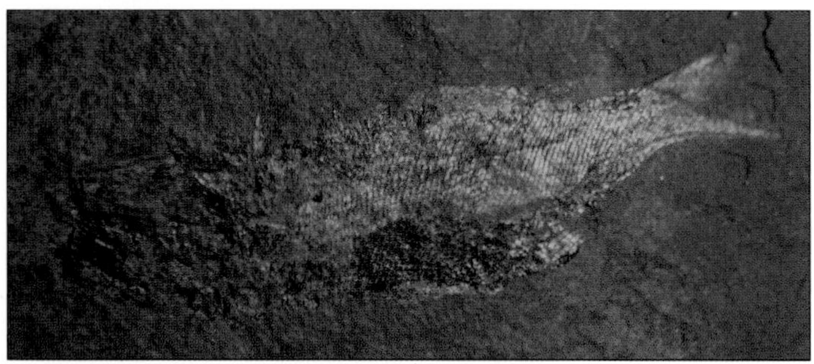

Aeduella blainvillei (Agassiz). A widely distributed paleoniscid fish from the Permian of France. Atun Region, central France. (Value range D)

Amblypherus macropherus. A paleoniscid preserved in an ironstone concretion. Permian (Rothlingendes) at Lebach, Saar Basin, Germany. *Courtesy of Dept. of Earth and Planetary Sciences, Washington University.*

Rhadinichthys alberti. A well preserved paleoniscid fish collected by the author from oil shale beds of Albert Mines, New Brunswick, Canada. Mississippian (Lower Carboniferous) near Fredericksburg, New Brunswick. (Value range C)

Rhadinichthys alberti. Specimen collected in the late nineteenth century from Albert Mines, New Brunswick, Canada. *Courtesy of Dept. of Earth and Planetary Sciences, Washington University, St. Louis.*

Ganopelus sp. A paleoniscid fish from a Lower Carboniferous freshwater limestone. Small fish such as these paleoniscids can occur in abundance in these slabby fresh or brackish water deposits. Ural Mountains, Russia.

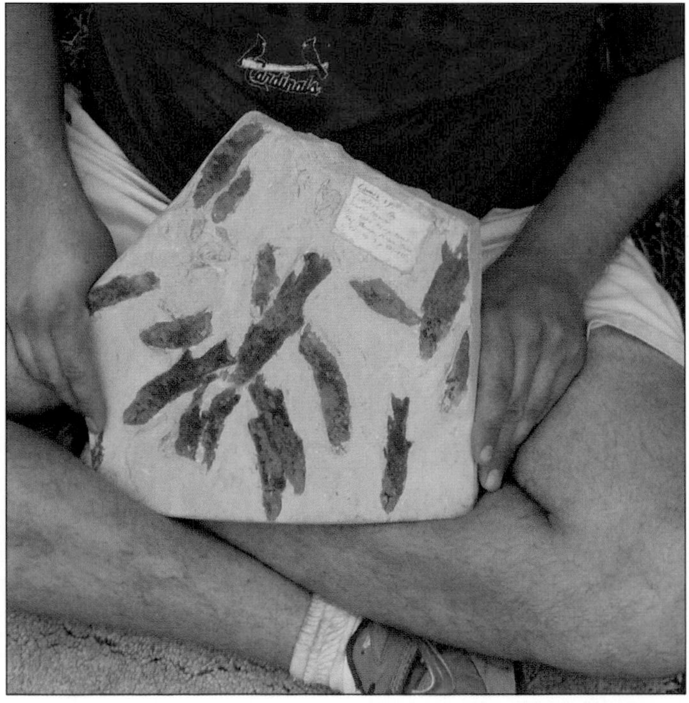

Lamnia sp. Clustered paleoniscids in sandstone formed in a river channel deposit. Lower Permian, Seymour, Texas.

Amphibians

Amphibians are characteristic of the late Paleozoic (Mississippian through Permian). They are believed to have evolved from lobe finned fish. Well preserved fossil amphibians are quite desirable fossils (and often pricey). Complete Paleozoic amphibian fossils are scientifically valuable and should go to science (or at least specimens found should be examined by a competent specialist). Trackways are probably the most common Paleozoic amphibian fossils. Often these are found on large slabs of sandstone that cannot be collected but are best collected by photography.

A typical Late Paleozoic Amphibian! Amphibians, laying "fish-like-eggs," have an unmodified "fish-like" pelvic girdle. Their vertebrae are also different from those of reptiles.

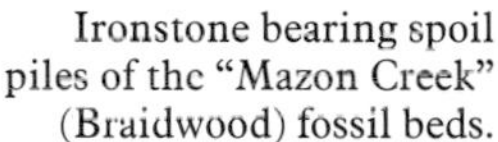

Ironstone bearing spoil piles of the "Mazon Creek" (Braidwood) fossil beds.

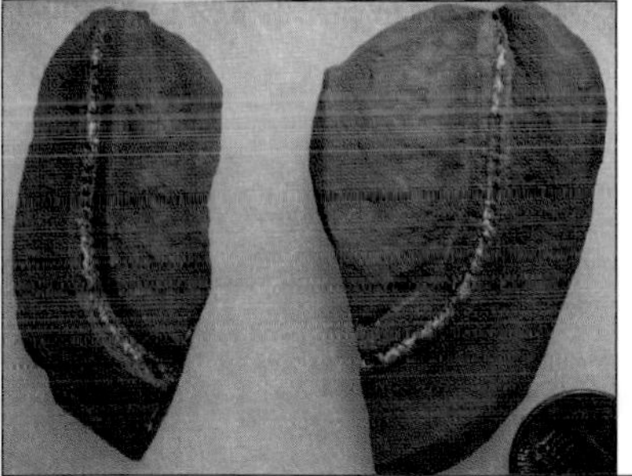

Aormerpeton mazonense. A primitive, legless amphibian in an ironstone concretion (nodule). Braidwood fauna, Coal City, Illinois.

Amblipterus sp. (Brachiosaur). Lower Permian (Rotliegendes). Brno (Brunn), Czech Republic. (Value range C)

Brachiosaurus petroli. Lower Permian (Rotliegendes). Odernheim Pfalz, Germany. (Value range F)

Brachiosaurus petroli. Lower Permian (Rotliegendes) Odernheim, Pfalz Germany.

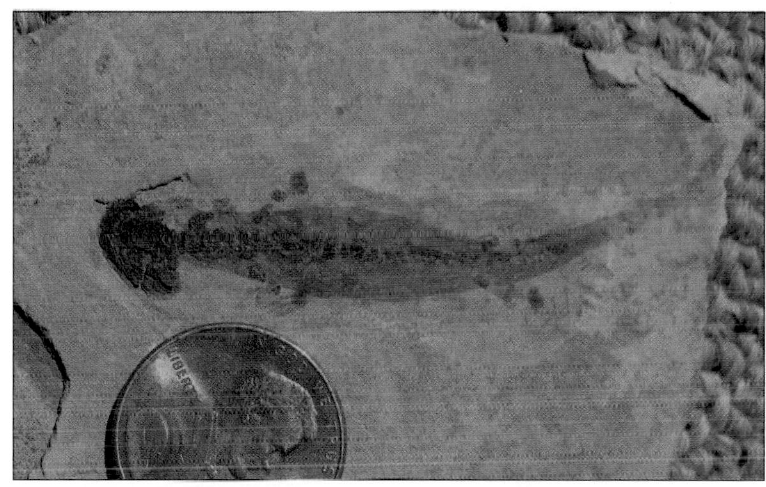

Brachiosaurus petroli. Lower Permian (Rotliegendes), Odernheim, Pfalz, Germany. A "doctored" poor specimen. The tail is just a brush mark and the vertebrae have been ground down. (Value range G)

Amphibian trackway. Alabama. A large number of these late Pennsylvanian trackways have come from shales above coal seams in the Black Warrior Basin of northern Alabama.

Amphibian trackway, Pennsylvanian, northern Alabama.

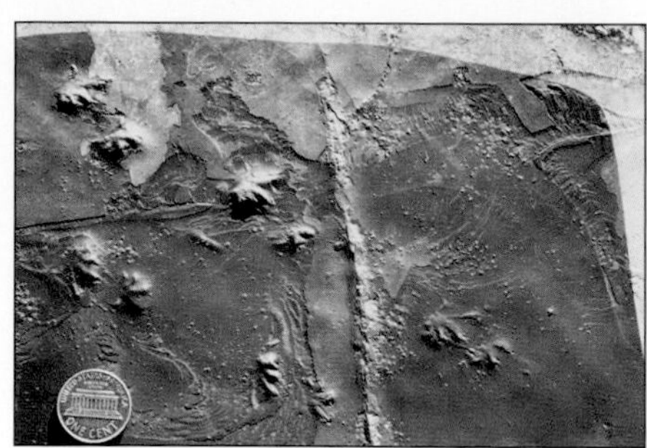

Close-up of the above trackway under different lighting.

Stegocephalian skull (cast). Permian. The stegocephalians were large amphibians with massive, bony skulls. Fragments of bone-head amphibians can be fairly common fossils in some fresh water Permian lake and stream deposits. Complete skulls are rare and usually require painstaking piecing together of the fragmented fossils. Once a specimen has been reconstructed, casts such as this can be made relatively easily. Clear Fork Formation, Lower Permian, Seymour, Texas. (Value range F for cast)

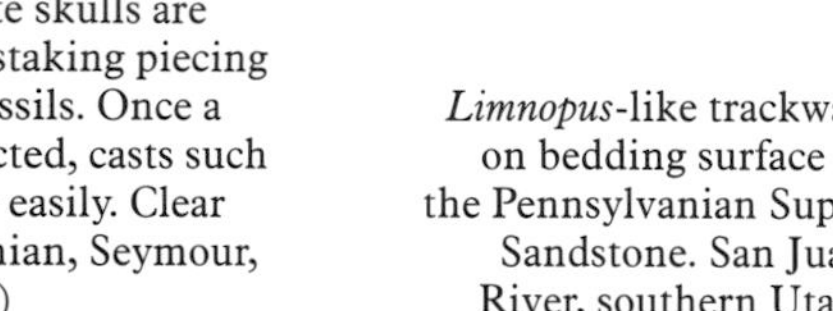

Limnopus-like trackway on bedding surface of the Pennsylvanian Supai Sandstone. San Juan River, southern Utah.

Stegocephalian skull fragments. Clear Fork Formation, Lower Permian, Seymour, Texas. (Value range F for group)

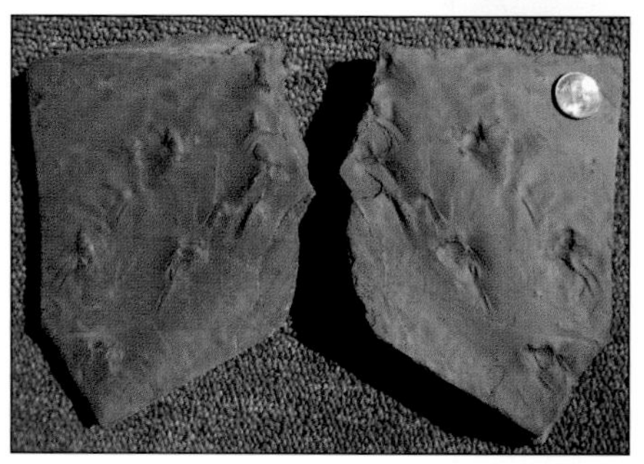

Batrachichnus delicatulus. Slabs (part and counterpart) made by a small crocodile-like reptile or a salamander-like amphibian. The genus comes from batrachian—an old term for amphibians. Permian, Abo Formation, Dona Ana, New Mexico. (Value range F)

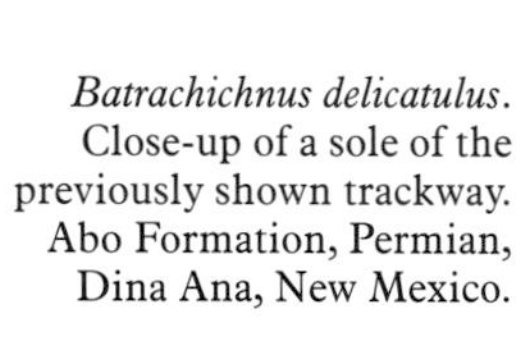

Batrachichnus delicatulus. Close-up of a sole of the previously shown trackway. Abo Formation, Permian, Dina Ana, New Mexico.

Redbeds, southern Utah. These red sediments have iron oxide present as the highly oxidized form—ferric iron. Red sediments such as this are characteristic of Permian and Triassic strata worldwide. Such redbeds usually contain few fossils. When they are present, they usually are tracks and trackways.

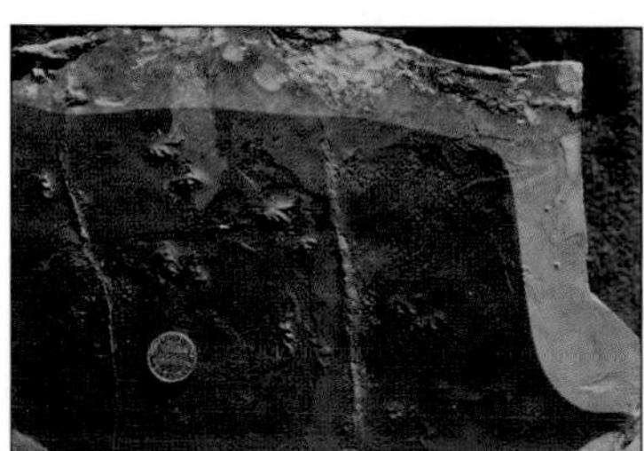

Limnopus sp. Natural trackway cast (sole cast) of a small amphibian. Upper Permian near Abilene, Texas.

Diplocalus sp. This peculiar boomerang-shaped skull is that of a Permian amphibian. (Value range G for cast)

Labyrinthodont amphibian (or early reptile teeth) with infolding of the tooth enamel on a jaw fragment. Lower Permian, Clear Fork Formation, Seymour, Texas. (Value range F)

Reptiles

Undoubted reptiles first appear in the Permian when (in part because of the existence of Pangaea and associated aridity) they became successful with their amniote egg. They are often associated with what are known as redbeds. Redbeds are believed to represent at least partial arid conditions, as well as an atmospheric oxygen level slightly over the 21% of today. Reptiles appear to have been favored by conditions of both the Permian and the Triassic Periods. Reptile fossils are equally divided between actual Permian skeletal remains and trackways which are found in redbeds, usually containing few other fossils.

Dromopus agilius. Tracks in Permian redbeds. Permian Abo Formation, Dona Ana, New Mexico. (Value range F)

Dimetropus nicolasi. A natural sole cast of what may be the track of the sail back reptile *Dimetrodon*. Permian Abo Formation (red bed), Dona Ana, New Mexico. (Value range F)

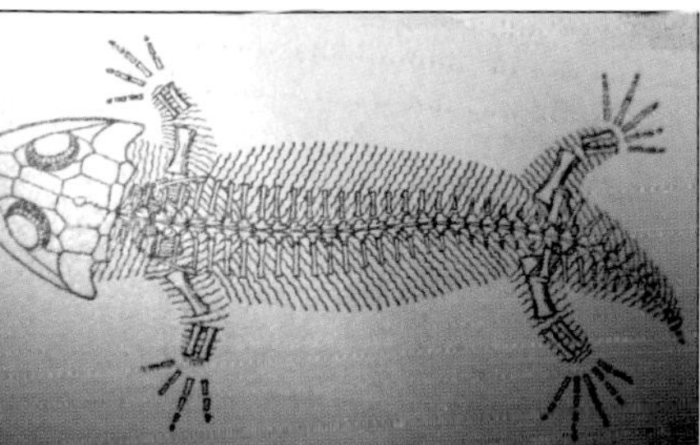

Reptile schematic! Laying amniote (yolk bearing) eggs, the pelvic girdle of a reptile is different from that of an amphibian.

Laoporus sp. Numerous small trackways of presumed reptiles locally occur on bedding surfaces of these sandstone slabs. It's believed that the makers were small mammal-like reptiles which made the tracks while "walking up leeward surfaces of sand dunes." These sand dunes now make up the Coconino Sandstone of the Colorado River where it cuts through the Colorado Plateau. Numerous specimens of these tracks also come from dimension stone quarries which work the Coconino Sandstone. (Value range F)

Puzzling reptile? trackways. Permian of New Mexico.

Slab of dune deposited Coconino Sandstone with *Laoporus* (track with heel) and *Chelichnus* (claw impressions without heel print). *Chelichnus* originally was named after turtle tracks when tracks like this were thought to be those of tortoises.

Large slab (two feet wide) of Permian Coconino Sandstone with *Laoporus* trackway. San Jaun River, southern Utah.

Boulder of Lower Permian sinkhole (karst) conglomerate from a quarry near Lawton, Oklahoma. Locally bones of primitive Permian reptiles are found in conglomerates which fill solution crevices developed in Ordovician limestone of the Arbuckle Mountains of Oklahoma. Most of these are from the mammal-like reptile *Captorhinus aquti*. About half of the white clasts are bones, the others are small clasts of Ordovician limestone.

Individual bones removed from the previous conglomerate with a weak acid and mounted. (Value range F)

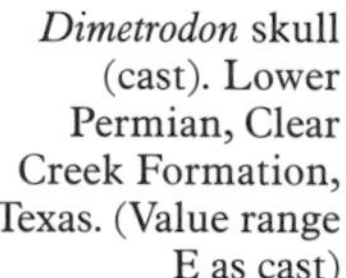

Dimetrodon skull (cast). Lower Permian, Clear Creek Formation, Texas. (Value range E as cast)

Dimetrodon toy models. These models often come with those of dinosaurs. They are **not dinosaurs** as they lived in the Permian Period of the Paleozoic and (most importantly) they were anatomically different from dinosaurs. Living in the Paleozoic, they also (obviously) predated dinosaurs by millions of years. *Dimetrodon* is a type of sail-back reptile, which is believed to be a theriodont or mammal-like reptile.

Captorhinus aquti. Reconstructed specimen of this mammal-like reptile made from bones derived from the previous conglomerate. Such a preparation, besides requiring considerable skill and anatomical knowledge, is very time consuming, hence such a reconstruction is quite pricey. (Value range A)

A fragment of a *Dimetrodon* dorsal spine. Lower Permian, Waurika, Oklahoma. Fragments of these reptiles, which can be recognized anatomically, are desirable fossils. (Value range F)

Top view of Captorhinomorph reconstruction.

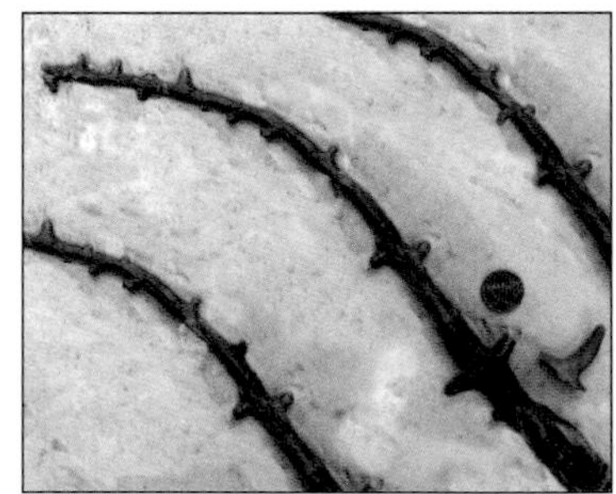

Edaphisaurus spines. Edaphisaurs were sail back mammal-like reptiles living contemporaneously with *Dimetrodon*. They are characterized by the cross members on the animal's dorsal spines. Lower Permian, Seymour, Texas. (Value range D)

Side view of Captorhinomorph reconstruction.

Bibliography

Hay, Andrew A., Don Auler, 1989. *Creature Corner, ESCONI, Keys to identify Pennsylvanian Fossil Animals of the Mazon Creek area.* ESCONI (Earth Science Club of Northern Illinois).

Lockley, Martin, 2002. *A Guide to the Fossil Foot Prints of the World.* Lockley-Peterson, Univ. of Colorado at Denver.

Palmer, Douglas and Barrie Rickards, 1991. *Graptolites, Writing in the Rocks, Fossils Illustrated.* Boydell Press. ISBN 0-85115-262-7.